The International Olympic Committee and the Olympic System

When the athletes enter the stadium and the Olympic flame is lit, the whole world watches and billions will continue to follow the events for the next 16 days.

Readers of this book, however, will watch forthcoming editions of the Olympic Games in a completely different light. Unlike many historical or official publications and somewhat biased commercial works, it provides—in a clear, readable form—informative and fascinating material on many aspects of what Olympism is all about: its history, its organization and its actors.

Although public attention is often drawn to the International Olympic Committee, the athletes, the host cities or even the scandals that have arisen, the Olympic system as such is relatively little known. What are its structures, its goals, its resources? How is it governed and regulated? What does the International Olympic Committee actually do? What are the roles of the National Olympic Committees and the International Sports Federations? What about doping, corruption, violence in the stadium?

In addition to providing a wealth of information on these subjects, the authors show how power, money, and image have transformed Olympism over the decades. They round off the work with thought-provoking reflections regarding the future of the Olympic system and the obstacles it must overcome in order to survive.

This book is an in-depth yet highly accessible read for anyone interested in the Olympic Games, in Olympism, and indeed sport in general.

Jean-Loup Chappelet, PhD, is Professor of Public Management at the Swiss Graduate School of Public Administration (IDHEAP) associated to the University of Lausanne, Switzerland.

Brenda Kübler-Mabbott i **REFERENCE** d translator for various academic instituti   ns.

D0226795

Routledge Global Institutions

Edited by Thomas G. Weiss
The CUNY Graduate Center, New York, USA
and Rorden Wilkinson
University of Manchester, UK

About the Series

The Global Institutions Series is designed to provide readers with comprehensive, accessible, and informative guides to the history, structure, and activities of key international organizations. Every volume stands on its own as a thorough and insightful treatment of a particular topic, but the series as a whole contributes to a coherent and complementary portrait of the phenomenon of global institutions at the dawn of the millennium.

Books are written by recognized experts, conform to a similar structure, and cover a range of themes and debates common to the series. These areas of shared concern include the general purpose and rationale for organizations, developments over time, membership, structure, decision-making procedures, and key functions. Moreover, current debates are placed in historical perspective alongside informed analysis and critique. Each book also contains an annotated bibliography and guide to electronic information as well as any annexes appropriate to the subject matter at hand.

The volumes currently published or under contract include:

The United Nations and Human Rights (2005)
A guide for a new era
by Julie Mertus (American University)

The UN Secretary General and Secretariat (2005)
by Leon Gordenker (Princeton University)

United Nations Global Conferences (2005)
by Michael G. Schechter (Michigan State University)

The UN General Assembly (2005)
by M.J. Peterson (University of Massachusetts, Amherst)

Internal Displacement (2006)
Conceptualization and its consequences
by Thomas G. Weiss (The CUNY Graduate Center) and David A. Korn

Global Environmental Institutions (2006)
by Elizabeth R. DeSombre (Wellesley College)

African Economic Institutions
by Kwame Akonor (Seton Hall University)

The United Nations Development Programme (UNDP)
by Elizabeth A. Mandeville (Tufts University) and Craig N. Murphy (Wellesley College)

The Regional Development Banks
Lending with a regional flavor
by Jonathan R. Strand (University of Nevada, Las Vegas)

Multilateral Cooperation Against Terrorism
by Peter Romaniuk (John Jay College of Criminal Justice, CUNY)

Transnational Organized Crime
by Frank Madsen (University of Cambridge)

Peacebuilding
From concept to commission
by Robert Jenkins (University of London)

Governing Climate Change
by Peter Newell (University of East Anglia) and Harriet A. Bulkeley (Durham University)

Millennium Development Goals (MDGs)
For a people-centered development agenda?
by Sakiko Fukada-Parr (The New School)

For further information regarding the series, please contact:

Craig Fowlie, Publisher, Politics & International Studies
Taylor & Francis
2 Park Square, Milton Park, Abingdon
Oxford OX14 4RN, UK

+44 (0)207 842 2057 Tel
+44 (0)207 842 2302 Fax

Craig.Fowlie@tandf.co.uk
www.routledge.com

The International Olympic Committee and the Olympic System

The governance of world sport

Jean-Loup Chappelet
and Brenda Kübler-Mabbott

Routledge
Taylor & Francis Group

LONDON AND NEW YORK

First published 2008
by Routledge
2 Park Square, Milton Park, Abingdon, Oxon OX14 4RN

Simultaneously published in the USA and Canada
by Routledge
270 Madison Avenue, New York, NY 10016

Routledge is an imprint of the Taylor & Francis Group, an informa business

© 2008 Jean-Loup Chappelet and Brenda Kübler-Mabbott

Typeset in Times New Roman by
Taylor & Francis Books
Printed and bound in Great Britain by
TJ International Ltd, Padstow, Cornwall

British Library Cataloguing in Publication Data
A catalogue record for this book is available from the British Library

Library of Congress Cataloging in Publication Data
Chappelet, J.-L. (Jean-Loup)
 International Olympic Committee and the olympic system: the governance of world sport / Jean-Loup Chappelet and Brenda Kübler-Mabbott.
  p. cm. – (Global institutions series; 27)
 Includes bibliographical references and index.
 1. International Olympic Committee. 2. Olympics. I. Kübler-Mabbott, Brenda. II. Title.
 GV721.3.C43 2008
 796.48068–dc22   2008003405

ISBN 978-0-415-43167-5 (hbk)
ISBN 978-0-415-43168-2 (pbk)
ISBN 978-0-203-89317-3 (ebk)

Contents

Illustrations

Figures

Tables

Boxes

Foreword

The current volume is the twenty-fourth in a dynamic series on "global institutions." The series strives (and, based on the volumes published to date, succeeds) to provide readers with definitive guides to the most visible aspects of what we know as "global governance." Remarkable as it may seem, there exist relatively few books that offer in-depth treatments of prominent global bodies, processes, and associated issues, much less an entire series of concise and complementary volumes. Those that do exist are either out of date, inaccessible to the non-specialist reader, or seek to develop a specialized understanding of particular aspects of an institution or process rather than offer an overall account of its functioning. Similarly, existing books have often been written in highly technical language or have been crafted "in-house" and are notoriously self-serving and narrow.

The advent of electronic media has helped by making information, documents, and resolutions of international organizations more widely available, but it has also complicated matters. The growing reliance on the Internet and other electronic methods of finding information about key international organizations and processes has served, ironically, to limit the educational materials to which most readers have ready access—namely, books. Public relations documents, raw data, and loosely refereed web sites do not make for intelligent analysis. Official publications compete with a vast amount of electronically available information, much of which is suspect because of its ideological or self-promoting slant. Paradoxically, the growing range of purportedly independent web sites offering analyses of the activities of particular organizations has emerged, but one inadvertent consequence has been to frustrate access to basic, authoritative, critical, and well-researched texts. The market for such has actually been reduced by the ready availability of varying quality electronic materials.

For those of us who teach, research, and practice in the area, this access to information has been particularly frustrating. We were delighted when Routledge saw the value of a series that bucks this trend and provides key reference points to the most significant global institutions. They know that serious students and professionals want serious analyses. We have assembled a first-rate line-up of authors to address that market. Our intention, then, is to provide one-stop shopping for all readers—students (both undergraduate and postgraduate), negotiators, diplomats, practitioners from nongovernmental and intergovernmental organizations, and interested parties alike—seeking information about most prominent institutional aspects of global governance.

The International Olympic Committee (IOC)

Most of the books in our series have so far concentrated on the more commonly recognized aspects of contemporary global governance. This book is something of a departure. While we do not embark on totally new terrain, by exploring the IOC we offer readers a book that deals with one of the less visible aspects of global governance.

At the same time, all statistics for newspaper readers, television viewers, and radio listeners indicate that sports are the number one interest in terms of popularity. Thus, this book fills a curious void in the contemporary literature on global governance. Moreover, since Jesse Owens's victories at the 1936 Olympic Games in Berlin, it has not been possible to argue that such sporting events do not have a political impact. So, this book also fills a curious void in political science, where athletics are not a serious topic.

As political scientists are aware, social orders are crafted and perpetuated by a variety of means. Formal political institutions are but one means; informal civil institutions are another. The IOC is one such institution; it is an organization that has been instrumental in garnering support for a form of international cooperation clothed in the resuscitation of the Olympic idea. In this, the IOC has been remarkably successful. It has consistently brought together nations of the world at times when they have stood as foes, contributing in some, albeit small, way to the cause of world peace; it has borne witness to some of the greatest triumphs in the face of adversity and repression (of which Jesse Owens's triumphs remain the most memorable); it has been a place where the repressed have sought to bring continuing injustices to the widest possible public attention (with Tommie Smith's and John Carlos's 1968 Mexico City black power salutes being perhaps the most controversial); it has been the occasion to indicate major dissatisfaction over interventions (with the US and other Western countries' boycott of the Moscow Olympics in 1980 being the most spectacular); and it has encouraged the creation of the Paralympics where differently abled athletes have been able to compete on the world stage.

The IOC has also had its fair share of controversy. The scandal surrounding Sydney's bid to host the 2000 Summer Games; the corruption scandal that erupted over the way the 2002 Winter Games were awarded to Salt Lake City (and the expulsion of members of the IOC that followed); the suspicions over the award of the 1998 Winter Games to Nagano (and particularly the entertainment expenses of the visiting IOC members); the accusations of misconduct by visiting members of the IOC to Toronto in 1991; and accusations of bias in the bidding process for host cities are just some of the most notorious.

The IOC is not an easy organization about which to write. Its relatively secretive and diffuse nature (spanning not only a formal organization but an entire movement) mean that few have a handle on both how the organization functions and the politics with which it has become infused. We were delighted, then, when Jean-Loup Chappelet and Brenda Kübler-Mabbott agreed to write this book for us. Jean-Loup is Professor of Public Management at the Swiss Graduate School of Public Administration (IDHEAP) associated to the University of Lausanne, Switzerland and a leading expert on the International Olympic Movement. He has an intimate knowledge of the IOC and of the Olympic movement; and he is one of the few scholars to have written widely on the subject. Brenda is, among other things, an author and translator who has had extensive experience with the IOC (having worked on IOC minutes as well as on the candidature files by cities wishing to host the Olympic Games). Together they make a first-rate team.

Needless to say, they have produced an excellent book. It comprises all the information necessary to gain a detailed understanding of not only the IOC but its role in global governance. As our readers will quickly discover, the book is clear, concise, authoritative, and meticulous. We know, and we are sure readers will agree, that it clearly deserves to be read by all interested in the International Olympic Movement as well as global governance more generally. We heartily recommend it and welcome any comments that you may have.

Thomas G. Weiss, The CUNY Graduate Center, New York, USA
Rorden Wilkinson, University of Manchester, UK
April 2008

Acknowledgments

We are grateful to a number of IOC members—including presidents—and senior and junior staff who have interacted with us over the years, answering our questions and further explaining many questions related to Olympism. Many thanks also to the numerous representatives of National Olympic Committees, International Federations, and Olympic Organising Committees who have helped us better understand the Olympic system. It is of course impossible to name them all because some of these relationships date from almost 40 years ago.

A special mention should be given to our fellow Olympic scholars. We are a small group of maybe 100 persons around the world, regularly meeting at Olympic Games and other Olympic events and congresses. We have learned a lot from reading their publications and having insightful discussions with them. Space constraints in the bibliography did not permit us to name as many of them as we would have wished.

We would like to thank the editors of Routledge's Global Institutions series, Professors Thomas G. Weiss and Rorden Wilkinson, for inviting us to write this book and providing very valuable feedback and encouragement.

Finally, we would like to thank our families, in particular Sophie and Chris, for having supported us during the several months we took to write this work—and for their understanding of a passion for the Olympic idea that we have shared since we first met in 1981.

Jean-Loup Chappelet and Brenda Kübler-Mabbott
Lausanne, Switzerland and Crest, France, December 2007

Abbreviations

ANOC	Association of National Olympic Committees (www.acnolympic.org)
AGFIS	General Association of International Sports Federations (www.agfisonline.com)
ASOIF	Association of Summer Olympic International Federations (www.asoif.com)
AIOWSF	Association of International Olympic Winter Sports Federations
CAS	Court of Arbitration for Sport (www.tas-cas.org)
EU	European Union (www.ec.europa.eu/sport)
FIFA	Fédération internationale de Football Association (www.fifa.com)
IAAF	International Association of Athletics Federations (ww.iaaf.org)
IF	International Sports Federation
IOC	International Olympic Committee (www.olympic.org)
ICRC	International Committee of the Red Cross (www.icrc.org)
IPC	International Paralympic Committee (www.paralympic.org)
NF	National Sports Federation
NOC	National Olympic Committee
OCOG	Organising Committee for the Olympic Games
TOP	The Olympic Partners
USOC	United States Olympic Committee (www.usoc.org)
UCI	International Cycling Union (www.uci.ch)
UN	United Nations (www.un.org/themes/sport)
UNESCO	United Nations Educational, Scientific and Cultural Organization (www.unesco.org)
WADA	World Anti-Doping Agency (www.wada-ama.org)

Introduction

The stadium, adorned with flags from throughout the world, is packed. On a central arena, thousands of performers present a rich, colorful spectacle to spectators both present and the millions throughout the planet watching it on television. At last, the parade of nations starts, beginning with the Greek delegation and continuing with those of every nation in the world, with that of the host country bringing up the rear. The world watches them, acclaims them, admires them. Then, the mood turns from festive to solemn, to dignified, as of the moment when a Head of State rises and proclaims a single phrase announcing the opening of sports competitions to celebrate a new Olympiad of the modern era. Bearers bring a white flag with five colored rings into the arena to the sound of the Olympic hymn, and it is raised high above the stadium. An athlete and an official take the Olympic oath. The world listens. Suddenly, a runner enters the stadium, holding aloft a torch that was lit by the rays of sun in Olympia, Greece, and then carried by a series of bearers, often for thousands of miles, before reaching what will be its unique home for sixteen days. The flame lights a cauldron that will burn, a visible and striking symbol of the sports competitions, for their entire duration. It will only be at the closing ceremony that this symbolic fire will be extinguished, marking the end of this, another edition of an event that has moved human hearts and souls for over a century. The world looks on, spellbound as the flame leaps forth, and then settles in to watch the athletes' exploits over the coming days: to share their joys, their sorrows, their emotions, their triumphs.

Who is not familiar with the Olympic Games, with their ceremonies, their symbolism, the athletes' achievements, and even some of the less glorious but highly publicized events surrounding them? But what about the system that has enabled the modern Games to go on from Olympiad to Olympiad since their renovation? Few individuals are aware of the workings of the International Olympic Committee (IOC), despite the fact that various journalists and writers have attempted to shed light on it—often in the form of highly controversial articles or works. Very few academic works exist, however, on what we shall call the Olympic system and more specifically on its governance. The aim of this book is thus to analyze how this system functions, how it is governed, and whether—and under what conditions—it will be able to survive in the twenty-first century. There can be no doubt that the major changes that have taken place in sport over recent decades and the problems such as doping, violence, and corruption all constitute a very real threat to the survival of this magnificent, unique event and the system currently behind its celebration.

The book begins (Chapter 1) with an overview of the Olympic system and its main actors organized in three categories: the established actors, the new actors and the regulators. We start by outlining the five pillars of the Olympic system (IOC, Organising Committees of the Olympic Games, National Olympic Committees, International Sports Federations, and National Sports Federations). All of these non-profit organizations could be likened to the five symbolic rings of the Olympic movement, but we interlink them in a different way. We continue with the new public and private actors (governments, sponsors, media, sport leagues) that have taken on an increasingly significant role in the system since the 1970s.

To conclude, we outline three recently founded, supposedly independent regulatory bodies that serve as "watchdogs" for the system in matters of doping and stakeholders' rights.

This overview, summarized in the form of a diagram comprising 11 rings, reveals the complexity of the relationships within the governance of Olympic sport.

Chapter 2 provides a more in-depth presentation of the central organization within the Olympic system, i.e. the IOC, a club of around 100 men and handful of women from about 70 nationalities. After a historical overview of its growth during the twentieth century under the leadership of only seven presidents, we describe the committee's organization and its administration in its present form, following the major reform that took place after the so-called Salt Lake City scandal in 1999 and the election of a new president in 2001. The tables include the IOC's organization chart (never previously published), and its revenues, expenses, and assets.

The next two chapters deal with two actors without which the IOC and the Olympic Games could not exist as we know them. Chapter 3 deals with the National Olympic Committees (NOCs), which are recognized by the IOC as its territorial ambassadors. Their mission is explained, and one of their main sources of financing—an organization called Olympic Solidarity—is presented. Chapter 4 deals with the International Sports Federations (IFs), their recognition and their mission. The General Association of IFs and the World Games (organized for non-Olympic sports) are briefly described.

Chapter 5 analyzes the main product and "cash cow" of the Olympic system, i.e. the Summer and Winter Games. It explains how, as of 1896, Pierre de Coubertin completely reengineered this ancient Greek religious gathering and the way in which it has evolved to become a massive global festival. Statistics of the Summer and Winter Games for the last twenty years are provided. The process for becoming a host city is explained, as are the structure and responsibilities of their Organising Committees (OCOGs). Finally, we explore the thorny and much-debated issue of the "gigantism" of the Games, concluding with some reflections on their future.

In Chapter 6, we review relationships between governments and the Olympic system. We start with the status of the IOC in Switzerland, the country that has hosted its headquarters since 1915. We then review the links between the Olympic system and the United Nations system, which have developed considerably over the last two decades. The question of sport within the European institutions is then briefly examined, including the involvement of the Council of Europe and of the European Union and their courts. Finally, a new legal framework inspired by those of the International Red Cross Movement is proposed with a view to improving cooperation between the Olympic system and governments.

The three current regulators of the Olympic system are covered in Chapter 7. The recent historical development and current functioning of the Court of Arbitration for Sport (created in 1983), the World Anti-Doping Agency (1999), and the IOC Ethics Commission (1999) are presented in detail. We also compare these regulators with similar bodies in other domains.

The concluding chapter provides reflections on the governance of the IOC and of the Olympic system. It then moves on to propose five principles that would be of benefit to all sport organizations when dealing with the myriad changes in world sport and continuing to promote this philosophy of sport that is Olympism.

The Olympic system has become extremely complex: power, money, and image have inevitably brought far-reaching changes on what was once a gathering of athletes from throughout the world. Our ambition here is to clarify its workings and to provide useful information on the organizations that run it, with particular emphasis on the International Olympic Committee. We believe that this work has a place between official publications issued by the organizations in question and the commercial works that tend to appear during the period running up to each edition of the Games. Beyond various historical works and those that are strongly biased, we felt that it was time to provide an overall view of what has become a global phenomenon reaching billions of people on every occasion that the Olympic flag flies over a stadium.

1 A brief overview of the Olympic system

This chapter takes the form of a brief presentation of the current actors within the Olympic system: the five established actors, the four new actors for whom the system has held considerable interest for some 30 years, and the three main regulatory bodies set up relatively recently.

The established actors

The entities that have contributed towards the preparation and running of the Olympic Games for over a century can be divided into five types of closely related actors within a robust structure. The overall term of "Olympic Movement" is used to encompass them all.

The central actor is the International Olympic Committee (IOC), founded by Pierre de Coubertin and his friends in 1894: it plays the leading role in the movement. The IOC recognizes the other actors, and partially finances them.

Despite its progressively expanding role and influence in the course of the twentieth century, the IOC's activities remain focused on the Olympic Games, to which it holds full legal rights thanks to the worldwide registration of the numerous trademarks related thereto (interlaced rings, flag, flame, motto, etc.). For the last 30 years, those rights have generated considerable, exponentially growing income.

The IOC's stated priority is to promote the Olympic movement and to reinforce the unity among its various entities (sport organizations) and individuals (athletes, coaches, fans, etc.) who accept the guidance of the Olympic Charter that it has drawn up. According to this charter, however, the IOC recognizes entities alone. Individuals (often volunteers) are thus only a part of the Olympic movement via their own organizations (e.g. athletes are members of their club, which is a member of their National Federation, which in turn is a member of the corresponding International Federation). The only exception to this indirect form of adhesion to the Olympic movement is that of the IOC members, since the IOC is above all an association of individuals: the men (and women since 1981) who are co-opted to this exclusive club. The Organising Committees of the Olympic Games (OCOGs) constitute a second type of actor. Despite not being permanent—their lifespan does not exceed the around ten years required to organize a Winter or Summer Games—they are central to the system and permit it to be self-financing thanks to the revenues inherent to organizing the Games. An OCOG is created by the public authorities and the National Olympic Committee of the country concerned in the months following the designation of the host city for the Games by the IOC. The OCOG is closely linked to the local, regional, and national governments of the relevant country for all kinds of organizational issues (construction work, transport, diplomacy, police, customs, etc.). The IOC is always working with three or four OCOGs of forthcoming Games at any given point.

The International Sports Federations (IFs) represent a third kind of actor. They govern their respective sport and disciplines on a worldwide level. A distinction is made between those whose sports are on the program of the Summer or Winter Games (35 in 2008), and those whose sports are not on the program but are nevertheless recognized by the IOC (29 in 2008). There are a further 25 IFs that are members of the General Association of International Sports Federations (GAISF), founded in 1967, but are not part of the Olympic movement (i.e. recognized by the IOC).

The Olympic IFs receive part of the broadcasting and marketing rights generated by the Games. The recognized IFs receive subsidies from the IOC. The IFs' activities are by no means restricted to the Games, but few of them organize world championships that are able to bring in major revenues of their own.

The National Olympic Committees (NOCs) represent a fourth type of actor in the Olympic system. They are the territorial representatives of the IOC, although since the IOC is not a confederation of NOCs they are independent from the IOC from a legal point of view. The IOC recognizes them as the sole entities entitled to qualify athletes from their territory to take part in the Games. In 2008, the NOCs number 205.

Like the IFs, the NOCs receive part of the rights from the Games. This distribution is, however, not carried out directly, but by means of an entity called Olympic Solidarity: a department within the IOC. The NOCs are often subsidized by their government although they are called upon to preserve their autonomy. To an increasing extent, they also serve as a "confederation of national sports federations," with Great Britain being a notable exception.

Since 1980, the NOCs have come together within a (world) Association of NOCs (ANOC), which encompasses five continental associations facilitating the distribution of Olympic Solidarity funds. Three of these continental associations govern continental games (Pan-American, Asian and African Games).

The National Sports Federations (NFs) are the fifth and last type of actor within the Olympic movement. They unite the clubs for a specific sport in a given country and thus the licensed athletes from that country. The NFs may be recognized on a national level by the NOC of their country and/or on an international level by the IF for their sport. In some cases, this double recognition is not obtained and the athletes concerned are thus not eligible to take part in the Olympic Games.

These five different actors can be shown in the form of five rings, arranged differently from the interlaced Olympic rings (see Figure 1.1).[1] The Olympic Charter, drawn up by the IOC, is the statutory basis for their actions while the athletes constitute their main *raison d'être*. The arrows denote the relationships among the autonomous entities that form the "classical" Olympic system.

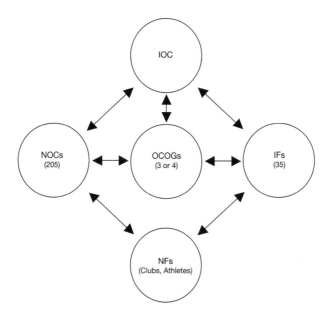

Figure 1.1 The classical Olympic system.

The new actors

All the actors within this system, including the IOC, are non-profit organizations in accordance with the legislation of the country in which they have their registered offices. Over the last 30 years however, these actors have, to an increasing extent, interacted with four further types of actors with a legal form that differs from their own.

Governments and inter-governmental organizations under public law constitute the first such actor. In recent years, the Olympic system has needed to tackle new questions of public order. In other words, the "sports order" that it has patiently built up during the twentieth century is increasingly confronted by national and international public authorities and by the legislation they edict. For example, the European Union (EU) and its member states have been particularly active regarding sport since 1995, when the European Court of Justice rendered its judgment on the famous "Bosman case" that caused upheaval within European soccer, a subject covered in Chapter 6.

The 1990s also represented a watershed for the Olympic system because of the rapid growth in problems related to doping, violence, and corruption within sport, which led governments around the world to become involved in issues that they had previously left the sports authorities to handle. (The Council of Europe, an inter-governmental organization comprising 47 European states, had been highly active in these areas since the 1970s.)

Multinationals active in international sponsoring and that maintain commercial relations with the IOC and the IFs represent another type of emerging actor within the extended Olympic system and within worldwide sport in general. Examples here are the twelve corporations belonging to the IOC's TOP (The Olympic Partners) marketing program (which includes Coca-Cola, Kodak, Visa, etc.) and the major broadcasters and television unions (National Broadcasting Corporation and its affiliates in the USA, the European Broadcasting Union, etc.). Given the broadcasting rights they pay to the IOC, the broadcasters could be considered as sponsors to the Olympic system in their own right. They even have the power to attract other financial partners since they convey the images of the Games to the world.

National sponsors are another type of new actor, and work with their NOC, NFs, and the OCOG (where applicable) by means of sponsorship contracts restricted to a national territory. In Switzerland, for example, the soft drinks manufacturer Rivella has been sponsoring the Swiss Olympic Association and several Swiss sports federations within the NOC. The regional and national media (written press, radio, television) also fall within this category if they sponsor the national sports movement in their region or country or buy broadcasting rights to their competitions.

National and international sponsors are usually limited, profit-making companies.

Finally, there is a fourth type of actor that has been emerging strongly over around the last 20 years, in cooperation or competition with the NFs and IFs: Leagues of professional teams or athletes. This category consists of international athletes' groups such as the Association of Tennis Professionals (ATP), the Women's Tennis Association (WTA), the Professional Golfers' Association (PGA) or the lesser-known Association of Surfing Professionals (ASP), Association of [Beach] Volleyball Professionals (AVP), and the Cyberathlete Professional League (CPL). Also included in this type are professional leagues for soccer or other team sports such as those present in most European countries and whose most prestigious clubs have attempted to set up continental leagues independently of the relevant European or International Federation (e.g. the "G14" uniting 18 major European soccer clubs or the ULEB Union of European Basketball Leagues).

Beyond Europe, the powerful American professional team leagues also belong to the above category. The National Basketball Association (NBA), the National Hockey League (NHL), the National Football League (NFL), the Major League of Baseball (MLB), and Major League Soccer (MLS) share a common objective, i.e. profit for their members, owners and/or shareholders. At times, the leagues cooperate with the classical Olympic system regarding the participation of their athletes at the Games.

All of the actors that we have just described, and that are peripheral to the classical Olympic system, are shown in the diagram of the extended Olympic system (Figure 1.2). The rings have been organized in this way in order to show that actors that were once distant from the Olympic system and not involved with it to a great extent or at all are today taking on a growing importance and establishing close links with the heart of the associative sports movement. The new actors are all external partners with which the classical Olympic system must now contend. Together, all nine types of actor constitute a new, expanded Olympic system.

Since a system is characterized more by its interactions than its elements, we shall now present these (new) forms of interaction, beginning with those between governments and the Olympic system.

In most countries, strong relations exist between the government and the NOC since the latter selects the team that will represent the country

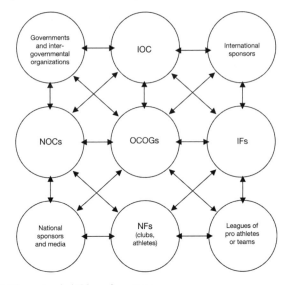

Figure 1.2 The extended Olympic system.

at the Games. Since the 1960s and the independence of former European colonies, taking part in the Games has been seen as a sign of sovereignty as strong or perhaps even stronger than being admitted to the United Nations (UN). The opening and closing ceremonies of the Games are, in fact, a unique opportunity for the over 200 countries and territories who take part to draw international attention to their existence, and in a peaceful, positive manner.

Interaction between an NOC and its government also exists on a level of the national sports policy, since the NOC of a country is often granted a specific role that is laid down within national legislation. This is the case, for example, in France, the USA, Australia, and Switzerland.

In a great majority of countries, however, the interaction takes the form of the NOC being dependent on the government, which attributes a subsidy, largely for operating costs, to it. This is notably the case in many developing countries whose ministers appoint the NOC executives, or at times occupy the posts in person. This approach is very much contrary to the spirit of the Olympic Charter, which states that NOCs must preserve their autonomy and resist all pressures of any kind, including but not limited to political, legal, religious or economic pressures (Rule 28.2.6). In practice, however, it is extremely rare for the IOC to withdraw recognition of an NOC temporarily on the grounds of public or political interference.

It would nevertheless appear that today many NOCs are succeeding in freeing themselves from financial dependency on their governments thanks to payments from Olympic Solidarity. This income, which reaches several thousand US dollars per year even for the smaller NOCs, is intended to cover normal operating costs and is granted in addition to provision of courses to train NOC staff and the financing of (minimum) eight athletes and officials to take part in the Games. Although the amount for operating costs may appear low, it nevertheless represents a fortune in many countries. Furthermore, by joining the IOC's TOP marketing program, the NOCs have the opportunity to earn commission in proportion to the value of the sponsoring market for their territory and the number of athletes they send to the Games.

If the Olympic Games take place on its territory, an NOC is closely involved right from the bid phase, and is entitled to participate in the OCOG. The local, regional and national governments must also become closely involved, since the Games have become a source of major changes in terms of developing land, economy and society. Hosting the Olympic Games also represents international prestige for a country. As already mentioned, the forms of interaction between an OCOG and the various levels of the state are mandatory for issues such as security, transport, customs, etc. Over time, OCOGs have thus become para-public entities within which the state—in the largest sense—plays a major role.

In the same way, the increasing importance of the Olympic Games and of sport in general has led to development in the area of relations between the IOC and governments. When the IOC was founded in 1894, Coubertin already stated a wish to see such relationships develop. His successors, however, imbued with a philosophy according to which sport had nothing to do with politics, did everything within their power to restrict such relations to a minimum. It was only as of the 1970s when it became necessary for the IOC to pay considerable attention to governments, notably because of the boycotts linked to the question of apartheid that targeted the 1972 Munich and 1976 Montreal Games. The boycotts were orchestrated by the Supreme Council for Sport in Africa (SCSA), the sports branch of the Organization of African Unity (OAU), and propagated to some extent by the United Nations Organization. The United Nations Educational, Scientific and Cultural Organization (UNESCO), which at the time was strongly influenced by tiersmondiste ideas, even imagined at one point that it could benefit from the IOC's difficulties to implement a new world sports order. An International Charter of Physical Education and Sport was thus adopted in 1978 within the framework of the Member States' first meeting of Ministers and Senior Officials Responsible for Physical Education and Sport (MINEPS).

The UNESCO's discomfiture in the 1980s, plus intensive diplomatic activity by the IOC President in office, overcame the threats despite the last vestiges of the cold war that had led to partial boycotts of the 1980, 1984, and 1988 Games in Moscow, Los Angeles, and Seoul respectively. The media and financial success of the 1984 and 1988 Games incited a great many cities to bid for the organization of subsequent Summer and Winter Games. Governments thus began to adopt more of a stance of applicants to the IOC prior to becoming its partners within the framework of operating the OCOGs.

In 1998, problems of doping in sport led several countries, notably the United States, Australia, and certain European Union states, to call for major reforms within the IOC with regard to the governance of world sport. Setting up the World Anti-Doping Agency (WADA) was the subject of intensive negotiations between the IOC and the aforementioned governments, with the outcome of parity representation within the agency on the part of the Olympic movement and governments.

At the end of the twentieth century, the IOC underwent upheaval because of a scandal surrounding IOC members rigging elections of host cities. This concerned the 2002 Games in Salt Lake City but also those of Atlanta (1996), Nagano (1998), and Sydney (2000). The uproar forced the IOC to restructure in 1999, under pressure from the sponsors, media and governments. The IOC President in office was also compelled to appear as a witness before the US Congress. During the same period, governments also realized that their relations with the Olympic system required strengthening and greater institutionalization, in a more balanced way.

Relationships between the broadcasters and the Olympic system date back to the 1960s, when the first broadcasting rights were negotiated, but really gained in significance in the 1970s and 1980s. As of the Munich and Sapporo Games (1972), the OCOGs began to receive a considerable portion of broadcasting income and initiated programs to obtain sponsorship. For their part, the NOCs also launched marketing programs with national sponsors, which subsidized their Olympic teams. Similarly, the national federations for the main sports began to sign agreements with national partners.

In 1985, the IOC founded "The Olympic Programme" (TOP), later to become "The Olympic Partners." Administered by an agency by the name of International Sport and Leisure (ISL) until 1992, it permitted the around 12 multinationals that had joined the scheme to be associated with the Winter and Summer Games for four years through their presence on the territories of all participating NOCs. In addition, the IOC authorized these same multinationals—against payment of a sum that today is of around 60 million US dollars—to use the Olympic rings and all the associated emblems and objects (posters, mascots, slogans, etc.) within their international communication operations, both prior to and during the Games.

The relations between the IOC and these multinationals thus became close, since the partners to the program provided considerable funding. Their influence has become clear within the higher echelons of Olympism, even if the IOC is reluctant to admit it. Coca-Cola, Kodak, Panasonic, and Visa have been part of this extremely exclusive club since the beginning. Some companies, however—including multinationals—prefer to deal with a specific OCOG alone. In such cases, they must negotiate with each NOC on whose territory they wish to advertize (except, of course, that of the country where the Games will take place).

Interaction between the IOC and its main broadcasters (or groups thereof) has also gained impetus since 1995, with the signature of contracts covering several Olympiads.[2] The European Broadcasting Union (EBU) enjoys special relations with the IOC because since 1956 it has been broadcasting the Games to all its member countries, and since 1992 including those in Eastern Europe. After a long relationship with the US network American Broadcasting Corporation (ABC) from 1964 through 1988, the IOC attributed the US broadcasting rights for the Summer Games—by far the most lucrative—to the National Broadcasting Corporation (NBC) as of 1992 and through 2012. The extent of the sums paid by the broadcasters makes them sponsors in their own right, and whose importance is at least equal to those within the TOP program.

In parallel to the development of closer relations between the IOC and international sponsors, the IFs (which today benefit from TOP financing whereas this was not the case when TOP was launched) have also developed sponsoring programs related to their own championships. The first of them to establish links with a series of multinationals, even before the IOC did so, was without doubt the FIFA (soccer), rapidly followed by the FIBA (basketball), and the IAAF (athletics). All of them received assistance from ISL, as did other IFs during the 1990s. Among the sponsors to the IFs are some of those who are also IOC partners (such as Coca-Cola) but also, at times, their competitors. The credit card company Visa sponsors the IOC, for example, whereas MasterCard sponsored the FIFA until 2006.

Sports leagues, the final category of new actors in world sport, maintain relations with the NFs, OCOGs, and IFs. As of the 1950s, the national federations of team sports created national leagues in order to organize national championships in their sports, some of which were becoming distinctly oriented towards professional athletes. The first case was that of soccer, for which most European countries have a national league in parallel to their national federation, which is nevertheless attached to the federation to some degree. Soccer was followed by basketball and, in certain European countries volleyball, ice hockey, handball, rugby, etc.

In North America, the major team sports had already created professional league structures prior to the Second World War. This was the case of baseball, American football, basketball and ice hockey. The Major Soccer League was created after the 1994 FIFA World Cup in the USA. Some sports even have several leagues per region or per level.

These North American leagues have no particular link to the national federations for their sport in the USA, which are often somewhat rudimentary. Fully independent and private, the leagues nevertheless maintained relations with the IFs for their sport as of the 1990s in order to permit their best (professional) players to take part in the Olympic Games under their country's colors. It was by this means that the US National Basketball Association (NBA) and the corresponding IF (FIBA) agreed for the US "Dream Team" to take part as of the 1992 Games, in close cooperation with the IOC and the Barcelona OCOG. The National Hockey League (NHL) interrupted its championships in 1998, 2002, and 2006 in order for its best players, from several North American and European countries, to take part in the Nagano, Salt Lake City, and Turin Games under the control of the International Ice Hockey Federation.

Although baseball has been on the Olympic program since 1992, no such agreement has been reached between the Association of Major League Baseball (MLB) players and the International Baseball Federation concerning the Summer Games, which coincide with the North American season. This fact might explain, at least in part, why baseball (and softball) were dropped from the Olympic program as of 2012.

Some of these professional leagues (the NBA and NHL in particular) even decided to compete with the relevant IFs by trying to create European versions of their championships, but so far without a great deal of success. The main difference from a purely sports angle between European and North American leagues is that American teams at the bottom of the table are not relegated to a lower league at the end of the season: it is a so-called "closed league system."

The idea of introducing a North American type of system in European soccer, involving the best clubs on the continent, was launched by the company Media Partners in 1998. To date, however, the notion has met with fierce opposition from the FIFA and the Union of European Football Associations (UEFA). The UEFA sees it to be in direct competition with the various European cups, and in particular the most prestigious of them, the Champions' League. This competition has in fact been reworked in order to better satisfy the major European clubs. The clubs have not formally abandoned the idea of creating other, potentially more lucrative, competition formats. Some 18 major European clubs such as Manchester United and Real Madrid have united under the name G14 (since they numbered 14 at the outset) in order to defend their interests and to develop projects for the future. They attacked the FIFA for abusing its dominant position before the Swiss Competition Commission, since both organizations have their registered offices in Switzerland. The G14 also supported the actions of a Belgian club regarding a dispute on a European Union level concerning the lending of club players to national teams. In 2008, the G14 decided to disband. It will be replaced by a larger European Clubs Association which will be recognized by UEFA.

Leagues of athletes are an extremely ancient notion dating from ancient times. For the time being, they have only become popular in some individual sports with high media impact, notably tennis, golf, surf, and beach volleyball. In other disciplines such as snowboard, figure skating, and alpine skiing, they have met with resistance on the part of the relevant IFs and eventually more or less disappeared.

Participation at the Olympic Games has been the subject of negotiations between athletes' leagues and the corresponding IFs. This was the case for snowboarders in Nagano (1998) and tennis players in Sydney (2000). Although tennis was reintroduced at the Games in 1988, the players were able to collect ATP and WTA points in the Olympic tournament for the first time in Sydney (2000). This permitted them to avoid being penalized in terms of points and rankings if they were absent from a circuit tournament scheduled to take place concurrently. One of the reasons for not including golf in the Olympic program until now is that the PGA players would not guarantee their golfers' participation.

Some athletes' unions also exist, notably in soccer, cycling, and athletics. To date, however, they have had little real impact on the relevant IFs, often due to a lack of unity.

This brief overview of interaction between the classical Olympic system and the four new, major actors within world sport reveals the extent to which the extended Olympic system has become a vast network that encompasses a broad range of partners: public, private, and associative, and national, international, and transnational. No single partner really dominates world sport. All of them govern jointly, but have varying degrees of power and differing resources, meaning the equilibrium is a precarious one. This equilibrium is, however, partially preserved by three regulators that appeared towards the end of the twentieth century in order to uphold—if possible—the values and interests of sport and of both amateur and professional athletes.

The regulators

The first sports regulator to be created—the Court of Arbitration for Sport (CAS)—was founded by the IOC in 1983 and began operations by mid 1984. The CAS is covered in detail in Chapter 6 but we shall summarize its function here.

The CAS was set up to resolve disputes concerning sport by means of arbitration. This made it possible to avoid turning to state courts, which were often slow, expensive, and not always well informed regarding the specific characteristics of sport and the Olympic system. The model adopted was that of the arbitration courts of international Chambers of Commerce. Curiously, however, the CAS handles far more cases that oppose an athlete with his or her federation (notably for questions of doping) than those between sports organizations and commercial enterprises.

This private court has two divisions: the Ordinary Arbitration Division handles disputes relating to sport submitted to it directly and voluntarily by the parties. The Appeals Division serves as a supreme court for all jurisdictional organs of the IFs and NOCs that wish to recognize it as such. The CAS seat is in Lausanne, but it has decentralized offices in Australia and in the USA. The applicable law is that of Switzerland unless the parties both agree to apply that of another country. The arbitration is based on the Swiss law on arbitration and on the CAS Code of Sports-related Arbitration. Its decisions have the same force as those issued by civil courts, and the parties formally undertake to apply them as of the moment that the arbitration agreement is signed.

The World Anti-Doping Agency (WADA) was founded in Lausanne in December 1999 following a recommendation by the World Conference on Doping in Sport held in February of the same year. The Conference, also held in Lausanne, was organized by the IOC, notably in response to the scandal surrounding the Tour de France cycling race in 1998. The race had been virtually halted by the "Festina Case," named after a team that systematically used doping. Like the CAS, the

WADA is covered extensively in Chapter 6 but we shall provide a short overview here.

The WADA's objective is to promote, coordinate, and supervise on an international basis the fight against all forms of doping in sport. Composed and financed equally by the Olympic movement and the world's governments, it has coordinated the development and drafting of the World Anti-Doping Code, which harmonizes regulations relating to doping in all sports and all countries. The code was adopted in 2003 at a conference uniting the parties involved and revised during a second conference in 2007, taking the first four years of implementation into account. Both the code and the existence of the WADA are validated by an international convention adopted by the member states of UNESCO in 2005, which are gradually ratifying it and thus incorporating it within their national legislation. In its code, the WADA mentions the CAS as the sole recourse for cases of doping that, in fact, have been a majority of cases the CAS has dealt with since it began its activity in 1984.

The IOC Ethics Commission—the third regulator—is also covered in Chapter 6 so we shall provide only a short summary of it here.

The commission was founded in 1999 following the discovery that several IOC members behaved improperly regarding the candidature of Salt Lake City to organize the Olympic Winter Games. It is charged with defining and updating a framework of ethical principles, including a code of ethics, which serve as a basis for investigating complaints raised in relation to the non-respect of such principles by IOC members, NOCs, candidature or organizing committees, and in general, people involved in the Olympic movement. The commission does not however deal with doping cases by athletes. Since the election of a new IOC President in 2001, the Ethics Commission has taken a central role in the functioning of the Olympic system, leading to the expulsion or resignation of five IOC members and the reprimand of several others.

The Ethics Commission is composed of nine individuals, no more than four of whom are IOC members and at least five prominent personalities known for their international reputation. These individuals are designated by the IOC President and ratified by the IOC Executive Board. The commission has been chaired by IOC members since its foundation. A Special Representative, who is a senior member of the IOC Administration, assists the commission as well as the Olympic organizations and collaborates with them to enhance ethical standards in the Olympic movement.

It must be pointed out that the Ethics Commission remains an IOC commission. As such it only takes conclusions and recommendations, which it submits to the IOC Executive Board. When it is charged with a complaint or a denunciation, the Ethics Commission undertakes a confidential investigation. A report drafted by the special representative is presented to the members of the commission and after deliberation, a decision is adopted by the means of conclusions and recommendations. This decision is delivered to the IOC Executive Board, through the IOC President, and remains confidential until the IOC Executive Board has reached a decision. The Ethics Commission cannot be considered as an independent body.

At the beginning of the twenty-first century, the CAS, the WADA, and the IOC Ethics Commission have become de facto regulators of world sport, but are nevertheless closely linked to the functioning of the Olympic system in terms of the men and women who make up their organs (see Figure 1.3).

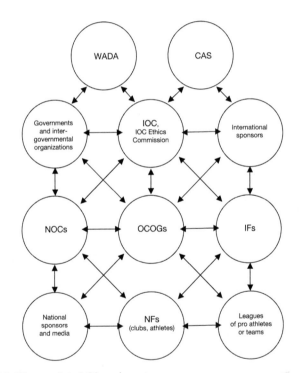

Figure 1.3 The regulated Olympic system.

2 The International Olympic Committee

This chapter gives an overview of the International Olympic Committee: its members, human and financial resources, and its governance structure. The IOC Administration, i.e. the staff who work daily in Lausanne, Switzerland, to further the goals of Olympism under the IOC members' supervision, is also outlined. The economics of the IOC are explained in the last section (revenues, expenditure and assets).

The IOC and its members

The IOC and its members—or the "cardinals of sport" as they are at times called—are described in the section below.

Structure and functioning

The International Olympic Committee is the non-governmental organization (NGO) that "manages" the Olympic Games. This responsibility—much envied today—was conferred on it by the Congress for the Renewal of the Olympic Games that took place in Paris on 23 June 1894, on the initiative of Pierre de Coubertin and some of his acquaintances from major sporting societies in France, England, and the United States plus a few from other countries (a dozen in total).

After the congress, Coubertin brought together fifteen of his friends within an "International Committee for the Olympic Games," of which he acted as the head of the secretariat. The chairman was Demetrius Vikelas of Greece because the first Games of the new era, in 1896, had been awarded to Athens. Coubertin had envisaged the start of the new cycle in Paris in 1900, where in fact the second edition was to take place. Since then, only the two World Wars have interrupted the four-year cycle.

The Games celebrated their centennial in Atlanta, United States, in 1996 and returned to their roots in Athens in 2004 before moving to

Beijing in 2008, and London in 2012. As of 1924, the Winter Games preceded their summer counterparts earlier in the same year until 1994, when it was decided to alternate the events. The Games—Winter then Summer—are now held at two-year intervals: Albertville 1992, Barcelona 1992, Lillehammer 1994, Atlanta 1996, etc.

To the public, the history of the IOC was closely linked to the Olympic Games for several decades because the committee remained barely visible beyond the actual event. Although the Games grew rapidly, they were organized by cities elected by the IOC several years previously, yet with little financial or logistical support from the committee being possible. It was only after the Second World War, with the emergence of the Cold War and the independence of former European colonies, that the IOC gained recognition on the international scene and became a genuine NGO approached by nation states with a view to being permitted to take part in the Games.

Today, the IOC presents itself as follows:

> The International Olympic Committee (IOC), created in 1894, is a non-governmental organization with volunteer members who represent its work around the world, and an administrative staff based in Lausanne, Switzerland. The IOC and its 205 National Olympic Committees (NOCs) worldwide promote the Olympic Movement, whose vision is to contribute to building a peaceful and better world by educating youth through sport. In addition to selecting the host city and coordinating the staging of the Olympic Games, the IOC and NOCs collaborate with a range of organizations and their members in the public and private sectors to place sport at the service of society. The main goal is to promote the values of Olympism, which include excellence, respect and friendship. For more information please visit *www.olympic.org*.

Despite its current role as a global institution, the IOC remains, as it was in Coubertin's time, an association of individuals—its members— who are supposed to represent and promote the IOC's interests in their countries and not vice versa. The men (and women since 1981) of the IOC have grown in number from 15 at its origins to 100 at the committee's centennial in 1994. In 1999, the maximum number of members was limited to 115 during a major reform that created two categories of them: there are 70 so-called "independent" members (maximum) and 45 who officiate as a result of the office they hold (usually president) of an International Federation (IF), a National Olympic Committee (NOC) or a member of the Athletes Commission (15 for each category). Certain independent members may also be, or become, the president of an NOC or IF.

Honorary members (former members affected by the age limit and with at least ten years of membership) and Members of Honor (who receive the distinction for their contribution to the Olympic cause) also exist, but do not have the right to vote.

All the members are co-opted (i.e. elected through secret ballots) by existing members following proposals by the IOC Executive Board, which first receives cooption proposals from the Nominations Commission (and from the IOC President prior to the foundation of the said commission in 1999). A candidate who was proposed for election has failed to be subsequently elected on a single occasion, in 2001.

Before being formally co-opted at the end of an edition of the Games, 12 members representing the athletes are first elected by the athletes participating in the Summer Games (eight members in total, over two successive editions) and the Winter Games (four, two per edition) by means of a vote organized at the Olympic Village. The vote is by secret ballot, and by simple majority. Every participating NOC may present one active athlete for the vote. These elected Olympians are the only truly democratic element within the IOC's supreme organ, the general assembly of the IOC members that in Olympic jargon is known as the "Session."

The purview of the IOC members co-opted by the IFs and NOCs is linked to their leading role within those organizations. If they leave office, they automatically lose their membership. Hein Verbruggen of the Netherlands, who was the president of the International Cycling Union (UCI) until 2005 had to be re-elected as an IOC member in 2006 in his capacity as a vice-president of the UCI. This representative role of certain members as opposed to other, "independent" members was a system that was begun in 1992 in connection with some IFs. It constitutes a fundamental change to the very nature of the IOC, in which all members were once supposed to represent the IOC and Olympism in their countries and not their organization in the IOC. Furthermore, it also grants the three central pillars of the Olympic movement (IFs, NOCs, and athletes) a certain degree of leverage.

Originally, IOC members were co-opted for life unless they were forced or chose to retire. An age limit of 75 was introduced in 1966, lowered to 72 in 1975 and then raised to 80 in 1995, thus permitting Juan Antonio Samaranch, born in 1920, to stand for the presidency again in 1997.

In 1999, following the scandal surrounding the awarding of the 2002 Games to Salt Lake City, the age limit was fixed at 70, and the period in office for independent members was restricted to eight years although reelection is possible, for a similar period in office, until the age limit.

All the reforms were voted in while preserving acquired rights, meaning that in 2008, the IOC still includes two life members (co-opted prior to 1966). The mandates of the existing members in 1999 were prolonged by eight, nine or ten years as long as they were not subject to the age limit before (following a draw of names and so that the members would not all be eligible for reelection at the same time).

In 2007, all the first members whose period in office was due to expire— and including the current IOC President—were reelected by a show of hands, which was a departure from the secret ballot instituted since 2000.

The IOC is a simple association under Swiss law with its registered headquarters in Lausanne (see Chapter 6 for more details regarding the IOC's legal status). Its statutes are known as the "Olympic Charter" and also contain all the rules applying to the NOCs, IFs and the Olympic Games. A preamble lays down the "General Principles" that provide a definition of Olympism and the Olympic Movement. The charter has evolved over the Olympiads: the name itself was only adopted in 1978. It underwent a major revision in 1990 since its method of constitution by means of successive amendments made by the Session meant it lacked coherence. Major modifications concerning the members were adopted following the major crisis of 1999. A complete revision was carried out in 2004.

As in any association, the IOC's general assembly (the Session) is the supreme authority. In 2004, 10 years after the IOC's centennial, the IOC consisted of 124 active members (112 men and 12 women) in the following categories: 81 independent, 18 for the IFs, 13 for the NOCs, and 12 for the athletes. The average age was 61. By the end of the 2007 Session, the number of members was exactly 115 as required by the Olympic Charter since 1999. See Table 2.1 for the origin of the members.

The socio-professional origin of the members has never, to date, been the subject of any kind of systematic study. When reading their official biography, it is possible to distinguish the following categories of member: those from reigning families, independent professionals

Table 2.1 IOC members per categories and continents (in July 2007)

	Independent	*NOCs*	*IFs*	*Athletes*	*Totals*
Africa	14	1	1	4	20
Americas	11	3	1	2	17
Asia	22	2	1	0	25
Europe	31	1	10	6	48
Oceania	3	1	0	1	5
Totals	81	8	13	13	115

(lawyers, physicians), (former) political figures, leading civil servants, judges, members of the military, industrialists, top-level athletes, and some teachers (notably of physical education).

Apart from electing or dismissing members, the main powers of an Ordinary IOC Session are as follows:

- To elect, by absolute majority, the IOC President for eight years and possibly to reelect him or her for four (a single reelection has been possible since the 1999 reform).
- To elect, by absolute majority, each member of the IOC Executive Board (including the four vice-presidents) for four years, and possibly for a second four-year period as vice-president (further reelections are subject to a waiting period of two years).
- To adopt or modify the "Rules" (articles) of the Olympic Charter (by two-thirds majority) and their bye-laws (by simple majority).
- To elect, by absolute majority, the Host Cities for the Olympic Games.

The IOC has only known eight presidents since its creation, thanks to the exceptional duration of the periods in office of three of them (20 years and above). Most of the presidents have come from "small" countries, and all except one was from Europe (see Table 2.2). Five of the eight belonged to the nobility (although the titles of Samaranch and Rogge were awarded following their election).

Since the Session meets only once a year (unless an Extraordinary Session is convened), major decisions are handled by the IOC's Executive Board, which meets four or five times a year. It is the real government of the IOC, and is chaired by the IOC President.

Created in 1921 with five members, the Executive Board consists of 15 members since 1999 of which four, in principle, are reserved for

Table 2.2 Table of IOC Presidents

Demetrius Vikelas	Greek	1894–1896
Pierre de Coubertin, Baron	French	1896–1925
Henri de Baillet-Latour, Count	Belgian	1925–1942
Sigfrid Edstrom	Swedish	1942–1952
Avery Brundage	American	1952–1972
Michael Morris, Lord Killanin	Irish	1972–1980
Juan Antonio Samaranch, Marquess	Spanish	1980–2001
Jacques Rogge, Count	Belgian	2001–2009*

Note

* Eligible for reelection in October 2009 for a maximum of an additional four years.

representatives of the athletes, the Summer IFs, the Winter IFs, and the NOCs. The members are usually the chairpersons of the IOC Athletes Commission, of the Association of Summer Olympic International Federations (ASOIF), of the Association of the International Olympic Winter Sports Federations (AIOWSF) and of the Association of National Olympic Committees (ANOC) unless these entities decide otherwise. The individuals are nevertheless formally elected by the Session, like the other members of the Executive Board, in order to protect the IOC from any kind of undesirable intrusion from the organizations concerned. Election to this executive body is much sought after, and there are seats available at each Session given the fact that the periods in office vary according to circumstances. The IOC members see the position as a source of power (since they are called upon to handle certain major issues) and of prestige (particularly as one of the four IOC vice-presidents).

Theoretically, the president wields little power, and his major decisions must be submitted to the following meeting of the Executive Board for ratification. According to the Olympic Charter, he may only appoint working groups and commissions (with the exception of the Executive Board and the Athletes Commission, whose members are elected).

At the end of Samaranch's presidency, over 30 commissions and permanent working groups were in place: Rogge reduced this number slightly to about 25. The commissions' titles are as follows: Juridical Affairs, Athletes, Nominations, Co-ordination of the Games (a separate commission for each of the coming three or four editions), Culture and Education, Television rights and New Media, Ethics, Women and Sport, Finance, Marketing, Medicine, Philately and Memorabilia, Press, Programme of the Olympic Games, Radio and Television, International Relations, Sport and Law, Sport and Environment, Olympic Solidarity, and Sport for All. The chairs of the various commissions—all entrusted to an IOC member—are highly sought after since they enhance that member's profile. The chairpersons of the most important commissions (Juridical Affairs, Finance, Marketing, Olympic Solidarity) are often members of the Executive Board.

In practical terms, however, the IOC President has numerous powers on a daily basis because he heads the IOC's administration. This provides him with a considerable degree of financial autonomy that permits him to spend major, non-budgeted sums that are then validated retroactively by the Finance Commission. The formula is thus of an executive presidency, brought in by Samaranch and taken over by his successor who, like Samaranch, lives in a suite at the Lausanne Palace

Hotel (although on a less regular basis). The role is a full-time one, however, and constitutes a change from the practices of former presidents who saw themselves more as "chairmen of a board of directors" (i.e. the Executive Board) who devoted relatively little time to Olympic affairs.

The IOC President nevertheless remains a non-remunerated official even though all the expenses related to carrying out his mission and his residence costs in Lausanne (notably his hotel suite and taxes), are borne by the IOC. That arrangement started with Samaranch and continued with the election of Rogge to the presidency in 2001, since the idea of a salary for the future president—discussed in 2000—had been abandoned. In 2004, the presidential residence costs amounted to US$397,000.[1]

Regular IOC members receive a *per diem* of US$1,400 during IOC meetings (US$3,000 for Executive Board members).

Roles and mission

The IOC's roles are laid down by the Olympic Charter. The Preamble and Article 1 thereof present the IOC as the "supreme authority of the Olympic movement," which is itself defined as all those individuals and entities that "agree to be guided by the Olympic Charter" and are specifically recognized by the IOC. Article 2 gives the IOC the mission "to promote Olympism throughout the world and to lead the Olympic Movement." Olympism is defined as a "philosophy of life, exalting and combining in a balanced whole the qualities of body, will and mind. Olympism seeks to create a way of life based on the joy of effort, the educational value of good example, and respect for universal fundamental ethical principles. The goal of Olympism is to place sport at the service of the harmonious development of man, with a view to promoting a peaceful society concerned with preserving human dignity" (Fundamental Principles 2 and 3).

These phrases, deep in meaning, were adopted in 1990 and at the time constituted the first official definition of the word "Olympism," a neologism developed by Coubertin to denote the ideology associated with the modern Games.

Today, the IOC sees itself as a "catalyst for collaboration."[2] It places more emphasis on its coordinating role within the Olympic movement than on one of authority, which is somewhat problematic to impose on its components, notably the IFs. In Article 3, devoted to its mission, the IOC assigns itself no less than 16 tasks concerning the development of top-level and mass sport and defending ideals for which it considers itself the guarantor, such as peace, fair play, ethics in sport, the fight against doping and all kinds of discrimination, the promotion of women, of athletes, of sustainable development and of Olympic education. This long list—a sort of "package" of concerns inherited from Olympic and sport history—would benefit from reorganization. The somewhat jumbled whole nevertheless reveals one extremely concrete task that is relegated to third position after the promotion of ethics in sport and support of the development of sports competition: "to ensure the regular celebration of the Olympic Games." For whatever it may claim, this is the principal task of the IOC, which gives rise to the four main responsibilities below:

1 To recognize one IF per "sport";
2 To recognize one NOC per "country";
3 To elect a city in charge of organizing the Summer or Winter Games every four years, and to monitor the Organising Committee for the Olympic Games (OCOG) responsible for doing so;
4 To distribute the revenues from the celebration of the Games, notably by means of Olympic Solidarity and other recognized entities.

In 2008, the IOC recognizes 35 Olympic IFs (28 for the Summer Games and seven for the Winter Games) and 29 others whose sport is not (yet) or no longer on the Olympic program. After 2008, baseball and softball will no longer be on the Olympic program but their Federations will not lose their status. The notion of "sport" is worthy of quotation marks since certain IFs in fact control several sports (known as "disciplines" in Olympic jargon).

The International Cycling Union (UCI) in fact governs road cycling, track cycling, mountain bike and BMX which are all disciplines present at the Summer Games and others which are not Olympic disciplines such as cyclo-cross or indoor cycling. At the Winter Games, The International Skating Union (ISU) supervises figure skating, speed skating and short track. On the other hand, there is an IF for curling alone and there are two separate IFs for baseball and softball, which are basically the same sport for men and women respectively. The role of the IFs is developed in Chapter 4.

In 2008, the IOC recognized 205 NOCs, with the last to gain admission to date being Montenegro in 2007. The use of the notion of a "country," like that of "sport" for the IFs, requires quotation marks since what it denotes has evolved over time. Today, according to its charter, the IOC only accepts independent states that are recognized by the "international community," which in practice means by the UN. The role of the NOCs is developed in Chapter 3.

The question of the venue of the Olympic Games and their organization is handled in Chapter 5. The redistribution of the IOC's revenues is covered later in the present chapter.

The IOC Administration

As we have seen above, the IOC is—on a legal level—an association of individuals who act on a volunteer basis and who meet at least once every year at a General Assembly known as a "Session." The Executive Board meets four or five times a year. Between those meetings, the daily running of the IOC is handled by an administrative staff. The administration's formal creation dates from the setting up of the Executive Board in 1921 under Coubertin's presidency. It was however his successor, Henri de Baillet-Latour of Belgium, who made use of this fledgling administration at the head of which, as of 1925, was the IOC's first real administrator, with the title of "secretary," André Berdez of Switzerland.

After the Second World War and until the 1960s, the IOC Administration consisted of two or three salaried employees under a "Chancellor": Otto Mayer, also of Switzerland, whose office was located in a jewelry store in the centre of Lausanne! Following his resignation, provoked by President Brundage after the 1964 Winter Games in Innsbruck, the IOC came to realize that it needed to create a more professional structure. This was also a period when it began to receive some revenues from successive OCOGs.

After several fruitless attempts, the Executive Board set up a joint directorship structure. One director, Arthur Takac, handled technical matters and sport and another, Frenchwoman Monique Berlioux, was responsible for the press and public relations. Berlioux rapidly took over as "general" director as of 1971, and remained in place until 1985 having worked with three successive presidents: Avery Brundage, Lord Killanin, and Juan Antonio Samaranch.

Monique Berlioux had gradually built up a staff of around 20: a number that rapidly grew to around 30 with Samaranch's election. One of the first decisions taken by the seventh IOC President was, in fact, to come and live in Lausanne and set up a personal staff there—to the great surprise of Berlioux, who with Brundage and above all with Killanin had become used to being accountable only to a president who lived elsewhere and was rarely present. Even though she had contributed significantly to his election to the presidency, Monique Berlioux found herself in a permanent situation of conflict with Samaranch. It was only at the Berlin Session in May 1985, however, five years after his election, that the IOC President was able to force his general director to resign, having accused her of failing to cooperate with the sports director at the time, Walter Tröger of Germany, who was co-opted as an IOC member a few years later.

Samaranch, who until that date had only been able to appoint the sports director and the director of Olympic Solidarity, was then able to set up an IOC Administration in the form he wished. Following a promise by the Swiss Government in 1981 to grant the IOC official status, Samaranch's objective was to bring in mainly Swiss staff. In October 1985, he had the Executive Board appoint an "Administrator-Delegate" in the person of Raymond Gafner, a Swiss IOC member who lived in Lausanne. Gafner suggested hiring Françoise Zweifel, his co-worker at the provisional Olympic Museum (of which Samaranch had placed him in charge as of 1982), as the Secretary General of the administration. In parallel, a number of directors were appointed (for finance and for juridical affairs, and then for press and for NOC relations). The organizational structure thus developed progressively. It was to a large extent based on recommendations by the consulting firm of McKinsey, yet its advice that an IOC member should not be in charge of the administration was ignored.

After the 1988 Games in Seoul, the Executive Board appointed a Director General from the "outside," in the person of François Carrard, a lawyer from Lausanne who had acted as the IOC's legal adviser ever since the end of Killanin's presidency. The "Administrator-Delegate," who was approaching retirement, remained in place but handed over his everyday operational responsibilities to Carrard and Zweifel. A Director of Marketing (formerly with ISL, the IOC's marketing agency) and a Director of Technology (close to IBM, an IOC sponsor at the time) were also appointed during that period. The organization chart that was to remain in place until the end of Samaranch's presidency was thus in place.

The president, now playing an executive role and acting as the genuine head of the administration, was able to count on two close subordinates, i.e. the Director General and the Secretary General, who shared the supervision of the various departments that were in turn headed by directors (sports, legal affairs, finance, marketing, etc.).

When Alain Coupat, a Frenchman who had been Samaranch's Chief of Staff since 1980, left in 1989, the Secretary General to a large extent took over that role.

Following the 1992 Games in Barcelona, an Ethiopian—Fékrou Kidane—was appointed to the position of the president's Chief of Staff and also headed an International Co-operation Department. Within the framework of the latter position, he negotiated numerous agreements with the UN system in which he had worked during the 1960s. An Internal Audit Director also appeared in 1997 with a view to mastering the expenditure by the administration, which was growing in terms of human resources despite the symbolic ceiling of 100 persons set by Samaranch. After the 2002 Games in Salt Lake City, the new IOC President, Jacques Rogge—elected a few months previously—undertook a reorganization of the IOC Administration based on several internal and external audits that he commissioned immediately following his election. A new organization chart was adopted at the Extraordinary Session held in Mexico at the end of 2002, and contained two new directorates: one for the Olympic Games (which was included in that for sport and required functional collaboration on the part of all the other directorates) and one for information management. The changes were facilitated by various departures: Françoise Zweifel had decided to leave her post as Secretary General following the Games in Salt Lake City, and both the Director of Finance and the Director of International Cooperation retired. The number of Swiss nationals holding key positions also dropped, and directors from other countries were appointed.

It was nevertheless a Swiss, Urs Lacotte, who succeeded François Carrard, the Director General from Lausanne, in 2003. Aged 49 at the time, Lacotte had previously been active in the military and in international trade. With the retirement of Carrard, who wished to pursue his work as a lawyer rather than become a salaried IOC employee (he had always worked by mandate), the prerogatives and tasks incumbent upon the Director General changed to become less political and more administrative, in line with President Rogge's wishes.

Box 2.1 The delicate sector of IOC communication

Communication—a particularly important issue for an entity such as the IOC that literally lives thanks to the image it portrays of the Games and of Olympism—has been given varying levels of focus since the Second World War. It can even be said that it was managed in a way that was nothing short of chaotic during Samaranch's presidency.

Historically, communication at the IOC was the task of the heads of the Administration, whether the individual concerned had the title of Chancellor or Director, and was also supervised by a Press Commission chaired successively by two future Presidents—Samaranch and Killanin—in the 1960s and 70s. This was, in fact, an excellent means for both men to enhance their profile in the media. The current Chairman of the Press Commission, Kevan Gosper of Australia, had a similar aim in mind at the end of the 1990s but finally decided not to run for the Presidency.

After the departure of IOC Director Monique Berlioux in 1985— who had always guarded her privileged contacts with the media extremely jealously—Samaranch nominated Michèle Verdier and José Sotélo, two individuals trained by the Frenchwoman a few years previously, to two key posts in 1987. Verdier became Director of Media Relations (a kind of spokesperson position but also in charge of accreditations and press facilities) and Sotelo became Director of the Press Review (an internal document that made it possible to monitor the publications by major press sources that concerned the IOC). These posts remained at a relatively subaltern level and their two holders left the IOC in 1999.

The Director General, François Carrard, who handled the intermediate briefings for the press on the occasion of meetings and who sat to the President's right at official press conferences during the 1990s, began to tackle the question of communication in earnest. After the Barcelona Games in 1992, the IOC nevertheless deemed it necessary to recruit a genuine Director of Communication in the person of Andrew Napier, of Britain. Napier was a specialist who had formerly worked for Ford, but only remained with the IOC for two years. After the 1994 Olympic Congress, he was replaced by Fékrou Kidane, also a former journalist, who thus combined the role of Director of Public Information with his numerous other tasks, notably that of Editor in Chief of the Olympic Review, the IOC's bi-monthly publication that has existed almost without interruption since its foundation.

In 1998, the IOC recruited Franklin Servan-Schreiber, a member of the famous French family of press magnates and above all an Internet specialist, in order to develop its communication by means of this new medium. But on the very day that the Executive Board approved Servan-Schreiber's Internet plan, the Salt Lake City scandal erupted. Hundreds of journalists began to call the IOC, night and day. Franklin Servan-Schreiber was catapulted into the role of the IOC's spokesman and a few weeks later became Director of Communication and New Media. Without really having any prior experience regarding Olympism, he was required to set up a completely new department and at the same time to handle an unprecedented media outcry.

The scandal was most virulent in the United States throughout the first six months of 1999, with three peaks: in January when the IOC published its enquiry report, in March when it excluded six members, and in June when it elected the Host City for the 2006 Winter Games. As of January, however, Servan-Schreiber was to receive assistance from the American public relations agency Hill & Knowlton, which delegated one of its managers to permanently second the new Director. The signing of a contract worth several million dollars with the agency that had advised the Union Carbide Corporation following the Bhopal disaster in India took place without Samaranch's approval, and meant severe criticism for the Director General during a meeting of the Executive Board. Carrard accepted the blame for the affair, even though the partnership had been strongly recommended by the TOP sponsors, most of which were American and wished to preserve the value of their investments in the Olympic image at any price.

Hill & Knowlton seemed particularly anxious to highlight one of the candidates for Samaranch's succession: Richard Pound of Canada, Chairman of the IOC's Enquiry Commission and its Marketing Commission. The group continued to work with the IOC until 2001, despite the fact that Franklin Servan-Schreiber had resigned from the IOC in December 2000 after seeing his powers severely curtailed and suffering from the consequences of poor relations with the Chairman of the Press Commission Kevan Gosper. On the eve of the Sydney Games, in fact, a televised documentary on the IOC was screened that was particularly detrimental to Gosper and that showed a Servan-Schreiber extremely willing to collaborate with the film crew.[3] Thereafter, the responsibility for the Communication Department was divided among three Directors from other, existing departments until the newly-elected President Jacques Rogge nominated a new Director of Communication, following the 2002 Winter Games, in the person of Gisèle Davis of Britain. Davis has been acting as the IOC's spokesperson ever since, and is one of the IOC's key Directors.

The Director General and the other directors are formally appointed by the IOC Executive Board on the proposal of the President. The current Director General is seconded by 12 directors in charge of 13 departments (see Figure 2.1). Two directors, however, occupy particularly key positions: the Chief of Staff, who handles all political questions and relations with the IOC members, and the Executive Director (the only director to have such a title) of the Olympic Games, who is in charge of the IOC's principal "product." These two directors and the Director General attend the meetings of the IOC's Executive Board, while all the others are called upon to present their reports only as and when needed. Under Samaranch, they all attended the entire meetings.

The directors hold a monthly management committee meeting, at times with the president, and have regular external one-day management seminars. Otherwise, they run their departments in a fairly autonomous manner. Staff units are, however, attached to the Director General for Human Resources and Corporate Development. The directors of the Olympic Museum and of Olympic Solidarity (the department that redistributes the sums due to the NOCs) have a greater degree of autonomy because they are geographically located outside the main headquarters in Vidy, and because of the nature of their activities. The director of Olympic Solidarity also heads the NOC Relations Department.

The IOC Administration has four locations in Lausanne (Château de Vidy and Olympic House on the shores of Lake Geneva, the nearby House of International Sport, the Olympic Museum in Ouchy plus two nearby mansions, and the Villa "Mon Repos" in central Lausanne, once used by Coubertin and that also housed the first Olympic Museum).

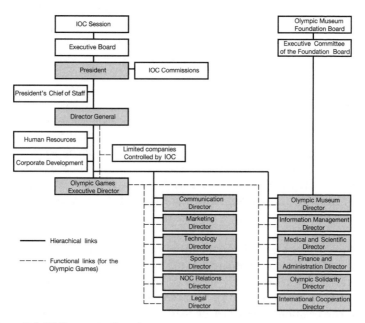

Figure 2.1 IOC organization chart.

The IOC's human resources have soared since the early days of Samaranch's presidency as a result of the multitude of tasks that the IOC took on during that period. Samaranch expressed the wish to restrict the IOC Administration to around 100 persons, not including the IOC Museum staff and many consultants. With the arrival of Rogge, the quantitative and qualitative growth of the administration continued, and in 2008 reached more than 400 persons from around 30 countries (see Table 2.3). This number includes all the employees in the "IOC Group," which were previously counted separately. In 2005, the average age of staff members was 37.5, and women represented 62 percent of the total.

In 2006, the "central operating and administrative costs" for the IOC amounted to approximately 83 million US dollars, with half accounted for by salaries and social charges.[4]

The great majority of the IOC's assets are shared between two foundations subject to Swiss law and that are controlled by the IOC and managed by the IOC Administration: the Olympic Foundation and the Olympic Museum Foundation. The latter owns the Olympic Museum. The Olympic Foundation accumulates the IOC's financial assets and owns several limited companies that are subject to Swiss law, of which two have a large number of employees: IOC Television and Marketing Services (formerly Meridian Management SA) and Olympic Broadcasting Services. The former, which provides services contractually promised to the IOC's sponsors, is managed by the IOC's marketing director and the second, in charge of producing the basic televised images of the Games, is headed by a former executive of the European Broadcasting Union. The two companies have boards of directors that are chaired by members of the IOC (respectively the chairmen of the Marketing Commission and the Commission for the Co-ordination of the 2008 Games). The Foundation Boards (the supreme governing bodies) of the IOC's two foundations consist of members of the IOC Executive Board and are chaired by the IOC President (for the Olympic Foundation), and the Honorary President for Life (Museum Foundation). All the legal entities (foundations and limited companies)

Table 2.3 Development of staff numbers at the IOC Administration

1968	1973	1976	1980	1982	1987	1994	2001	2003	2005	2007
12	18	21	27	48	78	139	208	297	326	407

Note
Including employees of the Olympic Museum (from 1982), Olympic Solidarity and the Marketing Department (formerly Meridian Management SA), yearly average in full-time equivalents

that are under the aegis of the association that is the IOC are known internally by the term "IOC Group."

There can be no doubt that the arrival of Jacques Rogge as the IOC President constituted a major turning point for the IOC on a management level, with the introduction of more solid structures and procedures and above all a change to a more technocratic style of management that is far more sensitive to questions of governance and risk management, yet less entrepreneurial and paternalist than that of the former president. A consolidation phase followed a strong period of expansion.

The economics of the IOC

The fact that, according to Rule 7 of the Olympic Charter, the IOC "owns" all the rights and data relating to the Olympic Games means that since the 1980s, it has been managing a flourishing economic business even though its legal status remains that of a non-profit organization, like most other national and international sport organizations. The constantly increasing funds at its disposal permits the IOC to promote the Olympic ideal and to assist the entire Olympic movement on a financial level. Since it has no need for governmental subsidies of any kind, the IOC also enjoys considerable independence from State powers.

The sources of the IOC's revenues

Today, the IOC's revenues are extremely high: for the period 2005–8 they will approach US$5 billion.[5] Nevertheless, its situation has not always been as comfortable. During the early days, the IOC was entirely financed by its founder, Pierre de Coubertin, who was moreover ruined by doing so and died in extreme poverty (although this was also due to bad investments he made during the "roaring twenties").

After Coubertin retired as its president in 1925, the IOC basically existed thanks to the membership fees paid, as is appropriate for an association—and to a lesser extent from (more or less) voluntary contributions from the OCOGs of the time and notably that for Berlin 1936. Since the members were rich, they paid their own expenses for attending IOC meetings or the Games, so the IOC had virtually no overheads.

This situation continued until 1972, when the membership dues were purely and simply discontinued. At the same period, the IOC began to benefit from substantial broadcasting rights for the Games. As of 1985, the IOC's revenues received a further boost thanks to its international marketing program (TOP).

At present, various percentages are also levied from the OCOGs' national sponsoring and licensing programs and their ticketing income. The IOC is now in possession of a considerable amount of capital, and also receives income from it that is invested in US dollars, Swiss francs and other currencies under the control of its Finance Commission. Part of its capital has been transferred in order to create the Olympic Foundation, which is covered later in this section.

Since 1960, the broadcasting rights have been paid by the television channels and networks for the exclusive transmission of the Summer and Winter Games on their territory or within the boundaries of their union. The IOC, however, only began taking part in negotiating the contracts concerned as of those for the 1972 Games. It has only been controlling the negotiations (and amounts paid) since those of 1992. Prior to 1972, the IOC received only meager amounts paid out of goodwill by the OCOGs signing the contracts, since the president at the time (Avery Brundage) did not really believe in the potential of television! Table 2.4 shows the amount (rounded) for television rights since 1960, in US dollars since most of the contracts were concluded in that currency.[6]

As one can see, the television rights are progressing constantly and today reach considerable sums. In certain cases, the IOC even shares the broadcaster's profits (revenue sharing). In the eyes of the broadcasters, however, the sums are justified because the Games remain one of the few televised events to attract large audiences and that incite the entire family to gather around the television set. In addition, the IOC has a "clean venue" policy, meaning that billboards and all kind of advertisements are banned in and around the Olympic arenas. These two factors therefore make it possible to sell slots for commercials at a very high price (around US$600,000 for 30 seconds in the United States for the Salt Lake City Games in 2002). Sponsors of the Games are almost forced to purchase these slots in large quantities or on the basis of an exclusive contract by product category (known as telecast sponsoring) if they wish to avoid their competitors deriving benefit from an association with the Games through the purchase of slots during telecasts of the Games (which in fact constitutes a form of ambush marketing).

This strong growth of the rights over the last 30 years is largely due to the competition between the three major American networks (ABC, CBS, and NBC), which are today joined by Fox when negotiations take place. The amounts paid by other parts of the world are far below those achieved for the US, although they are also increasing constantly thanks to growing competition among television channels. The proportion of the rights for the US is reducing in proportion to those for the rest of the world (from 78 percent in 1984 to 52 percent in 2008).

Table 2.4 Olympic Games broadcasting rights 1960–2012

Year	Winter Games	Amount	Summer Games	Amount
1960	Squaw Valley	0.05	Rome	1.1
1964	Innsbruck	0.9	Tokyo	1.6
1968	Grenoble	2.6	Mexico	9.7
1972	Sapporo	8.5	Munich	17.8
1976	Innsbruck	11.6	Montreal	32
1980	Lake Placid	20.7	Moscow	101
1984	Sarajevo	102.7	Los Angeles	287
1988	Calgary	325.5	Seoul	403
1992	Albertville	292	Barcelona	636
1994	Lillehammer	353		
1996			Atlanta	898.2
1998	Nagano	513.5		
2000			Sydney	1,331.5
2002	Salt Lake City	736.1		
2004			Athens	1,492.6
2006	Turin	833		
2008			Beijing	1,715*
2010	Vancouver	820**		
2012			London	1,181**

Notes
* Provisional
** Rights for the United States alone

The television company ABC obtained all Olympic broadcasting contracts for the USA from Grenoble 1968 until Calgary 1988. It was followed by NBC as of 1992 (except for CBS which broadcast the 1992, 1994, and 1998 Winter Games). Under Samaranch, these contracts were signed following secret tenders, sometimes for several editions of the Games. President Rogge has, however, imposed open tenders and for two successive editions of the Games (Winter, then Summer) at most.

Certain observers believed that Olympic television rights would reach a ceiling after 2008 and would suffer from the rising influence of the Internet as a medium. Broadcasting rights contracts signed by the IOC with NBC for 2010 and 2012 (including those for the new media) have nevertheless proved that for the time being, this is by no means the case despite a large drop in the 15–25 year old audience.

Since the beginning of Samaranch's presidency in 1980, the IOC endeavored to diversify its sources of income, i.e. it attempted to find "clients" other than television. A commission created for the purpose and chaired by Canadian member Richard Pound handled this issue, and proposed creating an integrated marketing program for the Olympic symbols known as TOP (The Olympic Programme, and later The Olympic Partners). TOP learned from previous, professionally organized marketing programs carried out by the OCOGs since 1972, which had suffered from two major shortcomings: they were mainly limited to the country hosting the Games, and they created no income for the IOC. With TOP, the IOC permits a company to purchase—simply by its signature—the right to be associated with the Winter and consecutive Summer Games (use of the Games' logos, hospitality possibilities, tickets, etc.), with the IOC (use of the Olympic rings), and with all NOCs in the world (use of their emblems). This facilitation is a major advantage for a multi-national that wishes to carry out a world campaign linked to the Games in the countries where it is present. This Olympic partnership is for a four-year period and includes two editions of the Games, or longer if the contract is signed for several Olympiads. This latter solution is becoming a trend similar to the case for television rights, and for example includes Coca-Cola which has signed until 2020. The partnership is of course exclusive and concerns a well-defined category of products such as all non-alcoholic beverages for Coca-Cola, including milk and mineral water. Such partnerships are much sought after thanks to the renowned Olympic symbol (the five interlaced rings), which is said to be the best-known logo in the world, above that of Shell, the McDonald's golden arches, and the Mercedes star, and well ahead of that of the Red Cross or the United Nations.[7]

The Olympic ideal, which evokes values such as peace, fraternity, and fair play, is also an excellent vector as long as it retains its purity. Some state that it is one of the world's most powerful brands. Since 1985, the IOC has been carrying out an ongoing study on the subject under the name of the Olympic Image Research Project.

Table 2.5 shows the evolution of the TOP program since its foundation. As we shall see later in this section, only a small portion of revenues from TOP remains with the IOC.[8]

The management of the two first TOP programs (1985–92) was entrusted to the limited company ISL (International Sport & Leisure) founded at the beginning of the 1980s in Lucerne, Switzerland by Horst Dassler (the owner of Adidas at the time) and his sisters. In 1989, the IOC created a marketing department within its administration and took over the negotiation of contracts with the Olympic partners while permitting ISL to service these once signed and to handle marketing relations with the NOCs. In 1993, the IOC canceled its agreements with ISL and transferred the work relating to the TOP sponsors, the OCOGs and the NOCs to a limited company under the name of Meridian Management, founded for the purpose by two specialists formerly with

Table 2.5 Evolution of the TOP Program

	Number of companies	Companies involved	Number of NOCs	Revenues (in million US dollars)
TOP I 1985–1988 Calgary Seoul	9	3M, Brother, Coca-Cola, Federal Express, Kodak, Panasonic, Philips, Sports Illustrated/Time, Visa	159	106
TOP II 1989–1992 Albertville Barcelona	12	3M, Bausch&Lomb, Brother, Coca-Cola, USPS-EMS, Kodak, Mars, Panasonic, Philips, Ricoh, Sports Illustrated/Time, Visa	169	192 (including ViK*)
TOP III 1993–1996 Lillehammer Atlanta	10	Bausch&Lomb, Coca-Cola, IBM, John Hancock, Kodak, Panasonic, Sports Illustrated/ Time, UPS, Visa, Xerox	197	376 (including 185 ViK*)
TOP IV 1997–2000 Nagano Sydney	11	Coca-Cola, IBM, John Hancock, Kodak, McDonald's, Panasonic, Samsung, Sports Illustrated/ Time, UPS, Visa, Xerox	199	579 (including 276 ViK*)
TOP V 2001–2004 Salt Lake Athens	10 (+ Swatch only for Athens)	Coca-Cola, Schlumberger-Sema, John Hancock, Kodak, McDonald's, Panasonic, Samsung, Sports Illustrated/Time, Visa, Xerox	202	663
TOP VI 2005–2008 Turin Beijing	12	Coca Cola, Athos-Origin, Manulife, Kodak, McDonald's, Panasonic, Samsung, Lenovo, Omega, Visa, General Electric, Johnson & Johnson	205	circa 866

Note
* ViK = Value in Kind

the OCOGs of Albertville and Atlanta (Laurent Scharapan and Chris Welton). The IOC owned 25 percent of the equity investment in this company, and 50 percent of the voting rights.

Meridian took over two essential tasks that were formerly attributed to ISL. The first was to ensure that the OCOGs supplied the counter-services to which the TOP sponsors were entitled in order to valorize their investment. The second was to negotiate with each NOC in order for it to remain a member of TOP (in exchange for services in cash or in kind) and could thus offer sponsors the possibility of using the acquired rights on the NOC's territory. This task naturally needed to be carried out in close collaboration with the IOC's marketing department which for its part focused on the positioning and development of the Olympic brand.

In 2001, after the election of President Rogge, the IOC decided to buy out the entire company, maintaining its former shareholders as its managing directors. The IOC member who chaired the Marketing Commission thus became the Chairman of the Board of Meridian. In 2004, the two managing directors were dismissed and in 2005, the company changed its name to IOC Television and Marketing Services SA (IOCTMS).

These developments clearly reflect the IOC's determination to control its marketing rights to the greatest possible extent and to maximize its income, notably by no longer paying commission or dividends to intermediaries.

Beside television rights and the TOP program, the IOC's other sources of revenues are not significant. They should nevertheless be mentioned, however, because they are developing progressively. We can make a distinction between revenues from the OCOGs' activities and those from the IOC's own commercial activities.

In addition to the (world) TOP program in which an OCOG's participation is mandatory, each OCOG develops its own, national sponsoring program in co-operation with the NOC of the host country (which holds the rights to use the Olympic rings on its territory and which receives a maximum of 10 percent of the revenues from the program set up by the OCOG). This program is particularly lucrative in host countries with a major domestic market such as China or the USA. Certain Chinese companies have paid more than TOP partners just to become national sponsors of the 2008 Beijing Games. A professional merchandising/licensing program has also been set up by the OCOGs since 1972.

In accordance with its contract with the host city (signed on the day the Games are awarded), the IOC must approve all contracts signed by the OCOG for the sponsoring or merchandising of the Games. At present, it receives 5 percent of the revenues this generates, in cash or in kind. This also applies to revenues from the sale of tickets for the competitions, which since 1996 are considerable (US$374 million for Sydney 2000). Interestingly, during the 1950s and 1960s, the IOC and IFs imagined they could finance themselves thanks to a tax on these tickets alone.

Finally, the IOC contractually reserves the right to 20 percent of the possible profits made by the OCOGs, but tends to reimburse this sum to them for the maintenance of the Olympic facilities.

As of the 1990s, the IOC has also been generating revenues independently of those from the Games and above and beyond interest on its assets. For instance, it organized a numismatics program for its centenary, it designated official suppliers for its administration in Lausanne (for example Mercedes for cars, Lufthansa for air transport, Mizuno for uniforms, Schenker for freight, etc.), and it organized the sale of historical images (photos and videos) of the Games and allocated the income to the Olympic Museum.

The IOC has also made some unsuccessful attempts at diversification in the form of several projects related to the notion of sport lotteries and Olympic theme parks.

For the period 2001–4, the Olympic revenues from the IOC and from the OCOGs of Salt Lake City and Athens can be estimated at over US$4.19 billion (compared with 3.77 billion for the period 1997–2000), of which around 50 percent consists of television rights and 40 percent of sponsoring. As we shall see later, only a small part of the revenues actually reaches the IOC.

The IOC's expenditure

Table 2.6 shows the total revenues, expenditure, and profit made by the IOC in 2004, 2005, and 2006 (the latest years for which an official report is available).

These annual snapshots nevertheless mean little when speaking of a structure organized around a four-year cycle. In 2003, for instance, the IOC recorded a negative balance of US$74 million. It is only after the Games (here, Athens 2004 and Turin 2006) that the IOC receives its portion of the revenues. It is therefore more significant to examine the IOC's expenditure on an Olympiad basis, i.e. by four-year period.

Table 2.7 presents the IOC's revenues, expenses, profits, and available funds from 1973 to 2000 (based on the 1996 US dollar exchange rate), by four-year period. This table has unfortunately not been published for the periods 2001–4 and following.

A considerable portion of the IOC's profits after payment of running costs is allocated to the capital of two foundations: the Olympic Foundation and the Olympic Museum Foundation. Created in 1993, these two foundations under Swiss law (Article 80 et seq. of the Swiss Civil Code) are fully controlled by the IOC.

The Olympic Museum Foundation manages an annual expenditure budget that has increased from US$13.6 million to US$16.6 million between 1995 and 2003 (and has almost doubled in Swiss franc terms). Half of this budget consists of salaries for the around 75 employees.

Table 2.6 Combined statements of activities for 31 December 2004 and 2006

	2004	2005	2006	Comments
Revenues				
Television broadcasting rights	1,492.6	0	830.8	
TOP program marketing rights	292.2	176.2	268.4	
Other rights	51.1	6.9	27.4	
Others	9.6	5.9	5.6	
Total revenues	*1,845.5*	*189.0*	*1,132.5*	
Expenditure				
Central operating and administrative costs	91.1	80.6	83.4	Of which 45.5 million in salaries in 2004
Olympic Games-related expenditure	68.3	0	34.6	Of which 24 million to the NOCs in 2004
Grants and subsidies	3.4	2.9	3.2	
Funds earmarked for allocation	57.0	0	33.1	Notably for WADA, ICAS, and recognized organizations
Olympic Solidarity program	38.7	44.9	51.8	Worldwide and continental programs
Special projects	1.6	0.7	0.9	
Distribution of broadcasting rights	1,095.6	0	613.6	Except to Olympic Solidarity
Distribution of TOP rights	270.7	137.1	238.8	
Total expenditure	*1,626.4*	*266.2*	*1,059.3*	
Excess of revenues (expenditure)	219.1	(77.2)	73.3	
Financial income, net	9.5	44.3	70.0	Despite 12 million exchange loss in 2004
Profit (loss)	*228.6*	*(32.9)*	*143.3*	

Around one-quarter of it is covered by operating revenues (200,000 entrances to the Museum per year, royalties for the use of historical images, shop, restaurant, sponsors, etc.). The balance comes from interest on the foundation's assets and (no doubt for a few years still) from a direct IOC grant.

Since 1993, the Olympic Foundation has been gradually building up reserves intended to permit the IOC to function for one Olympiad without major sources of revenues (i.e. if the Games are canceled and the related revenues are not received). President Rogge, following his election in 2001, demanded that savings be made and paid into the foundation.

As can be seen from Tables 2.7 and 2.8, the IOC's own capital is relatively modest compared to the billions generated by the Olympic Games. This is because the IOC, unlike other owners of major events (such as the FIFA for the football World Cup and UEFA for the European Football

Table 2.7 The IOC's revenues (expenses) and profits (losses) between 1973 and 2000

Years	1973 –76	1977 –80	1981 –84	1985 –88	1989 –92	1993 –96	1997 –2000
Revenues							
Total	17.9	28.9	92.9	131.0	175.6	230.9	345.8
Expenditure							
Administration	(9.4)	(15.0)	(32.0)	(46.9)	(67.4)	(99.7)	(119.5)
Other	0	(2.7)	(7.2)	(14.3)	(79.2)	(135.0)	(169.8)
Profits (loss)	8.5	11.2	53.7	69.8	29.0	(3.8)	56.5
Fund balance*	14.3	21.2	70.4	131.6	139.8	121.2	~105

Note
* On 31 December of each final year in the given four-year period.

Table 2.8 Allocation of revenues from the TOP III (1993–96) and TOP IV (1997–2000) programs in millions of US dollars

	TOP III	%	TOP IV	%
Summer OCOGs	169	44.9 %	221	38.2 %
(Atlanta 96 or Sydney 2000)				
Winter OCOGs	65	17.3 %	132	22.8 %
(Lillehammer 94 or Nagano 98)				
NOCs (except USOC)	62	16.5 %	93	16.0 %
NOC of the USA (USOC)	52	13.8 %	85	14.7 %
IOC	28	7.5 %	48	8.3 %
Total	*376*	100 %	*579*	100 %

Championships), shares its two main sources of revenue (television rights and TOP program) with its Olympic movement partners. The IOC thus only preserves around eight percent of the Olympic revenues generated over each Olympiad.

The sharing of the revenues (including those in kind) from the TOP program is carried out by means of contracts according to the following approximate ratio: 60 percent to the two OCOGs concerned (Winter and Summer Games), 30 percent to the NOCs (including almost half for USOC) and 10 percent to the IOC. Table 2.8 shows the precise ratios for the last two Olympiads, which are published figures.[9] For the periods 2001–4 and following, the IOC wishes to reduce the portion of the two OCOGs concerned to 50 percent and to increase that of the NOCs (except that for the US NOC, the USOC, which it would like to decrease).

As of the 1972 Games, the IOC imposed a distribution ratio for the television rights, which was roughly equivalent to two-thirds (66 percent) of the total amount for the OCOG and one-third for the Olympic movements, with this latter third itself divided into three equal portions (IOC, IFs, NOCs). This ratio has evolved considerably since the 1970s. From 1996 to 2002, the OCOGs received 60 percent of the television rights, and only 49 percent since 2004. There is some talk of reducing this percentage further without the absolute amount reducing, since the total amount from the rights continues to increase.

The allocation within the Olympic movement now takes into consideration the demands of the IFs (which contribute to the marketing success of the TOP program and obtain a special remuneration taken from the television rights and not the TOP revenues), and of the USOC (which theoretically could block broadcasting of the Games in the USA thanks to its control over the Olympic rings on its territory).

Finally, as of 2002, the World Anti-Doping Agency (WADA) participates in the distribution because it is, in theory, financed in equal proportions by the Olympic movement and the governments of the world (and the latter are not always inclined to pay).

Table 2.9 shows the distribution for the two last Olympiads in net amounts and percentages. The reduction in the OCOG's portion after Sydney mainly favored the IOC, which now takes Games-related subsidies to WADA and the NOCs out of its budget.

The Olympic IFs share their Olympic income among themselves according to discussions held within the Association of Summer Olympic International Federations (ASOIF). They are divided into five categories depending on their Olympic status and popularity. Each of the 28 IFs concerned received, at the end of 2004, the amounts mentioned in Table 2.10 out of about US$255 million available for the IFs.

The seven winter sports IFs share the income from broadcasting rights for the Winter Games according to another ratio decided by the Association of International Olympic Winter Sport Federations (AIOWSF): one that favors the so-called major sports (ice hockey, skating and skiing) over the smaller ones (biathlon, bobsleigh, curling, and luge). The amounts are however much higher in terms of absolute value than those for the summer IFs, who were four times more numerous (28 summer IFs in Sydney and Athens compared with 7 Winter IFs in Nagano and Salt Lake City).

Unlike the IFs, the NOCs did not adopt a distribution ratio because they are too numerous (202 in 2004). Since 1972, the sums due to them

Table 2.9 Redistribution of television rights

	Lillehammer 1994	%	Nagano 1998	%	Atlanta 1996	%	Sydney 2000	%	Athens 2004	%
OCOG	239.8	67.9	308.2	60	564.7	62.9	800	60	733.3	49.1
WADA (in 2000)	0		0		0		25	1.9	0	0
IOC	28.7	8.1	58.8	11.4	94.1	10.5	130.9	9.8	*268.8	18
Olympic IFs	27.8	7.9	65.4	12.7	114.2	12.7	189.7	14.2	253.7	17
USOC	29.5	8.4	37.5	7.3	45.6	5.1	70.5	5.3	101.2	6.8
Olympic Solidarity	20.3	5.8	30.0	5.9	56.4	6.2	88.7	6.7	135.6	9.1
Subsidies to NOCs (Games-related costs)	6.8	1.9	13.6	2.6	45.6	5.0	26.7	2.1	0	0
Total = Television rights	352.9	100	513.5	100	898.2	100	1,331.5	100	1,492.6	100

Note
* Including insurance premium for the cancellation of the Games (US$7.42 million).

Table 2.10 Distribution of 2004 broadcasting rights among IFs

Categories	Amounts received per IF
A: athletics	25.21
B: basketball, football, gymnastics, swimming, volleyball, tennis, cycling	12.22
C: handball, hockey, equestrian, rowing	8.12
D: archery, badminton, baseball, boxing, canoeing, fencing, weightlifting, judo, wrestling, modern pentathlon, softball, table tennis, shooting, sailing	6.75
E: taekwondo, triathlon	6.07

are managed by Olympic Solidarity, a redistribution institution whose objective is to assist the most needful NOCs via 21 worldwide programs (for the 2001–4 plan) intended for athletes, coaches, administrators, etc. Since 1984, Olympic Solidarity has been a separate IOC department and forms an integral part of the decision-making structure of the IOC Administration in Lausanne. It nevertheless has a separate budget and is managed by a commission chaired by the president of the Association of NOCs (ANOC) since 2002 (and before that, by the IOC President).

Table 2.11 shows the funds per four-year period that are available to Olympic Solidarity from the distribution of revenues resulting from television rights and the TOP program. Since 2001, around half of these funds are managed on a decentralized basis, in the continental associations of NOCs.

Although the distribution of the revenues between the IOC and the OCOGs is usually governed by detailed contracts, it is highly surprising to note that the allocation among the basic partners to the Olympic movement, i.e. the IOC, the IFs, and the NOCs (except USOC), are not the subject of contracts. They are the subject of negotiations on a goodwill basis from one Olympiad to another, without being specifically mentioned in the Olympic Charter and even though the Charter provides considerable details on many other subjects.

The IOC's assets

This presentation of economic aspects of the IOC would not be complete without a brief examination of its assets.

Table 2.12 presents the IOC's assets at the end of 2000 and 2004. It can be seen that under Rogge's presidency, the assets have tripled without a large increase in the restricted assets—funds preserved in trust for the NOCs and IFs until the end of the Olympiad. It means the IOC could continue to function despite the cancellation of one edition of the Olympic Games (and the subsequent loss of revenues).

Table 2.11 Olympic Solidarity budget between 1985 and 2008

Quadrennial plans	1985 –1988	1989 –1992	1993 –1996	1997 –2000	2001 –2004	2005 –2008
Number of NOCs concerned	167	172	197	199	202	205
Budgets	28.36	54.71	74.11	121.9	209.48	244

Table 2.12 The IOC's assets as at 31 December 2000 and 2004

Assets	2000	2004
Current	108.6	605.2
Non-current	110.9	296.3
Restricted	129.8	135.0
Total (rounded)	*349.3*	*1,036.5*

As of 1993, and as mentioned above, a large portion of the IOC's assets has been regularly transferred to the Olympic Foundation and the Olympic Museum Foundation. The supreme authorities (councils) of both have virtually the same members as the IOC's Executive Board. In accordance with their statutes, they are both chaired by the IOC President, but since 2001 the Museum Foundation has been chaired by Juan Antonio Samaranch, the IOC's Honorary President for Life.

The IOC has transferred ownership of the museum building and its fittings to the foundation of the same name, but lent it the collections, works of art and Olympic archives accumulated since Coubertin's time, free of charge. The construction of the Olympic Museum, between 1988 and 1993, cost around US$68.6 million, of which US$56.4 was financed by donations or sponsoring. As its name indicates, the objective of the foundation is to valorize and preserve the legacy of the Olympic movement thanks to a museum located in Lausanne and which houses an Olympic Studies Centre. The assets of this foundation stood at 8.4 million at the end of 2000.[10]

At the same date, the assets of the Olympic Foundation stood at US$166 million.[11] This Foundation holds the IOC's share capital in several limited companies linked to the organization of the Games (see below). Its objective is to achieve assets of approximately US$300 million that would serve as insurance for the IOC if the Games were not held or the IOC was faced with claims by third parties. Moreover, the IOC takes out insurance against the cancellation of the Games (with policies costing up to US$7.42 million for the 2004 Athens Games).

In addition, and in conjunction with the Greek government, the IOC created the International Foundation for the Olympic Truce in July 2000. This foundation, governed by Swiss law, is headed by the IOC President and the Greek Minister for Foreign Affairs. It is mainly funded by Greece. The foundation possesses little beyond its capital, which is also modest.

Like the IOC itself, these three foundations are exempt from direct taxation in Switzerland although they are required to pay Value Added Tax.

The IOC is moreover the owner of its administrative headquarters building in Vidy, built on land for which it benefits from a free lease granted by the City of Lausanne that runs until 2083. It also owns the "Villa du Centenaire" building that adjoins the Museum and that houses the offices of its Ethics Commission and formerly the Court of Arbitration for Sport.

Finally, the IOC controls the following companies, either directly or via the Olympic Foundation: 100 percent of the Meridian Management SA founded in 1995; 99 percent of Olympic Broadcasting Services (OBS) founded in 2001, which has produced the base signal for broadcasting the Games as of 2006; and 100 percent of Olympic Games Knowledge Services (OGKS) founded 2001 and intended to sell training and advice on the organization of the Games and major, multi-sports events (closed in 2005). When they were founded, these companies were co-owned by third parties but the IOC has preferred to gradually take total control of them. The boards of directors of these limited companies under Swiss law are chaired by IOC members. Moreover, the IOC controls the British companies Olympic Television Archive Bureau (OTAB), created in 1995 and managed by the Trans World International (TWI) agency, and Olympic Photo Archive Bureau (OPAB), created in 1996 and managed by the Allsport press agency (a division of Getty Images). The IOC is also a co-owner of the Lausanne International House of Sport SA where some of its offices are located.

At the end of the twentieth century, the IOC had reached a position of financial prosperity that its founder, Pierre de Coubertin, could without doubt never have imagined. This is due to the efforts of millions of volunteers and athletes who have made the Olympic Games what they are today: a unique and well-studied form of entertainment with an idyllic image. The IOC members, who are not paid for this role, have also contributed to this success and the Olympic movement as a whole has also derived considerable benefit from it.

On the other hand, and even if they are professionals, the main actors in the Olympic "show" are the athletes, and compete only for the glory of doing so whereas they receive prize money for taking part and for achieving results in many other competitions. A certain form of remuneration for athletes at the Games will no doubt have to be considered in the twenty-first century, and will obviously bring about considerable changes within the IOC's finances.

Another type of major Olympic actor has also contributed towards its wealth, yet without really being aware of doing so: the local, regional, and to an ever-increasing extent the national governments of countries that have hosted the Games. By means of candidatures that they have supported, the facilities they have built at huge expense for the Games, and often because of the organizational deficits they have absorbed, they have helped perpetuate the Olympic myth and thus to generate increasing revenues for the IOC.

The question that must be raised today is whether the Games should remain the exclusive property of the IOC (as the Olympic Charter drawn up by the IOC itself has been proclaiming since the 1980s). Do they not belong to humanity, as President Samaranch said at the beginning of his presidency? Should they not be a public good, a World Cultural Heritage, for which the IOC would only be the guardian for future generations? This, too, would constitute a fundamental change to the IOC's finances. It would seem, however, that the IOC has for the time being chosen to remain the monopolistic multi-national behind the Olympic show.

3 National Olympic Committees

The National Olympic Committees (NOCs) are the IOC's territorial representatives. They are however independent organizations under the laws of their own territory. Their main responsibility is to select and send a team for the Olympic Games. Before discovering the thrust of their mission, we explain how an NOC can be recognized by the IOC and thus enter the Olympic system. The final section of this chapter presents Olympic Solidarity, an IOC department dedicated to helping the NOCs fulfill their mission and that is funded by about one-third of the broadcasting rights of the Olympic Games.

NOC recognition

The IOC recognizes over two hundred National Olympic Committees throughout the world, with a maximum of one per "country." The notion of "country," however, requires quotation marks since it has evolved somewhat over the Olympiads. Today, according to the Olympic Charter, the IOC only accepts independent states recognized by the "international community" within the Olympic system, i.e. in practice those recognized by the United Nations (UN). Until the 1980s, the IOC recognized NOCs in around a dozen territories (often islands) that were to varying degrees dependent on other states: for instance Aruba, the Cayman Islands, Guam, the Netherlands Antilles, Puerto Rico, the Virgin Islands, etc. The policy dated from Coubertin's time. Under the slogan "All games, all nations," he permitted the participation of territories such as Finland and Bohemia that were annexed to Russia and the Austro-Hungarian Empire at the time of the first editions of the modern Games.

The objective pursued was clearly for the IOC to expand its territorial coverage throughout the world: in fact the number of recognized NOCs rose from 150 in 1984 to 199 in 2000, i.e. a 25 percent increase.

Oceania (with a view to the 2000 Games in Sydney) and the new republics born of the dissolution of the USSR in 1991 accounted for around 20 new NOCs during the 1990s. In 2008, the figure stood at 205 and thus higher than that of UN member states (192). The five latest NOCs to be recognized are those of Timor-Leste, Kiribati, the Marshall Islands, Montenegro, and Tuvalu. During the 1990s, many requests for recognition were made from potential NOCs in Anguilla, the Channel Islands, the Faroe Islands, Greenland, Kosovo, Montserrat, New Caledonia, etc.

The fact that the IOC now refers to UN recognition is notably because a few years ago, Juan Antonio Samaranch had to deal with the cases of Gibraltar and Catalonia. Both created a local NOC, which constituted a thorny issue for the Spanish IOC President. Today, some exceptions still exist. Palestine was authorized to participate in the Games as of 1996, even though its territory does not formally constitute an independent state. Similarly, Hong Kong was permitted to preserve its NOC when the former British colony was returned to China in 1997, while Macau was not allowed to have its own committee.

Beyond the criteria of the independency of the state concerned and recognition by the international community, it is relatively simple to constitute an NOC. The requirement is to bring together a minimum of five national federations of which three represent a sport on the program of the Olympic Games. An NOC is thus above all a grouping of national sports federations (around 20 on average). It also often includes various individuals. It is mandatory for any IOC members for the country concerned to be part of the NOC's executive office, and active athletes are also frequently involved. Most NOCs are non-profit organizations in accordance with the relevant national legislation on such entities. The NOCs' internal statutes must be approved by the IOC, but many are not in good standing.

A national governing body or national federation (NF) groups together local and regional sport clubs and associations of a sport and indirectly those holding a license for this sport or simply practicing it. Normally, it attempts to gain recognition by the international federation (IF) for its sport, which is necessary if it wishes to take part in international competitions sanctioned by that IF. The IFs' recognition criteria are usually less stringent than those of the IOC, and it is for this reason that some of them (athletics, basketball, football, volleyball) have a number of national federations that exceeds that of the NOCs within the IOC—for example the IF for football recognizes the Faroe Islands. It is for that same reason that new NOCs can still be created on the basis of uniting at least five NFs. The admission of a new NF to an already recognized NOC is more difficult since it can change the political and financial balance from which existing member NFs benefit. According to the Olympic Charter, the Olympic NFs must have the voting majority within the NOC's decision-making bodies for all issues relating to the Games.

There have been five major waves of NOC recognitions:

1 Prior to the First World War (1894–1914), certain NOCs were founded at the time when the concept emerged, notably to take part in the Games as of 1908 (as of which date an NOC was mandatory in order to take part). The countries involved were mostly European plus the United States, Canada, Australia, Egypt, and Japan. All five continents were represented for the first time at the Stockholm Games in 1912.

2 Between the two World Wars (1918–39), nearly all Latin American countries joined the Olympic system, as did three Catholic countries in Europe: Spain, Malta and Poland, and also India and the Philippines.

3 After the Second World War (1945–75), the Soviet bloc joined the Olympic system (the USSR in 1952) and it was the turn of former colonies to have their NOCs recognized: first those of the Arabian peninsula and Southeast Asia (during the 1950s) and later those of the Caribbean and Africa (1960s and 1970s).

4 The following decade (1976–88) saw the arrival of countries that had not been part of the system for political reasons, such as China or Vietnam, plus countries that had not achieved independence before such as the Portuguese colonies in Africa and certain Pacific and Caribbean islands.

5 After the fall of the Berlin Wall (1989), it was the turn of the new republics that had formerly been part of the Soviet Union and Yugoslavia, plus South Africa and Namibia, to join the system. All of them did so almost as rapidly as they gained independence and/ or international recognition.

In the twenty-first century, only a few territories are not included in the Olympic system and could potentially form part of it, such as Kosovo. Table 3.1 shows the number of NOCs per continent in 2007.

Table 3.1 Number of NOCs per continent in 2007

Africa	Americas	Asia	Europe	Oceania
53	42	44	49	17

The IOC may withdraw recognition of an NOC that does not respect its obligations as specified in the Olympic Charter. The two main reasons for suspending recognition are the total absence of autonomy from the government (e.g. Iraq in 2003, Afghanistan in 1999, and Venezuela in 1993) and non-respect for fundamental principles such as racial non-discrimination (violated, for example, by South Africa from 1960 to 1991 and Rhodesia—today Zimbabwe—from 1972 to 1979). In practice, these suspensions are very rare and increasingly imposed on the IOC by international politics.

In order to avoid penalizing athletes from the countries concerned, the IOC has in the past used the artifice of allowing "individual" or "Olympic" athletes from a territory experiencing difficulties to take part (e.g. Yugoslavia under embargo at the 1992 Barcelona Games, or Timor-Leste at the 2000 Sydney Games). This nevertheless remains an exception since the IOC's wish is for all athletes to participate via their respective NOC.

The NOCs' mission

Today, the NOCs have become the IOC's genuine correspondents in their respective territories. Their three main functions are:

1 To select and organize the national team for the Winter and Summer Games.
2 To promote Olympism, notably via the national education system.
3 To deploy all the IOC's policies on their territory (courses and grants organized by Olympic Solidarity, the fight against doping, education and culture, promotion of women, sport for all, protection of the environment, etc.).

Until the 1980s, only the first of the above functions was taken seriously in many countries. Since 1988, however, the NOCs' work has been facilitated since the IOC covers the costs of six to eight participants (six athletes at the Summer Games, four at the Winter Games plus two officials for each Games). As of 1996, quotas of athletes per sport and minimum performance criteria were progressively introduced by the IOC and the IFs, while nevertheless authorizing "invitations" or wild cards in order to preserve—artificially—the universal aspect of the Games. Moreover, the athletics and swimming federations permit one male and one female athlete to take part in the Games without meeting the minimum standards (as do the skiing and skating federations at the Winter Games). In 1999, the participation of an NOC at the Summer Games became mandatory, and failing to do so incurred the risk of losing IOC recognition. In 2004, the NOC of Djibouti did not comply with this obligation but was not suspended.

The second function is far more delicate since to achieve it, the NOCs must collaborate with their national education system and in particular the area of physical education and sport—a sector that is frequently controlled by the public authorities. Many NOCs have created national Olympic institutes or academies that attempt to spread the Olympic ideal and promote better sport management. This task is nevertheless rendered more difficult thanks to the lack of clarity surrounding the very notion of Olympism.

It is also within the framework of promoting Olympism that an NOC may accept a city within its country as a candidate for organizing the Games (see Chapter 5).

The third function—that of deploying the IOC's policies—is relatively new since it was only during the early 1980s that the IOC had sufficient financial resources to develop specific policies for the NOCs by means of an entity called "Olympic Solidarity" (see below). Many NOCs realized that this provided them with the possibility of holding programs independently of public funding and State controls and thus preserve their autonomy: an aspect demanded of them by the Olympic Charter yet one that proves delicate in most countries.

Moreover, many NOCs have other functions related to sport in the country: for example making statements on behalf of the sport sector, running facilities, organizing events, implementing anti-doping programs. This is notably the case for those NOCs that are confederations of all the NFs, as is increasingly common in Europe (with Great Britain as the main exception) and in the rest of the world (with the United States as the main exception).

To fulfill all these tasks, the NOCs need funding. Beyond government subsidies (either direct or via sport lotteries) and the (limited) aid from the IOC, the only other major source of revenues for an NOC is that of marketing its image and that of sponsorship for its national Olympic squad. Regarding marketing, the NOCs are permitted by the Olympic Charter to use the Olympic rings alone or incorporated within a distinctive emblem or logo on their own territory. This right may be sold for the exclusive use of one or several sponsors with the exception of those who are already IOC sponsors within the framework of the TOP program and who are thus sponsors of all the NOCs (see Chapter 2). In the United States, which is an extremely important market for sponsorship, the IOC must negotiate special deals with the American NOC (USOC) in this connection since US law grants ownership of the rings to the latter alone.

A (world) Association of National Olympic Committees (ANOC) was formally created in 1979 after much reluctance from the IOC to deal with previous groupings of NOCs. Its headquarters are in Paris. Its mission is to represent the interests of the NOCs and to explain their point of view in all matters relating to the Olympic movement and especially the Olympic Games (for instance, universality, mandatory participation, accreditation, and accommodation). Its main function is to bring together all the NOCs during general assemblies held every two years in conjunction with IOC Executive Board meetings. Each NOC has one vote in these assemblies under the principle "one country = one vote." Under its sole president since its creation—Mario Vásquez Raña from Mexico—the ANOC has never acted as a counter-power to the IOC but it helped its President to become an IOC member in 1991.

The ANOC encompasses five continental associations, some of them created before the ANOC itself. Today, each association holds its own multi-sports event and manages it in the same way as the IOC operates at an international level: The Panamerican Games have been held since 1951, the Asian Games since 1951, the African Games since 1965, the South Pacific Games since 1963, and the European Youth Olympic Festival Days since 1991. This European event is reserved for junior athletes below the age of 18 and has both summer and winter versions (as do the Asian Games). (Senior) European Games have never taken place given the extremely full sport calendar in the countries concerned. Frequently, the NOCs take care of preparing their national squad for the relevant continental Games.

Beyond this overall framework that applies to all NOCs, their situations vary widely from one country to another. One finds:

- Politically independent NOCs with significant resources of their own, beyond those made available by Olympic Solidarity or the state.
- Politically independent NOCs but without significant financial resources of their own considering the tasks at hand.
- NOCs controlled by national government on both a financial and political level.
- "Fantasy" NOCs that only emerge every four years with a view to symbolic participation in the Games.

The NOCs that belong to the first of the above categories are fairly rare: perhaps around 20 in the world. Examples are those of the United States, Australia, Belgium, Canada, Italy, and Japan. They have been able to develop marketing programs for their territory or benefit from a monopoly for sport or other lotteries (such as the Italian NOC, CONI, or the Japanese Olympic Committee). Those in the second category are mostly in Europe and number around 30. They also have a well-organized structure, often operating in premises that they own. Such NOCs were, for example, able to resist the boycott of the 1980 Moscow Games that was decreed by governments allied to the United States (such as the British NOC). Other examples are the NOCs of Austria, Brazil, France, New Zealand, Portugal, and Switzerland.

The great majority of NOCs belongs to the third category, where the power and authority lies mostly with the government. The NOC is thus to a large extent an "annex" to the Ministry of Sport, and the minister concerned is frequently the president of the NOC. This applied to former socialist countries but is still found in many African, Asian and Latin American countries. The situation should not be acceptable from the IOC point of view because NOCs must—according to the Olympic Charter—preserve their autonomy and resist all pressures of any kind. The situation is nevertheless evolving favorably thanks to aid from Olympic Solidarity in the form of cash or other assistance, which is making certain NOCs relatively "rich" compared with the economic level of their country.

Finally, there are around 30 "fantasy" NOCs that have virtually no activity during non-Olympic years, and that at times even offer their Olympic privileges (accreditations, marketing rights, tickets, etc.) to the highest bidders (often tourists or travel agencies, etc.). This was the case of the Ethiopian NOC at the 2006 Winter Games in Turin and of the NOC of Djibouti at the 2004 Summer Games in Athens.

Olympic Solidarity

The major source of financing for many NOCs comes from Olympic Solidarity. This entity manages the portion of the various television broadcasting and marketing rights for the Games that is allocated to the NOCs. The amounts have soared over the last twenty years, from US$28 million for the period 1985–88 to US$244 million for 2005–2008 (see Chapter 2).

The concept of Olympic Solidarity dates from the 1960s, and was initiated by Jean de Beaumont, a French IOC member who wished to provide assistance to NOCs that lacked resources by means of an International Olympic Aid Committee (1962). Olympic Solidarity was, however, only officially created under that name in 1971. It was able to launch its activities in earnest thanks to around one-third of the television rights for the 1972 Sapporo and Munich Games that the IOC allocated globally to all the NOCs.

Under the Presidency of Lord Killanin (1972–80), Olympic Solidarity was managed from the offices of CONI (the Italian NOC) in Rome, since the Chairman of the Olympic Solidarity Commission also chaired the Permanent General Assembly of NOCs, an ancestor of the Association of NOCs (ANOC), which was headquartered there. In 1982, Olympic Solidarity was moved to Lausanne but in separate premises. Anselmo Lopez, a Spanish banker and acquaintance of Samaranch, was nominated as the director. Since 1996, this post has been combined with that of NOC relations within the IOC Administration, and is today held by Pere Miró, a Catalonian, who has a staff of around 20.

Olympic Solidarity is officially supervised by an IOC commission that until 2001 was chaired by the IOC President (Juan Antonio Samaranch). Since the election of Jacques Rogge, however, it has been chaired by the president of the ANOC, Mario Vásquez Raña, who is as such an *ex officio* member of the IOC Executive Board. This reform—symbolically important—coincided with a strategic move to distribute funds on a continental level, under the aegis of the continental associations of NOCs. The idea was to give more responsibility to the NOCs regarding how the funds were controlled, and less to the IOC. Several worldwide Solidarity programs are, however, still managed from Lausanne.

In 2007, Olympic Solidarity was running around 20 programs that can be divided into six major categories:

1 Courses for athletes, coaches, administrators, sport physicians, journalists, etc. (to train such individuals in a given country with a view to enhancing the practice and administration of sport, ideally and if applicable in co-ordination with the IF concerned).
2 Individual scholarships for athletes and coaches in order to improve their skills. The scholarships are generally spent outside the participants' countries in recognized centers and universities, notably with a view to taking part in the Games.
3 Subsidies for the administrative activities of an NOC and assistance regarding its management, in the form of higher training for their executives (for example, the MEMOS program)[1] or consulting by foreign experts.
4 Payment of travel and equipment expenses for six to eight athletes and officials at the Summer or Winter Games if they qualify for such aid (the accommodation expenses at the Olympic Village are paid for by the OCOG).

5 Contribution towards the organization of sports events recognized by the IOC such as the Olympic Day Run or the establishment of a national Olympic academy or museum.

6 Travel and accommodation expenses for various NOC delegates at Olympic conferences and meetings such as the ANOC General Assemblies, the continental forums and training sessions held at the International Olympic Academy in Olympia.

By the time Samaranch's presidency began in 1980, the percentage of participating NOCs whose athletes obtained medals at the Games had been dropping sharply at each successive edition of the Games (see Table 3.2). The Olympic Solidarity scholarship program for promising athletes made it possible to slow down this tendency while considerably increasing the number of NOCs taking part in both the Summer and Winter Games. Today, just over one-third of NOCs taking part in the Summer Games and just below one-third of those taking part in the Winter Games leave with one or several medals. Nevertheless, considerable disparities still exist between the continents, with Africa and Oceania achieving far fewer successes than Europe, which accounts for over half of the medals won at the Summer Games and even more at the Winter Games.

Table 3.2 Proportion of participating NOCs having obtained medals at the Summer and Winter Games between 1980 and 2006

Summer Games	NOCs present	NOCs with medals (gold)	% medal winners
Moscow 80	81	36 (25)	44
Los Angeles 84	140	47 (25)	33
Seoul 88	159	52 (31)	39
Barcelona 92	169	64 (37)	38
Atlanta 96	197	79 (53)	40
Sydney 2000	199	80 (51)	40
Athens 2004	201	74 (56)	37

Winter Games	NOCs present	NOCs with medals (gold)	% medal winners
Lake Placid 80	39	19 (11)	48
Sarajevo 84	49	17 (11)	34
Calgary 88	57	17 (11)	30
Albertville 92	64	20 (14)	30
Lillehammer 94	67	22 (14)	33
Nagano 98	72	24 (15)	33
Salt Lake 2002	77	24 (18)	31
Turin 2006	80	26 (18)	32

The influence of Olympic Solidarity nevertheless remains relatively insignificant in terms of medals obtained, since other factors are more decisive. Studies carried out prior to the Sydney Games and repeated since then have revealed that the number of medals obtained by an NOC at the Summer Games could be predicted, with a high degree of accuracy, according to four factors: the gross domestic product per capita of the country concerned (more than its total population figures); the results at the previous edition of the Games; strong governmental support (such as previously, in Eastern Europe, and nowadays in China); and the fact of being the host country.[2]

In summary, the NOCs constitute an extremely heterogeneous world: one with which even the IOC is not fully conversant and that would merit further investigation. There appears to be a feeling among some members of the IOC Administration that the NOCs are something of a "nuisance," and that it would be more appropriate for work to be focused more strongly on the "core product" that is the Olympic Games and also on relations with the IFs.

The NOCs nevertheless constitute an essential tool for the diffusion of Olympic ideals throughout the world and as such should deserve to be more carefully nurtured and supported by the IOC.

4 International Sports Federations

An International Sports Federation (IF) is a group of National Sports Federations (NFs) and continental federations, at times completed by individuals, that wishes to promote and develop a specific sport or a group of sports disciplines on a world level. Its objective is to represent all those practicing the said sport, notably those holding licenses from the national federations, and even if the individuals in question are not usually members of "their" NF but at most members of their own local sports club.

A total of nearly 150 sports or disciplines have been identified throughout the world, and there are around 100 IFs that belong to a parent association: the General Association of International Sports Federations (GAISF), presented at the end of this chapter. The around 50 sports that are not represented in the GAISF (such as the Brazilian sport of capoeira or the winter sport of snowshoe) rarely have a world-level parent organization or have one that is almost unheard of (such as the World Armsport Federation, for arm wrestling).

In order to enter the Olympic system, an IF must be recognized by the IOC in ways explained in the first section of this chapter. We briefly present the IFs' mission in the second section. The major IFs have been the subject of various works, although there are few overall descriptions of their huge responsibilities within world sport with the exception of the book by John Forster and Nigel Pope.[1]

IF recognition

The IOC recognizes some 60 IFs, and a maximum of one per "sport" at world level. The notion of "sport" requires quotation marks in the same way as we spoke of "countries" in connection with the NOCs, since certain federations control sports that are extremely varied. The International Swimming Federation (FINA), for example, handles (speed) swimming but also diving, water polo, and synchronized swimming, all aquatic disciplines that are present at the Olympic Games, yet it does not cover underwater diving or lifesaving. The World Underwater Federation (CMAS) is a federation in its own right, and notably organizes free diving or fin swimming competitions. The FINA does not, moreover, handle lifesaving, which also has its own federation: the International Life Saving Federation (ILS). The CMAS and the ILS are both federations that are recognized by the IOC but their sports are not on the Olympic program. The International Ski Federation (FIS) controls six "disciplines" (downhill and cross-country skiing, freestyle, snowboard, ski jumping, and the Nordic combined event). The biathlon, however, has its own IF, the International Biathlon Union (IBU). All these "sports" and "disciplines" are on the Olympic program but ski mountaineering is not, although numerous competitions are held (such as the "Glacier patrol" in Switzerland).

In 2008, some 35 IFs have the privilege of seeing their "sport" included at the Olympic Games on the basis of its worldwide practice on at least four continents (for summer sports) or three continents (for winter sports). They are 28 for the Summer Games and seven for the Winter ones. According to the Olympic Charter, sports that are eligible for the Winter Games program must take place on snow or ice (see Box 4.1).

Box 4.1　List of International Olympic Federations

The order of the list is that of the Olympic Charter, and corresponds to the names of the sports in French. Many of the IFs' official names and most acronyms are also in French alone, since that was the most widely-used international language when most of the IFs were created. The year corresponds to the first time the sport was included on the Olympic program, even if the IF in question had not yet been officially created or was known under another name.

Summer

International Association of Athletics Federations (IAAF)—1896
International Rowing Federation (FISA)—1896
International Badminton Federation (IBF)—1992
International Baseball Federation (IBAF)—1992
International Basketball Federation (FIBA)—1936

International Boxing Association (AIBA)—1904
International Canoe Federation (ICF)—1936
International Cycling Union (UCI)—1896
International Equestrian Federation (FEI)—1900
International Fencing Federation (FIE)—1896
International Football Association Federation (FIFA)—1900
International Gymnastics Federation (FIG)—1896
International Weightlifting Federation (IWF)—1896
International Handball Federation (IHF)—1936 and 1968
International Hockey Federation (FIH)—1908
International Judo Federation (IJF)—1964
International Federation of Associated Wrestling Styles (FILA)—1896
International Swimming Federation (FINA)—1896
International Union of the Modern Pentathlon (UIPM)—1912
International Softball Federation (ISF)—1996
World Taekwondo Federation (WTF)—2000
International Tennis Federation (ITF)—1896–1924 and 1988
International Table Tennis Federation (ITTF)—1988
International Shooting Sport Federation (ISSF)—1896
International Archery Federation (FITA)—1900–1920 and 1972
International Triathlon Union (ITU)—2000
International Sailing Federation (ISAF)—1900
International Volleyball Federation (FIVB)—1964

Winter

International Biathlon Union (IBU)—1960
International Bobsleigh and Tobogganing Federation (FIBT)—1924
World Curling Federation (WCF)—1998
International Ice Hockey Federation (IIHF)—1924
International Luge Federation (FIL)—1964
International Skating Union (ISU)—1924
International Ski Federation (FIS)—1924

From 1972 through 1984, 21 sports featured on the program of the Games. Under Samaranch's presidency, however, the number grew progressively to reach 28 for Athens in 2004 and for Beijing in 2008. Under Rogge's presidency, however, the IOC decided to revise the list of sports on the program every two years, and thus the list of "Olympic IFs," while maintaining the maximum number of sports at 28.

In 2005, two sports were removed from the program of the 2012 London Games (baseball and softball) without others being added (rugby sevens and squash had been envisaged). In 2007, all the seven sports planned for the 2010 Vancouver Winter Games were maintained. A highly detailed review of the 28 summer sports and seven winter sports and corresponding IFs was published by the IOC before its 2005 and 2007 decisions.[2] It is currently the best source of information available on all the Olympic IFs and five recognized IFs (golf, karate, roller sports, rugby, and squash). These reviews were the basis of the IOC decisions concerning sports on the program beyond their mere worldwide extent of practice mentioned in the Olympic Charter (Rule 46).

Since 2007, adding or removing a sport requires a vote by the majority of the IOC members while in Session, based on a report that takes into consideration the Olympic history of the sport, its universality, its popularity among television viewers, its requirements in terms of facilities, its respect for ethics, its anti-doping work, etc. For the inclusion of an Olympic discipline or (medal) "event," however, the IOC's Executive Board may take the relevant decision without referring the issue to the Session. It was by such a decision that trampoline was organized for the first time at the 2004 Athens Games (as a gymnastics event), and that BMX will be included at Beijing 2008 as a cycling event, replacing another. Similarly, snowboard and skeleton were added to the Winter Games as skiing and bobsleigh events respectively. This avoided increasing the number of summer or winter IFs and thus sharing the Olympic revenues over a larger number thereof. The IOC is even considering the possibility of accepting skateboard as a cycling event at the 2012 London Games!

Table 4.1 shows the number of events per sport and disciplines at the 2008 Summer and 2006 Winter Games. During the last 20 years the number of women's events has been slowly increased to approach that of men's events, and at present parity is frequently achieved.

Whether or not they are accepted as Olympic federations, the IFs have an existence beyond that of the Olympic Games. They have two major functions with relation to their sports: the adoption and diffusion of universal rules, and the co-ordination of a world calendar. They have thus contributed significantly towards rendering sports competitions more international during the twentieth century, and also towards the globalization of sport in general.

The creation of the first IFs arose from the need to centralize the organization of the first modern sports that appeared in the second half of the nineteenth century, and to unify their hitherto extremely heterogeneous rules. Three so-called Olympic IFs in fact existed before the IOC,

Table 4.1 Events per sport at the 2008 Olympic Summer Games and 2006 Olympic Winter Games

Sport	Men's events	Women's events	Mixed events
Summer Games Beijing 2008			
Aquatics, swimming	17	17	0
Aquatics, diving	4	4	0
Aquatics, water-polo	1	1	0
Aquatics, synchronized swimming	0	2	0
Archery	2	2	0
Athletics, track events	12	12	0
Athletics, field events	8	8	0
Athletics, combined events	1	1	0
Athletics, road events	3	2	0
Badminton	2	2	1
Baseball	1	0	0
Basketball	1	1	0
Boxing	11	0	0
Canoe-kayak, flatwater	9	3	0
Canoe-kayak, slalom	3	1	0
Cycling, track	7	3	0
Cycling, road	2	2	0
Cycling, mountain bike	1	1	0
Cycling, BMX	1	1	0
Equestrian, jumping	0	0	2
Equestrian, dressage	0	0	2
Equestrian, eventing	0	0	2
Fencing	5	5	0
Football	1	1	0
Gymnastics, artistic	8	6	0
Gymnastics, rhythmic	0	2	0
Gymnastics, trampoline	1	1	0
Handball	1	1	0
Hockey	1	1	0
Judo	7	7	0
Modern pentathlon	1	1	0
Rowing	8	6	0
Sailing	4	4	3
Shooting, rifle	3	2	0
Shooting, pistol	3	2	0
Shooting, shotgun	3	2	0
Softball	0	1	0
Table Tennis	2	2	0
Taekwondo	4	4	0
Tennis	2	2	0
Triathlon	1	1	0
Volleyball, indoor	1	1	0

(Table continued on next page.)

Table 4.1 (continued)

Sport	Men's events	Women's events	Mixed events
Volleyball, beach	1	1	0
Weightlifting	8	7	0
Wrestling, freestyle	7	4	0
Wrestling, Greco-Roman	7	0	0
Totals (302 events)	165	127	10
Winter Games Turin 2006			
Biathlon	5	5	0
Bobsleigh	2	1	0
Bobsleigh, skeleton	1	1	0
Curling	1	1	0
Ice hockey	1	1	0
Luge	2	1	0
Skating, figure skating	1	1	2
Skating, speed skating	6	6	0
Skating, short track	4	4	0
Skiing, cross country	6	6	0
Skiing, ski jumping	3	0	0
Skiing, Nordic combined	3	0	0
Skiing, Alpine skiing	5	5	0
Skiing, freestyle skiing	2	2	0
Skiing, snowboard	3	3	0
Totals (84 events)	45	37	2

which was founded in 1894: the International Gymnastics Federation (FIG) created in 1881, and the International Rowing Federation (FISA) and the International Skating Union (ISU), both founded in 1892.[3]

As of the early twentieth century, the renovation of the Olympic Games led to the creation of more new IFs. Those governing sports that came to take on considerable importance, such as cycling (UCI, created in 1900), football (FIFA, 1904), swimming (FINA, 1908) or athletics (IAAF, 1912) were thus created prior to the First World War. Those for other major sports followed prior to 1950: for example skiing (FIS, 1924), basketball (FIBA, 1932), amateur boxing (AIBA, 1946), and volleyball (FIVB, 1947). More recently, newer sports have also become organized within a worldwide federation: for example surfing (ISA, 1976), triathlon (ITU, 1989) or karate (WKF, 1970).

Three major waves of IFs created can thus be identified:

1 Prior to the First World War for most classical sports (athletics, rowing, swimming, football, gymnastics, skating, etc.);

2 From 1920 to 1950 for most of the other Olympic IFs (badminton, canoe, hockey, ski, etc.);

3 From 1970 to the present for all the "new sports," many of which are not on the program of the Games (except taekwondo and triathlon), but nevertheless members of the GAISF (see later in the chapter for more details of the GAISF).

The history of the IFs is to some extent marked by their relations with the IOC. Although on the whole these relations can be considered as extremely good today, this was not always the case in the past. Although few in number and badly organized at the first Games in 1896, the IFs grew in number, became organized, and also gained awareness of their potential power as of the beginning of the twentieth century. Since their technical competence meant that they became essential to the organization of the Olympic Games, for which they approved/sanctioned the competitions, they began to claim a special status within the heart of the international administration of sport. Early in the 1920s, Coubertin went as far as thinking that they were hatching a "plot" to take over the Games. The relations between the IOC and the IFs thus evolved against the backdrop of a constant attempt to seek consensus: although the Olympic Games needed the IFs, many of them would have had little impact without the Games since the Olympic competitions represented the only large-scale international showing of their sport.

The problem of amateurism—today obsolete—was long the subject of extremely delicate relations between the IOC and the IFs. The interpretation of amateur status was more stringent within the IOC's rules than in those of certain IFs, and led to the temporary removal of sports from the Olympic program such as shooting (1928), football (1932)[4], tennis (from 1928 to 1984), and golf (absent since 1904). This same question of amateurism moreover led to profound and lengthy conflicts with the International Ski Federation (lasting from the end of the 1930s until the beginning of the 1970s!) and the International Ice Hockey League (now Federation). Today, all the IFs have removed the word "amateur" from their official titles with the exception of that for (three-round) boxing in order to distinguish it from the many entities that govern professional (ten-round) boxing but that are not recognized by the IOC.

Tension between the IOC and the IFs reached a climax under the IOC presidency of Avery Brundage in the 1960s and early 1970s before dissipating to some extent.

During the same period, sports events took on a far more international character whereas before, as mentioned above, the Olympic Games were one of very few truly international competitions for many sports. As of the 1970s, the IFs introduced an increasing number of world championships and world cup events or continental meetings. These events, like the Ski World Cup or the Volleyball Grand Prix, had a considerable effect on the general public. The World Swimming Championships were created in 1973, and the World Athletics Championships in 1983. The cycle of these international meetings became increasingly frequent: for athletics and skiing they were held every two years instead of every four and for some sports they even became annual. Today, there are few IFs that do not hold world championships. For Olympic sports, tennis is a significant exception. At the beginning of the twenty-first century, however, world championships are becoming more and more difficult and expensive to organize. To better showcase their sport, many IFs are considering the circuit format, i.e. competitions returning to the same cities every year.

This multiplication of international events no doubt contributed towards dissolving the tensions with the IOC, since it gave the IFs more independence. In the long term, however, it also meant that certain powerful IFs gained an additional possibility for putting pressure on the IOC.

Today, although a small number of IFs (e.g. the FIFA, the UCI or the IAAF) would be in a position to strike out on their own, since their world championships have a planetary impact that is comparable to or even greater than that of the Games, the others are fully aware that the Olympic Games remain the only real showcase for their sport in terms of its image—not to mention the broadcasting rights that all the IFs receive from the Games.

All these elements, plus constant dialogue that was intensified as of the 1980s thanks to President Samaranch and his successor, today mean that there is a certain degree of equilibrium within the Olympic Movement that contributes towards its unity.

The IFs' mission

All the IFs take the form of a non-profit organization (usually an association) in accordance with the legislation of the country where their headquarters are located. Around 30 of them are headquartered in Switzerland, with around 20 being located in Lausanne, close to the IOC headquarters.

The scope and influence of the IFs varies considerably. A great deal depends on the media impact of the sports in question, IOC recognition, and the number of national federations (and indirectly the number of license holders). Consequently, there are major disparities between the powerful IFs (FIFA, IAAF, UCI, FIS, ISU, etc.) and lesser-known ones, but also between those governing a single sport and those responsible for several. The differences nevertheless have very little effect on the IFs' internal organization structures, which are essentially identical for all.

There are also various powerful continental federations such as the Union of European Football Associations (UEFA) or the European Gymnastics Union (UEG).

At the peak of the organizational pyramid of each IF there is usually a legislative or decision-taking organ and an executive organ. The former, usually known as a Congress or General Assembly of the IF, is the supreme body that defines its policy. It consists of all the recognized national federations (one per country, usually giving the right to one vote). Its role is significant, and consists of drawing up or modifying the statutes, electing the members of the executive body, adopting rules, defining the calendar of events, admitting new members, and approving the budget. The legislative body usually meets annually or at times less frequently, which provides the executive organ—responsible for implementing the policy decided upon by the Congress—with considerable leeway and power.

The executive organ is usually known as the IF's "Council" or "Executive Committee." Elected by the relevant congress and/or designated by the continental federations (more rarely), it meets several times a year and is tasked with directing, managing, and representing the IF. It normally comprises a relatively small group of individuals: a president (only two women are Olympic IF presidents in 2007), one or several vice-presidents, a treasurer, a Secretary General and several other "simple" members. It is increasingly common (and above all within the larger IFs), for the council also to coordinate various consultative committees. These handle certain specific, specialized areas (medicine, legal affairs, technical aspects, leisure sport, etc.) or a geographical zone.

The council's powers are at times difficult to distinguish from those of the administrative entity and can give rise to confusion. This "grey area" can even become more blurred if the chairman of the council exerts considerable influence within both the legislative and executive bodies, and runs the administration without a secretary or Director General as the second in command. In other cases, a Secretary General is the administrative director and also a member of the council, and thus has the greatest powers within the federation (e.g. in the International Basketball Federation, FIBA, where the chair rotates between continental confederations). Beyond the chairman and Secretary General, the administrative entity consists of the heads and employees of the administrative departments (technical, finance, marketing, communication, etc.). Held by volunteers or non-existent a few years ago, these posts are now becoming more professionalized, particularly in the larger IFs. Table 4.2 shows the approximate number of employees at the IFs based in Lausanne and the surrounding area in 2007. It should be noted that these are small or even extremely small organizations in terms of staff.

The financial resources of an IF are generally as follows (by order of their historical emergence):

• Annual fees paid by the affiliated national federations recognized by the IF (today, these are marginal).
• The proceeds of fines and penalties paid by national federations or teams taking part in competitions held under the aegis of the IF (large sums for team sports).
• Fees received for international competitions organized with the IF's patronage (at times).
• Television rights for international competitions organized by the IF (to an increasing extent).
• Marketing rights for international competitions with the IF's patronage or for the IF itself (sponsorships).
• Payment by the IOC of part of the television rights for the Olympic Games (vital for most Olympic IFs).

Table 4.2 Employees of IFs based in Lausanne and surrounding area (2007)

Federation	Sport	No. of employees
AIBA	Boxing	6
FAI	Aeronautics	5
FEI	Equestrian	10
FIE	Fencing	5
FIH	Hockey	11
FILA	Wrestling	4
FINA	Swimming	14
FISA	Rowing	10
FITA	Archery	9
FIVB	Volleyball	21
IBAF	Baseball	7
ICF	Canoe	4
ITTF	Table tennis	6
ISU	Skating	10
UCI	Cycling	45

It is easy to imagine that the nature of these sources of revenues leads to major rifts between the Olympic and non-Olympic federations but also between those whose sport is attractive to the media and the others. Television and marketing rights today represent an exponential source of funds for IFs governing sports with a high media impact such as football, volleyball, basketball, and ice hockey (for team sports) and athletics, cycling, figure skating, and skiing (individual sports). Those federations able to benefit fully from this attractiveness to the public—meaning a slice of the "cake" offered by the media and the sponsors—see their influence growing continually. Others, however, are condemned to play a more modest role on the world sport scene (canoe, curling, luge, modern pentathlon, etc.). The revenues thus obtained are for the most part redistributed to the national federations via various programs such as advanced training for athletes, coaches and judges, equipment, or the construction of sports facilities. Since 1990, the IFs have therefore taken on an additional role: that of obtaining financial income in order to continue promoting the development and the financing—at least partially—of their members. On this subject, Forster and Pope speak of an "ends-means inversion"[5] whereby the IFs no longer live off their members' fees but mainly from television and marketing rights from their event(s). The coexistence in the same IF of both a regulatory arm and a marketing arm has been criticized by the European Commission for risk of conflict of interests.

Each IF is the central international entity for the sport in question. Within the Olympic system the IFs are the most autonomous structures within world sport and those most independent of the IOC. As already mentioned, the fact that they are tasked with the technical responsibility for the competitions and the running of them at the Olympic Games means that they are vital for the organization of the Games. It is also their responsibility to define the international selection criteria for the athletes at the Games in collaboration with the IOC, which latter wishes to limit the number of athletes. The FIFA, for example, only permits players aged below 23 to take part in the Olympic tournament and the IAAF has threatened to operate a similar system under the presidency of Primo Nebiolo of Italy (1981–99). Inversely, the IOC alone may include or withdraw a sport on the Olympic program: a subject on the IOC's agenda one year after each set of Games since the arrival of President Rogge.

Relations with the IOC remain somewhat ambiguous: each party has its prerogatives within a system where consensus and the objective of preserving common interest have so far made it possible to maintain a balance. It is this same objective that leads the IFs and the IOC to remain united when confronted with commercially motivated assaults on the part of the private actors on the sport scene (the media, sponsors, agents, etc.).

Within their respective sports, the IFs have "monopolistic powers" over the national federations (NFs) affiliated to them. Without recognition of the national federation by the IF of the sport in question, an athlete cannot envisage international-level competition. To take part in the Games, it is also necessary for the NF to be a member of the relevant NOC. This double affiliation is not always automatic: the IFs are tending to accept as many national federations as possible to increase their geographical coverage, while many NOCs prefer to restrict the number of NFs for political reasons (voting rights, notably) and economic ones (sharing of the governmental subsidies).

Beyond recognizing their NFs, the IFs have appropriated other tasks of a legislative, executive or legal nature, and principally:

• To promulgate and control the application of worldwide rules on sports practice (at times with the assistance of an autonomous entity such as the International Football Association Board for the FIFA or the Royal and Ancient Golf Club of St. Andrews for the IGF).
• To set the length and organization methods of competitions.
• To define standards for sports facilities, equipment and material.
• To classify competitors by category (notably age or weight).
• To establish and endorse the list of world and continental records (in some sports only since most sports do not have such records).
• To draw up medical regulations aimed at protecting athletes and to fight against doping (today within the framework of the worldwide anti-doping code that nearly all the IFs have signed).
• To attribute and control international competitions (at a world, continental and regional level), and at times organize them.
• To train and accredit international judges and referees.
• To promote the development of their sport worldwide.
• To co-operate with the Organising Committees for the Olympic Games (OCOGs), with Olympic Solidarity and with other pertinent organizations;
• To levy sanctions on athletes, officials and NFs that do not respect the rules of the sport in question.

By controlling the application of the various rules and by penalizing those who infringe them (by means of fines, suspension or even exclusion), the IFs have considerable legal power: not only over the national federations affiliated thereto but also over the licensed athletes within those federations, since the statutes and rules of the national federations may not contradict those of the IF concerned. Beyond this requirement, the IFs do not intervene, in principle, in purely national questions and only exert their authority over the international aspects of their sport. This is already a major aspect, however, since all the NFs must respect the international statutes and all individual athletes must be members of an association affiliated to an NF—directly or through their club—if they wish to take part in international competitions. It is therefore accepted that the IF chooses to impose its views on its affiliated national federations (particularly regarding technical and legal aspects) as a result of its aim to unify, standardize and protect the sport to the greatest possible extent. Any such federation that chose to ignore the IF's directives would inevitably penalize and isolate its own athletes.

This powerful sovereignty of the IFs is counterbalanced by the fact that an IF is, after all, only a confederation of all its national federations, which are often closely linked to their national government. This situation means that sports are sometime exposed to attempted political interference (particularly from the public sector) or commercial interference (from the private sector). These attempts often go beyond a purely sport-related framework and threaten to affect the IFs (which do not benefit from a real international status) on a legal terrain where their independence could in the future become seriously affected. This, then, is the complexity surrounding the autonomy of sport organizations. In Chapter 6 we shall handle the increasingly frequent phenomenon of confrontations between IFs and civil tribunals or national and European laws.

On another level, however, it cannot be denied that the IFs have long been the "structures representing the unified wishes of the competitors" according to French scholar Gérald Simon. Their current power is the result of this monopoly, which is rarely contested and even then unsuccessfully. Examples that could be cited are that of the International Snowboard Federation (which contested the control of snow surfing by the International Ski Federation in the 1990s), of the World Skating Federation (which disputed control over figure skating with the International Skating Union following judging scandals at the 2002 Salt Lake City Games), or even "federations" that have long been dissidents such as those for karate and taekwondo. The case of boxing, which has one IF recognized by the IOC (International Amateur Boxing Association, IABA) and several professional federations, remains exceptional, and does not favor the sport's transparency or appeal.

The importance that elite sport has taken on today, and particularly on an economic and social level, tends to favor the emergence of other representative structures (groups of athletes, parallel circuits, athletes' unions, owners of teams or tournaments) and—by diluting it—to threaten this unified determination on the part of the sports sector. As an example, and without mentioning the major professional sports leagues in the United States, we could cite athletes' leagues such as the Association of Tennis Professionals (ATP),[6] the Women's Tennis Association (WTA) or the Professional Golfers' Association (PGA) that have far more influence than the respective IFs concerned: the International Tennis Federation (ITF) and the International Golf Federation (IGF). On the other hand, we could also cite the Professional Surfers Association (which competes with the International Surfing Association recognized by the IOC), the Professional Association of Diving Instructors PADI (which competes with the World Underwater Federation, CMAS), the Association of (Beach) Volleyball Professionals (which fought a lengthy battle with the FIVB), and a group of athletes that has now disappeared: the World Indoor Soccer League (which attempted to compete with the FIFA-supported sport of futsal). Certain sports even have an athletes' league before having an IF, such as the World Riders Association (roller skating) and the Cyberathlete Professional League (computer games).

The General Association of International Sports Federations (GAISF)

More than just a grouping of IFs, the GAISF sees itself as a genuine forum for the sports sector to handle technical, scientific and educational aspects of sport. In 2007, it has 104 members including sports federations as such but also organizations as diverse as the International Federation of Sports Medicine (FIMS), the International Timekeeping Federation (FIC), the International Association for Sports and Leisure Activities (IAKS), Panathlon International (a mostly European network of service clubs similar to the Rotary clubs), the European Broadcasting Union (EBU), the International Catholic Federation for Sports and Education (FICEP), and the Commonwealth Games Federation (CGF). This diversity is in line with the priority objectives defined by the GAISF in its statutes: promoting information and rapprochement among the various sport organizations (among IFs of course but also among its full and associate members) and coordinating and protecting their common interests.

At a very early stage, the IFs felt the need to become grouped together in order to collaborate and act as an efficient counterweight to the IOC. Under the initiative of the International Cycling Union (UCI) and its General Secretary Paul Rousseau, a permanent bureau for the

IFs was already created in 1921. The bureau was behind the organization of the first regular meetings between the IFs and the IOC, but from which non-Olympic IFs were excluded at the time. It took 40 years for a really active association of the IFs to see the light of day. In fact, the 1960s were a period of growing divergence between the IFs and the IOC, incarnated by President Avery Brundage. The IFs criticized Brundage's inflexibility regarding amateur status and his lack of interest in consensus within the Olympic movement. On the initiatives of IF presidents Roger Coulon (wrestling), Thomas Keller (rowing), W. Berge Philips (swimming), and Williams J. Jones (basketball), the General Assembly of International Federations (at the time abbreviated to GAIF) was founded in Lausanne in April 1967 in the presence of 26 International Federations, both Olympic and non-Olympic. Berge Phillips became its president for two years and Coulon the Secretary General. The headquarters were established in the offices of the International Federation of Amateur Wrestling (FILA) in Lausanne. Thomas Keller of Switzerland became president in 1969 and remained in office for nearly 20 years.

The IOC of Brundage the paternalist was by no means favorable to this new entity uniting the IFs and that allowed non-Olympic federations to have their say. Initially, it refused to recognize the GAIF on the pretext that it did not include some of the major sports (notably athletics and football). The real reasons behind the refusal, however, were more a case of the potential threat that the young GAIF represented to the IOC's supremacy.

The GAIF was a flexible group of organizations with common interests in which each member preserved full independence. Those who hesitated at first soon joined, and the association grew rapidly: the FIFA and the IAAF joined in 1968 and 1978 respectively. The new moral authority of the IFs, the GAIF became the GAISF in 1976. A year later and on the initiative of Horst Dassler, the head of Adidas, it moved from Lausanne to Monaco as though distancing itself from the IOC's scope of influence. This was the beginning of a new era that saw the IFs take their individual and collective destiny firmly in hand.

Under the presidencies of Lord Killanin and later of Juan Antonio Samaranch, the IOC's attitude towards the GAISF evolved considerably and took the form of a determination—constructive and indeed tactical—to collaborate with IFs that were becoming even more demanding but equally essential. An Olympic Congress was held in Varna (Bulgaria) in 1973. Such a meeting of the entire Olympic movement, and one that had been specifically requested by the GAISF and had finally been accepted by Brundage, had not been held since 1930. The congress was organized thanks to the work of the IOC's

Tripartite Commission, a new entity that united three representatives of the IOC, three of the NOCs and three of the IFs. The commission continued to exist (under the name of Commission for the Olympic movement during Samaranch's presidency) and was to play a major role in the evolution of relations within the Movement. Finally, and following the 1973 Congress, the IOC withdrew the word "amateur" from the Olympic Charter: another symbolic step within a rapprochement with the IFs.

When Samaranch came to office in 1980, major progress had thus already been accomplished. The new IOC President nevertheless needed to establish a rapport with the complex individual who had been the real driving force of the GAISF: Thomas Keller. While Samaranch defended the unity of the Olympic movement (and the IOC's leading role therein), Keller defended the IFs' right to a certain supremacy, and wished to reduce the IOC's scope to the Olympic Games alone. In the background, the issue of the allocation of the exponentially increasing revenues from television rights was at stake. To remove the threat that the GAISF president's inclinations represented, Samaranch very adroitly opted to divide in order to conquer: he initiated the creation of the Association of the International Olympic Winter Sports Federations (AIOWSF) in 1982 (under the presidency of Marc Hodler of Switzerland, who had run against him for the IOC presidency), and the Association of Summer Olympic International Federations (ASOIF) in 1982 (under the presidency of Primo Nebiolo of Italy, an opponent of Keller). This diluted the GAISF's means of bringing pressure to bear on the IOC, in particular with regard to television rights to the Games, and also weakened Keller's position. The latter, aware that the wind was turning, left office as the president of the GAISF in 1986. His successor, Kim Un Yong of Korea, was far more cooperative. He came from an IF that was recognized by the IOC alone but whose sport was not yet on the Olympic program. Such IFs moreover were to form their own entity, the Association of Recognised International Sport Federations (ARISF).

Today, the unity of the Olympic movement is a reality in whose perpetuation the diversification of the IFs' activities beyond the Games plays a part. With Kim Un Yong's resignation in 2004 because of corruption charges in Korea, the presidency was taken over by Hein Verbruggen, who presided over the International Cycling Union (UCI) at the time. Verbruggen gave some of the GAISF's former luster back to it. For example, he developed the traditional annual meeting of the GAISF, and gave it a new name, SportAccord. Thanks to the parallel meeting of the IOC Executive Board, this made it a crucial date on the calendar of sport administration as an opportunity for leaders, consultants, suppliers, and organizers to come together.

Like the IFs, the GAISF is a non-profit organization. Its highest organ is the General Assembly that takes place annually (during SportAccord). Like the IFs, it also has an executive body with extensive power, the GAISF Council, whose main function is to apply the policy defined by its members. The council, whose members are elected for four years, consists of eight individuals: the chairman, elected by the General Assembly, two members designated by ASOIF, one by AIOWSF, two by ARISF and two (one from the IFs and one from the associate members) designated by other sport federations/organizations that belong to none of the other entities mentioned. Each organization or group applies its own procedures for designating its representatives. Two vice chairmen and a treasurer are elected from among the council members.

The GAISF's administration is operated from Monaco, by an administrative secretariat that was long headed by Jean Claude Schupp of France (from 1992 to 2004) but now under Christine Dominquez, also of France. There is little to say regarding the GAISF's finances, which depend on the membership fees paid by its members and contributions from various sponsors wishing to benefit from its network. The GAISF receives no revenues from television rights since it does not organize sports competitions on its own behalf. Its SportAccord Congress, however, is organized by an independent entity based in Switzerland and since 2003 has been producing significant revenues. It should be said that the ownership of Sportel, an annual meeting of sports broadcasters in Monaco, has escaped the GAISF despite the fundamental role it played in creating the event. Similarly, the publication of an international sport calendar is now in the hands of a British company (Sportcal.com) after a far more ambitious attempt with the company Worldsport.com failed in the early 2000s following the crash of many dot.com companies.

Box 4.2 The World Games: the (very) poor relation of the Olympic Games

Contrary to what is often believed, the GAISF is neither the organizer nor instigator of the World Games: a planetary competition held every four years and attracting some of the disciplines that are not represented at the Olympic Games. It was in fact a member of the GAISF, the International World Games Association (IWGA), that was responsible for launching the event.

In 1980, 12 IFs whose sports were not on the Olympic program decided to unite within a Council for the World Games (later to become IWGA). Their objective was to create a multi-sports competition on a world scale that could attract media attention and enhance the impact of sports that remained marginal among the general public. Kim Un Yong of Korea, president of the International Taekwondo Federation, played a major role in the foundation of the IWGA and in the organization of the first World Games, in Santa Clara, United States, in 1981. This initial experience met with major financial obstacles but managed to remain on the calendar. As the various editions came and went, the World Games gained importance slowly but surely. After London (Great Britain, 1985) they met with encouraging popular success in Karlsruhe (Germany, 1989). In 1992, in The Hague (Netherlands), they benefited from daily (recorded) television broadcasts on the American cable channel ESPN. In 1997, in Lahti (Finland), the Games were opened by Juan Antonio Samaranch and the number of athletes reached 2,600 (for 30 sports on the program, of which 5 were demonstration sports) as opposed to 1,865 athletes and 18 sports in Santa Clara. Most importantly, the Finnish television channel YLE broadcast 30 hours of competitions, of which 15 live. And finally, the prestigious marketing company IMG and its production company Trans World International (TWI) handled the sale of television rights outside Finland.

The 2001 World Games in Akita (Japan) and those of 2005 in Duisburg (Germany) confirmed the ongoing progress of a competition whose total budget is today in the order of US$6 million. Admittedly, the World Games remain little known by the general public and do not (yet) benefit from significant promotional resources, but the media showcase they managed to become in Lahti and then in Akita and Duisburg made known some sports that today feature on the Olympic program: taekwondo, triathlon, badminton, and softball first featured at the World Games. In 2009, the eighth edition of the World Games will be held in Kaohsiung (Taiwan), and constitutes a somewhat weak attempt by the Formosa regime to respond to the 2008 Beijing Games. Nevertheless, at a time when the overcrowded program of the Olympic Games is confronting the IOC with major logistical problems, why not envisage the World Games as becoming, in future, the mandatory gateway to the Olympic Games?

To summarize, it is possible to say that as is the case for the NOCs, there is a considerable diversity underlying the unifying face of the IFs: a diversity that is changing, that is little known, and that would merit more in-depth investigation. The IFs represent sport as it is today. It is moreover interesting to note that their number has more than doubled since the 1970s, and that certain IFs are in competition with rival entities. It is likely that the IFs will take on an increasingly important role in the governance of world sport during the course of the twenty-first century.

5 Organising Committees of the Olympic Games

After a very brief overview of the history of past Olympic Games and the selection of their location, we shall present the role of the Organising Committees of the Olympic Games (OCOGs)—as they are officially known—as well as some of the challenges facing the Olympic Games in the twenty-first century.

A brief overview of the Olympic Summer and Winter Games

Since the middle of the twentieth century, the modern Olympic Games have been by far the largest regular, peaceful gathering on the planet. No universal exhibition, no cultural or religious festival has the same universal impact. The Games have a history that is more than one hundred years old, a tradition that spans millennia. In our era, they have regained the importance they enjoyed in ancient times for over 12 centuries. Since 1896, and despite all the problems they have raised, they remain a unique symbol of international cooperation and as such merit preservation as a major legacy of mankind's cultural heritage.

Our intention here is not to recall the entire history of the ancient and modern Games, nor to retrace the exploits of their many heroes. A great number of both academic and more popular works already exist on those topics. It is nevertheless important to stress that the very aspect of performance conveyed by the Olympic Games to a large extent explains their success—both in our time and in history—on a sociocultural and economic level.

The modern Games did not reach their current pinnacle immediately. It is possible to distinguish five periods, each of around 20 years, which mark their gradual ascension.

The first, from 1896 through 1912, is that of their difficult early days. After a highly successful launch in Athens in 1896, the Games suffered from being integrated within the Universal Exhibitions from 1900 through

1908 (in Paris, St. Louis, and London respectively), since this reduced their visibility and scope despite the British achieving more exposure than the French or the Americans. The great success of the Stockholm Games in 1912 (which for the first time united countries from all five continents) permitted the modern Games to survive the interruption caused by the First World War (during which the 1916 Games scheduled in Berlin were canceled).

The second period, from 1920 through 1936, is that between the two World Wars. It saw the birth and anchoring of most of the Olympic symbols and ceremonial features we know today and that form part of the image of the Games: the interlaced rings invented by Coubertin, the athletes' oath, the medal ceremony, the Olympic flame, and the torch relay from Olympia, the Olympic Village, etc. From Antwerp in 1920 through Los Angeles in 1932, and including Paris in 1924 and Amsterdam in 1928, the Games became increasingly important compared with other multi-sports events such as the Workers' Olympiads or the World Women's Games that took place regularly during the same period. In 1936, the Berlin Games were lavishly organized by the Nazis in order to glorify their regime in the eyes of the world. This same regime, however, prevented the holding of the 1940 Games (attributed to Tokyo and then to Helsinki) and those of 1944 (symbolically attributed to London) as a result of the Second World War.

The third period, spanning the years 1948 through 1968, marks the internationalization of the Games, which were held outside Europe and North America for the first time and staged in Melbourne in 1956, Tokyo in 1964 and Mexico in 1968. The editions of 1948, 1952, and 1960 took place in Europe, in London, Helsinki, and Rome respectively. An informal rotation between the continents then emerged. New countries resulting from the end of colonization in Asia and Africa took part in the Games for the first time. The Cold War intensified the importance of the Olympic confrontations, with the Eastern European countries—and the Soviet Union at their head after first taking part in 1952—carrying off the vast majority of medals.

The fourth period, from 1972 through 1992, was characterized by strikingly improved technological sophistication related to the Games (international broadcasting, cutting edge sports facilities and equipment) and by an accentuation of political problems. The 1972 Munich Games barely escaped an African boycott—a phenomenon that seriously impacted on those of Montreal in 1976—but were gravely affected by Palestinian terrorists who took most members of the Israeli team hostage and assassinated many of them. At the initiative of the United States, the 1980 Moscow Games were boycotted by nearly half of the National Olympic Committees (NOCs) that could have taken part, on the pretext of the invasion of Afghanistan by the USSR six months earlier. The 1984 Los Angeles Games were in turn boycotted by all the Soviet bloc countries with the exception of Romania. The USSR and Eastern European countries took part in the 1988 Seoul Games, but a few of their allies (Cuba, Ethiopia, etc.) maintained their boycott. The 1992 Barcelona Games were the first edition to be free of boycotts for 20 years, and even marked both the first participation of Palestine and the reintegration of South Africa after its exclusion since 1960 because of the apartheid regime. Following the fall of the Berlin Wall, the Soviet Union took part in Barcelona as the Commonwealth of Independent States and Germany again took part with a single team.

The fifth period, as of 1996, has seen the Games reach a size that renders their logistical organization extremely perilous, and makes government involvement absolutely essential. Barcelona paved the way for this gigantism, but it was the "Centennial Games" in Atlanta, in 1996, which were to encounter major difficulties in the area of transport, information technology, and security. Moreover, the organizers of Atlanta 1996 sought to achieve every possible form of commercial revenues and savings regarding resources because they lacked genuine support from the city government or the State of Georgia. On the other hand, the 2000 Sydney Games took place without incident, and particularly thanks to the full involvement of the State of New South Wales. Those of Athens in 2004 benefited from a similar level of governmental support, as will those of Beijing in 2008. The latter two Games appear to represent a pinnacle in terms of logistics and governmental involvement in their organization.

Table 5.1 provides some key figures relating to the organization of the Summer Games from Moscow 1980 through Beijing 2008. Most of the figures are increasing. Over seven Olympiads, the number of participating countries has more than doubled (from 81 to 205 NOCs), as has the number of athletes (from 5,217 to 10,625), notably thanks to a continual increase in the number of female competitors. The number of events has increased by one-third (from 203 to 302), and that of sports (from 21 to 28) by one-quarter. Television rights have multiplied by almost 20 times during the period in question (from US$88 million to US$1,715 million), and media representatives attending the Games have more than doubled (from 7,960 to 17,231). These figures bear witness to the gigantic proportions the event has taken on, and a problem to which we will return at the end of this chapter.

The Olympic Winter Games have been held in parallel to the Summer Games since 1924: for the most part in Europe or North America with

Table 5.1 Some key figures on the development of the Olympic Summer Games 1980–2008

	Moscow 1980	Los Angeles 1984	Seoul 1988	Barcelona 1992	Atlanta 1996	Sydney 2000	Athens 2004	Beijing 2008
Teams								
NOCs present / recognized	81 /145	140 /159	159 /167	169 /172	197 /197	199 /199	201 /202	Approx. 205/205
NOCs with medals (gold)	36 (25)	47 (25)	52 (31)	64 (37)	79 (53)	80 (51)	74 (56)	
NOC teams without women	24	45	41	35	26	9	9	9
Sports								
Number of sports	21	21	23	25	26	28	28	28
Events on the program	203	221	237	257	271	292	301	302
Men's events	134	144	151	159	163	166	166	165
Women's events	50	62	72	86	97	115	125	127
Mixed events	19	15	14	12	11	11	10	10
NOC Teams								
Male athletes	4,092	5,230	7,150	7,060	7,006	6,834	6,296	
Female athletes	1,125	1,567	2,477	2,845	3,624	4,192	4,329	
Team officials	3,093	4,323	5,323	7,155	5,698	5,474	6,075	
Doping cases	0	14	10	5	2	11	27	

(*Table continued on next page.*)

Table 5.1 (continued)

	Moscow 1980	Los Angeles 1984	Seoul 1988	Barcelona 1992	Atlanta 1996	Sydney 2000	Athens 2004	Beijing 2008
Other personnel								
Journalists & photographers	3,860 (from 74 NOCs)	3,840 (from 105 NOCs)	4,930 (from 108 NOCs)	4,880 (from 107 NOCs)	5,954 (from 161 NOCs)	5,300 (from 187 NOCs)	5,231	
Broadcasting personnel	4,100	4,860	10,360	7,950	9,880	Approx. 11,000	Approx. 12,000	
Number of volunteers		33,000	27,200	34,600	47,466	46,967	39,494	
Revenues								
Tickets sold	5,268,000	5,720,000	3,306,000	3,812,000	8,384,290	7,000,000	3,599,000	
Total TV rights (million US$)	87.9	286.8	398.7	635.5	898.2	1,331.6	1,488	> 1,715
Broadcasting countries	111	156	160	193	214	220	> 200	
Worldwide sponsors	0	0	9	12	10	11	11	12
(Grand) National sponsors	35	35	13	24	34	32	11	19
Official suppliers and providers	290	64	55	25	65	60	12	15
License-holders	6,972	65	63	61	125	104	n.a.	

the exception of the Japanese cities of Sapporo (1972) and Nagano (1998). Of the 20 editions from 1924 to 2006, ten took place in the Alps. Until 1992, the Winter Games were held during the same years as the Summer Games, but as of the 1994 Winter Games in Lillehammer they have been held on even-numbered years between editions of the Summer Games, which maintain their original cycle. Until the 1984 Sarajevo Games, the Winter Games were relatively small but gained importance—with their program and number of participants increasing sharply—as of Calgary in 1988. After Nagano in 1998, Salt Lake City in 2002, and Turin in 2006, the Winter Games will take place in Vancouver, Canada, in 2010, demonstrating the IOC's increasing tendency to attribute them to larger cities rather than mountain resorts. In 2014, the Games will be held in Sochi (Russia), a seaside resort of 300,000 inhabitants located fairly close to the high mountains of the Caucasus. Sochi was the largest city among the three finalist candidates, the other two being Pyeongchang (Korea) and Salzburg (Austria).

Table 5.2 shows some key figures for the organization of the Winter Games from Lake Placid in 1980 through Turin in 2006. As for the Summer Games, most of the figures are rising sharply. Over the last quarter of a century, the number of nations taking part has doubled (from 39 to 80 NOCs). The number of events has increased by a little over 50 percent (from 38 to 84), as has the number of athletes (from 1,072 to 2,508), notably thanks to the participation of more female athletes. The number of sports on the program has nevertheless remained extremely stable (with curling as the only addition from 1998). The television broadcasting rights have multiplied by nearly 40 (from US$21 million to US$832 million), while the number of media representatives attending the Winter Games has more than doubled (from 3,803 to 9,408) although the total remains less than half of that for those covering the Summer Games. Although they are roughly twice or three times smaller than the Summer Games, the Winter Games are also beginning to be affected by gigantism and thus require a fairly large city to organize them, if only for questions of accommodation and transport infrastructures.

Candidatures and elections of Olympic host cities

Elections for the city that will organize the Summer or Winter Games have always been one of the main prerogatives of the IOC members. The election procedure has nevertheless evolved considerably over the Olympiads.

Table 5.2 Some key figures on the development of the Olympic Winter Games 1980–2006

	Lake Placid 1980	Sarajevo 1984	Calgary 1988	Albertville 1992	Lillehammer 1994	Nagano 1998	Salt Lake City 2002	Turin 2006
Teams								
NOCs present/recognized	39 /143	49 /154	57 /167	64 /171	67 /194	72 /198	77/202	80 /205
NOCs with medals (gold)	19 (11)	17 (11)	17 (11)	20 (14)	22 (14)	24 (15)	24 (18)	26 (18)
NOC teams without women	10	16	17	19	22	17	19	19
Sports								
Number of sports	6	6	6	6	6	7	7	7
Events on the program	38	39	46	57	61	68	78	84
Men's events	24	24	28	32	34	37	42	45
Women's events	12	13	16	23	25	29	34	37
Pairs events	2	2	2	2	2	2	2	2
NOC Teams								
Male athletes	839	1,000	1,110	1,312	1,215	1,389	1,513	1,548
Female athletes	233	274	313	489	522	788	886	960
Team Officials	920	1,417	917	1,888	1,821	1,468	> 2000	2,704
Doping cases	0	1	1	0	0	0	7	1

Table 5.2 (continued)

	Lake Placid 1980	Sarajevo 1984	Calgary 1988	Albertville 1992	Lillehammer 1994	Nagano 1998	Salt Lake City 2002	Turin 2006
Other personnel								
Journalists & photographers	1,272	2,373	1,939	2,091	2,333	2,586	2,661	2,688
Broadcasting personnel	2,531	4,653	4,361	3,623	5,534	5,737	6,069	6,720
Number of volunteers	6,703	4,040	9,526	8,647	9,054	24,000	22,000	16,400
Revenues								
Tickets sold	433,000	434,000	1,338,000	913,000	1,212,000	1,275,000	1,525,000	930,000
Total TV rights (million US$)	20.7	102.7	325.5	294	353	513.1	737.8	832
Broadcasting countries	40	33	64	86	120	160	160	> 160
Worldwide sponsors	0	0	9	11	8	11	10	11
(Grand) National sponsors	included among suppliers	included among suppliers	12	12	9	8	21	5
Official suppliers and providers	228	184	37	25	17	18	31	47
License-holders	165	140	40	12	35	127	69	32

During the entire first half of the twentieth century, notably during Coubertin's presidency, the designation of the host city was frequently by tacit approval and often for two editions of the Games at a time (Paris 1924 and Amsterdam 1928, for example), or a case of substitution if a city withdrew (such as the replacement of Chicago by St. Louis in 1904, London by Rome in 1908, and Tokyo by Helsinki in 1940—although the 1940 Games were canceled and Helsinki organized an edition in 1952).

After the Second World War, major cities of the world (such as Rome, Mexico City or Montreal) and countries undergoing reconstruction (Japan with Tokyo, Germany with Munich, Korea with Seoul) became interested in the Games and presented their candidature to host them, often on repeated occasions. After the financial disaster of the 1976 Montreal Games (whereby the city fell into major debt) and the political failure of the 1980 Moscow Games (which were widely boycotted), the flow of candidatures dwindled. Los Angeles was the only city interested in holding the 1984 Games, and Lake Placid (also in the United States) the only candidate for the 1980 Winter Games (once Vancouver, Canada, withdrew only a few days before the election). Moreover, after a referendum that mixed financial and ecological concerns, Denver (United States) withdrew from its commitment to organize the 1976 Winter Games, and was replaced by Innsbruck (Austria) just three years prior to the Games. Innsbruck had already organized the 1964 Winter Games. Certain sources began to predict that the Olympic Games were doomed to die out.

Against all expectations, the 1984 Los Angeles Games achieved considerable profits, which boosted the number of candidatures for subsequent Games. There were five of them for the 1992 Summer Games, six for 1996, five for 2000, eleven for 2004, ten for 2008, nine for 2012 and seven for 2016 (see Figure 5.1). A similar enthusiasm can be observed for candidatures for the Winter Games that are to an increasing extent seen by cities as an interesting promotional opportunity, independently of whether or not they are elected.

Faced with this large number of candidatures, the IOC was obliged to put in place a more and more stringent procedure. First of all, it demanded increasingly comprehensive candidature dossiers from candidates, based on detailed specifications and organized in around 20 chapters. In the past, it had only requested responses to a vague questionnaire and some architectural sketches. In addition, and as of the 1992 Games, it created a commission to evaluate the candidatures, which visited the cities and produced a report for the IOC voting members.

As of the 2002 Winter Games, for which there were nine candidate cities, the IOC set up a pre-selection procedure that eliminated the

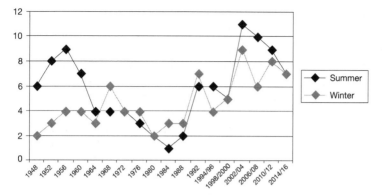

Figure 5.1 Evolution of the number of candidatures for the Summer and Winter Games 1948–2016.

candidatures that were considered the weakest, on the basis of a mini-dossier (without evaluation visits). The IOC Executive Board thus only kept four cities in contention for the final vote by all IOC members for 2002, five cities for 2004, 2008, and 2012, and just three for 2010 and 2014. The Evaluation Committee only visits the pre-selected cities, compares the various proposals and sets out its preferences but in carefully muted terms. The IOC members are renowned for not really taking into account the technical recommendations and focus on their political and personal judgment of the candidatures. The vote takes place by means of a secret ballot, meaning the members are accountable to no-one. On several occasions, the results have been a surprise when considering the quality of the dossiers presented (for example those by candidates for the 1996, 1998, 2006, 2012, and 2014 Games).

In parallel to the reinforcement of the administrative procedures surrounding the elections, the IOC has found it necessary to impose increasingly stringent ethical rules on its members and on candidate cities. As of the explosion in the number of candidatures during the mid-1980s, the cities in question attempted to influence the IOC members in ways that were ethically questionable. A fairly significant number of IOC members accepted favors from the cities or even demanded them for themselves or their entourage: valuable gifts of all kinds, study grants, free vacations, air tickets, paid internships and jobs or even cash, etc. These practices were revealed and made public in the media as of 1986, on the occasion of the election of the 1992 Olympic cities. They probably even existed before that date (notably regarding the election of Seoul over Nagoya for the 1988 Games) but in a more discreet way.

In 1986, the pitched battle between Barcelona (where President Samaranch was born) and Paris for the 1992 Summer Games and the equally hard-fought struggle between six resorts for the 1992 Winter Games provided an almost untouched terrain for lobbying groups of all kinds and led to a significant waste of resources. It was during this period that invitations to visit the cities began to be issued to IOC members and that representatives of the candidature committees visited the members (on the pretext of presenting the candidature file). Invitations of a third type, on "neutral ground" were also issued: for example at a sports event or an Olympic meeting of some kind. Such invitations often involved lavish expenditure.

As a result of these questionable experiences, the IOC decided to impose the first rules for candidate cities and its own members as of 1987. For example, the possibility of holding receptions was restricted and the value of gifts was limited to US$200. The rules were drawn up by a Swiss IOC member, Marc Hodler, who was responsible for ensuring that they were applied. Notably, his duties involved meeting representatives from the candidate cities following each vote so that they could inform him about violations to the rules or questionable cases. Few cities dared do so either because they were not fully innocent of such practices themselves, or they wished to present a subsequent candidature. Some of them nevertheless came forward, either in confidence or by means of press articles or publications. This was the case of the Swedish city of Falun, which had lost against Lillehammer, Norway for the 1994 Winter Games and of Toronto, Canada (beaten by Atlanta for the 1996 Summer Games) and even Sydney, Australia, which had won a narrow victory against Beijing for 2000 and whose head of the candidature openly admitted various questionable aspects of the lobbying by the Australian city, including the use of "agents" in charge of obtaining votes or grants to African NOCs awarded on the eve of the vote.

The IOC bore the revelations in mind to a limited extent, and progressively reinforced the "Hodler rules" while never penalizing a city or a member despite several debates on the subject within the IOC Executive Board. Finally, in December 1998, the practices were suddenly and widely exposed in the media and were the subject of a worldwide scandal that led to a major crisis within the IOC.

The cause was the publication of the fact that those in charge of the 2002 Salt Lake City candidature—currently the organizers of those Games—had given a study grant to the daughter of an IOC member (the member had since died but voted when Salt Lake City was elected in 1995). Marc Hodler seized the opportunity to make staggering statements to the international media present in Lausanne for an Executive Board meeting. He criticized Salt Lake City, but also other host cities and the famous "agents." The Italian automobile constructor Fiat was even accused by this Swiss lawyer of having provided irregular support to the resort of Sestrières, Italy with a view to obtaining the 1997 World Ski Championships. These accusations took place while Turin—with Sestrières and supported by the Italian automobile manufacturer Fiat— was a candidate for the 2006 Winter Games.

Beyond the ethical aspect, the deeply held reasons that led to Hodler's statements were linked to his multiple functions within world sport: he was in charge of ensuring that the candidate cities applied the relevant rules, and was also the head coordinator within the IOC for the Salt Lake City Games, president of the International Ski Federation between 1954 and 1997 and last but not least, a member of the Sion (Swiss) candidature for the 2006 Winter Games, to be attributed seven months later in June 1999.

Hodler's words led to the creation of no less than four enquiry commissions regarding the attribution of the 2002 Winter Games, created respectively by the IOC, the Salt Lake City OCOG, the United States Olympic Committee, and the United States Congress. Investigation procedures were also engaged in relation to Sydney 2000, Nagano 1998, and, following a battle over the ownership of the archives, to Atlanta 1996. Curiously, nothing took place with regard to Athens 2004 although the Mayor of Rome, which city had lost to the Greek capital in 1997, stated that votes had been bought and that the attribution of the 2004 Games should be reviewed.

The various enquiry commissions reached the conclusion that the "Hodler Rules" had been infringed regularly. Around 30 IOC members in office (out of 104 in 1998) were implicated to varying degrees. Four of them resigned of their own accord, six were dismissed following a special Session in March 1999, ten were officially reprimanded with varying degrees of severity, and around ten were placed in question by the media but escaped any form of action by the IOC.[1]

In parallel, the IOC began to study structural reforms that led to new rules being issued in December 1999. For the 2006 Games, which were to be attributed six months later, the candidature process was modified on a temporary basis (pre-selection of two finalist cities out of six candidates one hour prior to the election as such by all IOC members). The system proved unsatisfactory, however, and was later modified. It was decided that the pre-selection would be carried out by the IOC Executive Board (whose composition was itself modified to include representatives of the IFs and NOCs within the framework of the structural reforms within the IOC) on the basis of a technical report drawn up by a working group from the IOC Administration and its experts. Moreover, the NOCs of cities wishing to put forward a candidate are required to ensure that the said cities had genuine potential for organizing Olympic Games. A city may only, under this new system, draw up its candidature dossier and receive the IOC Evaluation Commission. Visits by IOC members to the candidate cities and visits by representatives of the said cities to the members are no longer permitted. Contacts between cities and members during meetings on neutral territory are subject to tight controls. controls. International communication activities are strictly curtailed.

The new procedure for attributing the Games is better than those that preceded it, but nevertheless does not guarantee an end to corruption or methods of influencing votes. A great many things can take place even if visits are forbidden: members can still vote according to their personal or other interests that have nothing to do with the quality of the candidatures. The publication of the individual votes (and not just of the results) following the elections would provide additional transparency.

As is the case in any parliament, it would be logical to know who voted for which candidate. Since—according to the principles behind the IOC's foundation—it is individuals who vote (rather than delegates of organizations or governments and according to instructions), the best guarantee of an honest vote lies with the choice of the individuals in question, or in other words on the quality of the members elected by their peers. A Nomination Commission for IOC members has moreover been created as a result of the 1999 reforms (see Chapter 2). With the pre-selection of candidate cities by the Executive Board, however, the IOC is in principle able to avoid any risk of seeing the Games attributed to a city that has major logistical shortcomings.

Organising Committees of the Olympic Games (OCOGs)

Once the Olympic Games are attributed seven years prior to the event, an extremely detailed host city contract, of around 100 pages, is signed by the IOC, the host city and the NOC. The host city and the NOC notably confirm their formal commitment to create an OCOG within eight months. The OCOG then becomes the main stakeholder under the contract and also the IOC's main dialogue partner throughout the organizational phase. It has around six years in which to organize the Games on the basis of the undertakings made by the Candidature Committee and summarized in the candidature dossier.

Naturally, many changes always take place between the time that the undertakings are presented in the dossier and the Games, as a result of numerous economic and political factors. The Games have taken on such importance over the last few Olympiads that regional and national governments have been obliged to make major contributions to their organization in addition to those on the part of the OCOG and the host city. These contributions are not only financial but also take the form of services on a state level (police, customs, security, transport, etc.), despite the fact that according to tradition, the Games are always attributed to a city and not to a country.

The socio-political issues at stake in connection with the Olympic Games are considerable today. It could be said that the Games have become a genuine public policy aiming to develop the city and its region, or even the country as a whole, for a period of around 10 years (if the candidature phase is included). In a word, the aim is to develop infrastructures and external image, i.e. the city and region's competitiveness in comparison with others.

Nowadays behind every candidature, the objective is to obtain a positive social and economic impact without endangering the environment, meaning that the Games quite naturally fall within a given territory's problematic of sustainable development (i.e. a balance between the social, economic and environmental impacts). Since the 1990s, the IOC has been focusing on the fact that the Games and their venues should not harm the environment and moreover should contribute towards the rehabilitation of urban wastelands and provide a legacy for the host region. Sustainable development thus offers both justification to any candidature and constitutes an objective to strive for once the Games have been attributed. The candidatures by Sion (Switzerland) and Turin (Italy) for the 2006 Winter Games were the first to place considerable emphasis on sustainable development. This concept is at present a reference framework for the actions of OCOGs, and most of them state it openly as a priority.

Given this framework of public policy, the legal form of an OCOG is increasingly becoming that of a government agency (such as for Sydney 2000), a company whose executives are appointed by a prime minister (Athens 2004), an association dominated by the public authorities (Albertville 1992) or a quasi-public foundation (Turin 2006). Purely private OCOGs (such as Atlanta 1996 or Los Angeles 1984) are progressively disappearing. Over recent Olympiads, the OCOGs have often been completed by a second, purely public organization in charge of constructing the necessary facilities: the Olympic Co-ordination Authority for Sydney 2000, the "Agenzia" for Turin 2006 and the Olympic Delivery Authority for London 2012. These entities are often the subject of ad hoc legislation that also foresees exceptional measures for organizing the Olympic Games: for security, transports, and for publicity (to prevent ambush marketing). For instance the British parliament passed the London Olympic Games and Paralympic Games Act a few months after the election of this city for the 2012 Games.

An OCOG is a highly unusual organization in that it has neither a past (apart from the brief candidature phase, during which the executives are at times different from those of the operational phase) nor a future because by definition its main activity ceases a few days after the closing after the Games. Once the Games are over, it needs only to close its accounts and draw up an official report. The OCOGs thus grow in terms of staff from a few employees upon their creation to around one or two thousand by the time the Games are held. The staff is again reduced to a few dozen a few months later and the organization is finally dissolved around one or two years after the Games. Around six months prior to the Games, an OCOG must thus manage the transition from a classical functional organization (finance, human resources, information technology, marketing, communication, etc.) to a decentralized field operation divided into as many units as there are competition venues or logistical areas (Olympic Village, media centers, accreditation, etc.). This change from a functional organization chart to one by site or venue is delicate since it represents a move from the planning stage to the operational one while also changing the hierarchical relations. It is this operational organization that must also handle the around 40,000 volunteers required for the millions of daily tasks (reception, controls, competition management, etc.) to be carried out for the duration of the Games. Without these volunteers, which appeared in large numbers for the first time in Los Angeles 1984, the practical organization of the Games would no longer be possible and their atmosphere much less lively. Recruiting and training these individuals—mainly in tasks requiring relatively low skills—is one of the OCOG's essential responsibilities: the volunteers are the "face" of the Games for most visitors.

The work of the OCOGs is increasingly monitored by the IOC, via a so-called Coordination Commission but to an even greater extent by means of regular visits by the chairman of that commission and the IOC directors in charge of the Games, of sport or of other specific areas. It is during these visits, which are prepared by experts, that the OCOG's progress is charted and that organizational problems—which never fail to arise—are resolved, often by approaching the highest levels of the state concerned or of the IOC. After long considering the OCOGs as "franchisees" of the Olympic franchise attributed by the IOC as the franchisor, the IOC is now increasingly considering them as partners working towards the success of a common project with multiple stakeholders. It is however extremely difficult for an OCOG to have a view going beyond its own lifespan and to adopt the IOC's long-term perspective, since the IOC must ensure that the Olympic system continues from one Olympiad to another.

To further complicate the challenge faced by an OCOG, the Paralympic Games have been taking place around ten days after the Olympic Games, at the same facilities as the latter, since 1988 for the Summer Games and 1992 for the Winter Games. These Games are owned by the International Paralympic Committee (IPC), an organization born during the 1980s by grouping together several entities involved in sport for athletes with various disabilities (with the exception of the blind and the mentally handicapped, for which two other entities and separate games exist). Since the end of the 1990s, the IOC and the IPC have concluded several agreements that have led to the Paralympic Games being integrated within the Olympic system to an increasing extent. The president of the IPC is a member of the IOC by virtue of his office, and representatives of the IPC sit on several IOC commissions. The Organising Committee for the Paralympic Games is now a unit within an OCOG, etc. Of course these Games do not have such an impact as their Olympic counterparts but virtually double the organizers' tasks, who need to maintain virtually all their structures in place for them, although to a reduced extent. The Paralympic Games nevertheless make it possible to integrate disabled athletes, in line with Olympic ideals, but without including specific events during the actual period of the Games, as was the case from time to time in the past.

In 2007, the IOC decided to establish Youth Olympic Games (YOG) on the model of the European Youth Olympic Days organized since 1991 by the European Olympic Committees on the initiative of Jacques Rogge, who was their president at the time. In 2007 these European Days took place in Belgrade, Serbia, for summer and Jaca, Spain, for winter.

The first edition of the YOG, reserved for athletes aged between 12 and 17, will take place in 2010 in Singapore. They are aimed at fighting young people's lack of interest in Olympic sport and television broadcasts thereof, also at building an internet community around the practice of sport.

These new Games could also be termed the "Spring Games." They are an opportunity to spread the Olympic ideal and values to countries that cannot organize the regular Games because of the size they have reached. On the other hand, however, they may dilute the uniqueness of the Olympic event unless they include sports and disciplines which really attract young people.

Box 5.1   Regional and other multi-sport games

In addition to the Olympic Games, there are numerous multi-sport competitions using a similar format, usually held at four-year intervals, but organized around either a geographical area (continental or sub-continental) or based on affinities. These events are governed by entities similar to the IOC (apart from the X Games which are owned by a cable television company in the Disney Group of companies). Below are some of the most important of these, by age (although some events had precursors):

- The Central American (and Caribbean) Games (organized since 1926 by the Organización Deportiva Centroamericana y del Caribe (ODECABE)),
- The Commonwealth Games (organized since 1930 by the Commonwealth Games Federation)
- The Asian Games (organized since 1951 by the Asian Amateur Athletic Federation then by the Olympic Council of Asia)
- The Pan American Games (organized since 1951 by the Pan American Sport Organization)
- The Mediterranean Games (organized since 1951 by the International Committee of the Mediterranean Games)
- The South East Asian Games (organized since 1959 by the South East Asian Games Federation)
- The Summer University Games (organized since 1959 by the International University Sport Federation (FISU))
- The Winter University Games (organized since 1960 by the International University Sport Federation (FISU))
- The (South) Pacific Games (organized since 1963 by the Pacific Games Council)
- The All African Games (organized since 1965 by the Supreme Council of Sport in Africa, then by the Association of National Olympic Committees of Africa)
- The International Children's Games (organized since 1968 by the Committee of the International Children's Games)

- The World Games (organized since 1981 by the International World Games Association) (see Chapter 4)
- The Gay Games (organized since 1982 by the Federation of Gay Games)
- The Military World Games (organized since 1985 by the International Military Sport Council (CISM))
- The Francophony Games (organized since 1989 by the Conference of Youth and Sport Ministers of the French speaking countries)
- The Summer X Games (organized yearly from 1994 by Entertainment Sport Programming Network Incorporated)
- The Winter X Games (organized yearly from 1997 by Entertainment Sport Programming Network Incorporated).

The gigantism of the Olympic Games

The question of the size and cost of the Olympic Games has long been a subject for discussion: possibly even since ancient times, since some chroniclers complain of Olympia being overcrowded during the events. As far as the modern Games are concerned, their size has increased constantly since the beginning of the twentieth century, and we can consider that major problems inherent to logistics have confronted the host cities since the 1960s. It was also around the same time that the Games ceased to be accessible to medium sized towns or "small" countries. Greece, which organized the 2004 Games, remains the smallest country to host the Games since Finland (Helsinki, 1952).

A topic for debate within the IOC since the 1970s, the problem of gigantism has become central since the turn of the century. It should be said that both the 2004 Summer Games in Athens and the 2006 Winter Games in Turin beat all records in terms of size, and that the financial difficulties facing both Vancouver 2010 and London 2012 could one day discourage candidates from coming forward—a phenomenon resembling that following the severe financial failure of Montreal 1976. The issue is thus an important one for the Olympic system, since the Games must not become an undertaking subject to too many risks or even a "mission impossible." Moreover, they should not be exclusively reserved for a minority of wealthy cities and countries because of the resources they call upon. It would be a positive move if the Games could be organized in South America (Rio de Janeiro is a candidate for 2016) or in Africa (the football World

Cup—easier to organize than the Games—will be held in South Africa in 2010).

Fully aware of the issues at stake, and soon after his election to the IOC presidency, Jacques Rogge initiated a study commission to fight against the gigantism of the Games and improve their organization. The ad hoc commission, chaired by Richard Pound of Canada, called for suggestions on the part of the public by means of a questionnaire available on the IOC's web site. The commission's 117 recommendations, submitted in 2003, above all focus on sporadic savings or improvements that are somewhat marginal. They were progressively implemented by the OCOGs, and will all be in place by London 2012.

A genuine solution or improvement to the issue of gigantism requires in-depth reflection on the sport program and the very format of the Games. The said format is based on three major principles of classic tragedy: units of time, place and action.

The unit of time means that the Olympic competitions currently take place over 17 (16 until 1992) days, including the opening ceremony, although some football or ice hockey matches often take place prior to the opening. Without returning to a system whereby the competitions take place over several months (which was the norm prior to the 1928 Games), the idea of increasing the competition period to three weeks (i.e. four weekends) could be envisaged for the Summer Games. The Winter Games period could also be extended, in order to manage delays caused by bad weather more efficiently. Longer Games periods would facilitate logistics without adversely affecting their media impact to any major degree. Certain television company executives have moreover expressed the wish to see the competitions take place over four weekends in order to make their investments in the broadcasting rights more profitable. For the time being, however, the IOC has rejected that option.

The unity of place means that the Games are always officially attributed to a city and not to a country, unlike the case for the football World Cup or other major events.

In fact, however, the Games have long taken place over an entire region, and the preliminary matches of the football tournament often take place in three or four cities located a considerable distance away from the Olympic city, where only the final phases take place. For instance, the 2008 Olympic football tournament took place in Qinhuangdao, Shenyang, Tianjin, and Shanghai, in addition to the finals in Beijing. Would it not be possible to extend this model to the other seven team sports on the program, which represent one-quarter of all the competitions? It could doubtless also be applied to other sports organized as tournaments, such as badminton or tennis. Spreading the events geographically would permit more efficient use of existing facilities in the host country and considerably alleviate the problems of accommodation and transport without changing the spirit of the Games. This was the model chosen by Los Angeles in 1984, where the competitions were held throughout southern California. Such a solution nevertheless meets with strong opposition on the part of the IFs concerned, who all wish to be in the heart of the Olympic host city. Even the FIFA, after a final close to but not within Atlanta in 1996, now demands that the football final takes place in the main Olympic stadium. The NOCs are also against such a model, which would require them to multiply the number of team officials.

The unity of action is linked to the content of the Olympic program, which should be examined from the angle of the sports represented but also from that of the disciplines and events within each sport. The work of revising the program has been entrusted to a special IOC commission since the late 1960s and which, after a long period of inactivity, began to make recommendations once again as of 2002.

From the sport point of view, it can be said that the Winter Games respect the unity of action more closely than their summer counterparts. The Olympic Charter states that the sports represented must take place on snow or ice. There are seven at present (biathlon, bobsleigh, curling, ice hockey, luge, skating, skiing). Skiing alone unites six disciplines (alpine, cross-country, jumping, Nordic combined, freestyle, snowboard) and over half of the winter events. Today, there are only very few sports or disciplines that could be added to the winter program: ski alpinism, ski orienteering, snowshoe, winter triathlon, luge on a natural run or sled dog races. The IOC Programme Commission has nevertheless recommended that nothing—with the exception of a few events such as skicross—be added for Vancouver 2010. No new sports can thus be added to the program, far less dense than that of the Summer Games, before those of Sochi 2014 at the earliest.

Since the winter program is in fact relatively "light," the transfer of certain sports such as basketball or fencing from the Summer Games has been widely discussed within the IOC since the 1960s and 1970s. The idea nevertheless met with opposition from the IFs concerned and above all from the Winter Sports Federations, which share the revenues from the television rights and sponsoring. Although the revenues only represent half the amounts received for the Summer Games, they are shared by 7 IFs only (as opposed to 28).

Today, the Winter Games are not held in the same year as the Summer Games and have also gained in importance and visibility, so the question of their program could be reexamined, notably for indoor sports wishing to join the Olympics or those for whom the season is mainly during winter. Futsal (indoor football) evoked such a possibility in 2001. Bowling wished to hold an unofficial competition during the 2002 Winter Games but the IOC did not permit it. Despite similar pressures, a bridge tournament was organized during the 2002 Salt Lake City Games. Transferring sports or accepting new ones would require even larger Winter Olympic cities, with vast indoor facilities. Certain IOC members are favorable to such a reform, although the IOC President and the IOC Programme Commission have clearly rejected it. It would no doubt change the very nature of the Winter Games and moreover threaten them, in turn, with a slide towards gigantism. After Salt Lake City (2002) and Turin (2006), this already seems to be a genuine danger.

The unity of action of the Summer Games is far more difficult to achieve given the diversity of the sports on the program: most of the sports in fact virtually reproduce, at the Games, the program of their respective world championships. The number of events for which medals are awarded rose from 198 in Montreal (21 sports) to 302 in Beijing (28 sports), and particularly because women's events have now been included in all sports except (for the time being) in boxing. (See Table 4.1 in Chapter 4, which gives a breakdown of events by sport and discipline.)

The IOC President wishes to preserve the limits reached, in his opinion, at Sydney 2000. His Programme Commission proposed removing three sports in 2002 (baseball, softball and modern pentathlon) and possibly including two others. In 2005, the IOC Session did in fact remove baseball and softball but preserved modern pentathlon: perhaps out of respect for Pierre de Coubertin, who invented the sport in 1912. No other sport obtained the two-thirds majority when voted upon, although the Executive Board proposed five of them for acceptance (golf, roller sports, rugby sevens, squash, and karate) and squash and karate came close to reaching the required number of votes. Including those two sports born on other continents could, however, have constituted progress regarding the fact that very few sports on the program did not originate in Europe.

In 2007, the IOC modified that Olympic Charter so that as of 2009, a simple majority will be sufficient to add or remove a sport from the program. The change also specifies a minimum of 25 sports and maintains the maximum, arbitrarily, at 28.

The various Olympic sports have greatly differing effects on the size of the Games. Can modern pentathlon with around 60 athletes logically be seen in the same light as rowing and its 550 competitors? What does golf cost compared with baseball, since most cities have a golf course but few have baseball pitches?

One genuine potential measure to reduce the size and above all the cost of the Games would be to remove certain disciplines, notably those that require particularly costly facilities that are not subject to much use: such as the slalom in canoe, the equestrian three-day event and, at the Winter Games, long-track speed skating or ski jumping. They could be replaced by more modern sports that are less expensive to organize, such as skateboarding or snowshoe. Regarding disciplines, it should be noted, the decision falls within the scope of the IOC's Executive Board alone.

Removing events could also be envisaged. The IOC Programme Commission has proposed, for example, removing almost half of the wrestling events, and permitting the International Federation to choose between the Greco-Roman style and freestyle (a proposal that was not retained). An effort could be made to reduce events in some of the five sports classified by weight category, which range from 12 (too numerous for boxing) to four (not sufficiently numerous for taekwondo). On the other hand, possibilities of removing events that are too similar in other sports (e.g. 50 and 100 meters in swimming) are limited, and would in fact have little impact on the size of the Games since a sport facility can easily be used for a few more events (in which athletes who are already present often compete). The objective is more one of remaining at around 300 events and only accepting new ones if other, older ones are removed. Here, too, the traditional events should make way for those that are more popular among young people. It was for this reason that the IOC decided to introduce cycling BMX at Beijing 2008 and ski cross at Vancouver 2010 (while citing the Disney X games as a reference!).

The unity of action of the Summer Games is without doubt placed at a disadvantage as much by an excessive number of preliminary competitions as by too many events. Without wishing to move to a program consisting of finals alone, such as that of the now defunct Goodwill Games (organized four times from 1990 to 2001 by the Turner Broadcasting System) or invitation athletics meetings, it would nevertheless be possible to reduce the number of preliminary sessions by considerably reducing the number of athletes. The IOC has already imposed a limit of 10,000 competitors as of the Atlanta Games— always slightly exceeded (10,625 in Athens)—in order to be able to house them at all the Olympic village. Athletics, however (20 percent of the athletes in Athens), swimming (10 percent) and, at the Winter Games, skating, and skiing, do not have an imposed quota while modern pentathlon is satisfied with a grand total of 32 men and 32 women. In Sydney and Athens, this made it possible to organize pentathlon over a single day for each gender (as opposed to five in the past), meaning a considerable logistical saving.

If such quotas develop, they must of course be implemented without destroying the universality of the Games, i.e. the possibility for each country—notably those with fewer resources—to send some athletes who do not meet the strict minimum performance criteria. In Athens, however, the origin of the athletes was still considerably weighted towards Europe (50.3 percent of the participants) as opposed to America (18.4 percent), Asia (17.1 percent), Africa (7.8 percent) and Oceania (6.3 percent). The NOCs would only be more willing to accept these quotas—a development that would inevitably reduce their Olympic delegation—if their youngest athletes (who do not reach the minimum standards and are often added to the team to gain experience) had an opportunity to take part in the Youth Olympic Games, recently initiated by the IOC (see earlier in this chapter).

Similarly, the development of the World Games, reserved for non-Olympic sports and that have taken place every four years since 1981 (the last edition being in Duisburg, Germany, in 2005) should be encouraged in order to avoid having to add new sports to the Olympic Games or to provide an alternative to those forced out of the program to make way for more popular sports. The Youth Games or the World Games, like the Paralympics, would benefit from being more integrated within the Olympic system.

Beyond the suggestions made above, aimed at reducing the size of the Games by modifying their format or their program, it is always possible to focus on the organizational methods and efficiency of the structures put in place, i.e. the possibility of organizing Games that use fewer human or financial resources for the same result (while remaining in line with the IOC's objectives).

Regarding human resources, and apart from the athletes and their support staff (two for every three athletes), four large categories should be examined in detail: the OCOG volunteers, the media, the sub-contractors and the spectators. The other categories of "participants" are too small to have a major impact on logistics, transport, and accommodation at the Games, and notably that of the "guests," who represent less than 1 percent of those accredited.

The number of Olympic volunteers increased from 34,000 at Barcelona in 1992 to 47,000 for Sydney in 2000, i.e. an increase of 38 percent and one that is out of proportion with the development of the sport program. The volunteers are admittedly the "face" of the Games and contribute towards their atmosphere, but many are under-occupied and nevertheless require transport, food and clothing, etc. The quality of the volunteers should be more important than their quantity in order to organize the best possible Games.

The category of the media is traditionally divided between representatives of the written press and those from radio and television. Contrary to what is often believed, the number of journalists from the written press (including photographers) is stabilizing at around 5,000, i.e. around one for every two athletes. A decrease in their number was even recorded between the 1996 Atlanta Games and those of Athens in 2004. Representatives of radio and television are however constantly increasing in number: around 8,000 in Barcelona and 12,000 in Athens. This soar in numbers of around one-third is difficult to explain even if the number of broadcasting hours and countries is on the increase. Reducing this category would of course be a sensitive issue, since those involved belong to the channels and broadcasters that have bought the broadcasting rights. Even so, these individuals require ever-larger media villages, plus more transport and accreditation facilities, etc. Ceilings should thus be specified in future contracts with broadcasters.

The category of sub-contractors includes all non-OCOG personnel and volunteers working at the Games for a company providing products and services needed. Those in question range from individuals working at beverage stands in a stadium to the head of an official supplier, technicians who repair photocopiers or a sponsor's head of marketing. In Barcelona, over 23,000 persons were accredited under this category, and a total of around 75,000 in Sydney. It would therefore be useful to study, in detail, the use of these accreditations and notably to see if they are too generously made available to sponsors.

Paying spectators are not accredited, but nevertheless require logistical services in proportion to their number, which has been increasing considerably over recent Olympiads. There were 3 million spectators in Seoul and Barcelona and 6.7 million in Sydney (with a peak at 8.4 million in Atlanta). The sale of tickets of course constitutes a major source of revenues for the OCOG, proportional to the number of events. The presence of spectators nevertheless represents a logistical burden in terms of transport, reception facilities and temporary or permanent seating. Increasing the number of these facilities and services leads to the creation of stadiums that prove too large for the local population after the Games or even remain only partially filled during the first week of Olympic competitions. It is possible to organize Games that are equally successful using smaller facilities that are easier to use afterwards. The public can also follow the Games on giant screens in the centre of the Olympic city, which would contribute towards creating a lively atmosphere.

There is considerable room for maneuver regarding spectators, but this also depends on the willingness to make concessions on the part of the International Federations, which have to date been demanding ever larger spectator capacities. It would seem that the Athens OCOG took the issues we have mentioned to heart, since they "made do" with 3.6 million spectators, although the figures could once again soar for Beijing.

Concerning financial resources, it should be noted that a great deal of money is spent on organizing the Games in order to compensate for two intangible assets that are not easily available: time and information. It is clear that planning the Olympic tasks according to a schedule can considerably reduce costs. For several Olympiads, the IOC has been attributing the Games seven years in advance, but it is vital that the first years are not lost as a result of useless discussion. Such a situation can be avoided by the better preparation of candidatures, and by a better transition from the candidature stage to that of the actual organization (notably by keeping the same teams in place), but also by reutilizing certain solutions that have proved their worth at other editions of the Games. Notable examples of such solutions are those related to information and communications technology, which are among the major areas of expenditure for an OCOG (in the order of US$400 million).

In this respect, the IOC is faced with two very different options: it could take over certain sections of the organization itself (or most of it as UEFA has done for the European Football Championships since 2004), or outsource them in the long term to reliable partners. By founding the company OBS (Olympic Broadcast Services), it has chosen to take over, indirectly, the fundamental role of the audio and video signal provider for all broadcasters of the Games worldwide as of 2008. By signing a contract with Swatch AG, however, it has decided to sub-contract—through value in kind sponsorship—the processing of the results of Olympic competitions until at least 2010. These developments will both lead to substantial savings in two major sectors of the organization. In the same order of ideas, sectors such as temporary constructions, ticketing, security or Internet provision could be the subject of similar strategic partnerships. In reintegrating the administration of the company OGKS (Olympic Games Knowledge Services), created in 2002, within the IOC Administration, it would appear that the IOC wishes to keep knowledge sharing and expertise related to organizing the Games within its custodianship and thus, in the long term, to avoid reinventing the wheel for each new edition of the Games.

The future of the Games

After the 2004 Athens Games and above all after Turin 2006, the IOC began to reflect on the future of the Olympic Games. It now considers that the Games possess four other fundamental components in addition to the sport competitions as such. The first is the torch relay from Olympia, which takes place over several weeks prior to the Games, in the host country and frequently with many international stages. The second is the Opening, Closing, and Medal Ceremonies. At the Winter Games since 1980, the medals have all been awarded in the center of the host city during the early evening. The third is the cultural program, consisting of exhibitions and artistic performances. The program is a mandatory feature of the Games since the art competitions were discontinued after 1948 but is one that is often overshadowed by the sport competitions, despite its excellent quality. The fourth and final component is that of the street activities organized in the host city, including broadcasts of the competitions and concerts. Since Sydney, these have been united under the name of "live sites."

These four components of the Games have of course existed for many Olympiads, but the IOC now wishes to highlight them: on the one hand to distinguish the Games from simple world championships and on the other to increase their attractiveness for spectators and sponsors in particular. Here, the football World Cup serves as both an example and a competitor, since FIFA has succeeded in making it a highly successful event that is extremely attractive not only to companies providing financial support for it but also for the population of the host country. The Games in Athens and Turin both suffered from a certain degree of indifference on the part of spectators, notably those from the region, and resulted in deserted stadiums during the preliminary competitions—whereas the matches of the 2006 football World Cup were all sold out. Similarly, the Olympic sponsors are dissatisfied with the on-site possibilities they are granted for advertising their association with the Games, and particularly compared with what is available elsewhere, such as in the stadiums and cities for the 2006 football World Cup in Germany. The IOC has always applied a "clean venues" policy that forbids any publicity within the Olympic venues and restricts it severely in the areas around them. The Olympic sponsors thus find themselves corralled into special villages where they remain among their own number, and with little interaction with the public. Recent organizers of the football World Cup have, however, succeeded in bringing fans and sponsors together at festive venues: for Berlin 2006, Adidas even created a temporary, one-third scale model of the stadium used for the final to house its guests and spectators wishing to watch the broadcasts on giant screens. The future of the Games will thus inevitably call for a better "Olympic experience" for those who attend. If not, fans of the various sports will prefer to remain at home and watch them on television— where, it must be said—they have a vastly superior view thanks to the close-ups, slow-motion extracts, commentaries, etc. that can only become even better with the advent of high-definition television. This tendency to watch the Games on television is of course compounded by the price of tickets and of accommodation in the Olympic city, which will become increasingly excessive for the "average fan." The security measures implemented are also dissuasive since they make access to an Olympic venue a complex and time-consuming affair.

Paradoxically, the Olympic experience will increasingly take the form of elements other than simply attending a competition. It will need to incorporate festive and cultural elements that attract the local, regional and national population and that contribute towards a good Olympic atmosphere, and also be accompanied by outstanding decorative elements throughout the host city rather than at the Olympic sites alone. During the 2000 Games in Sydney, and although the stadiums were filled, many inhabitants came together to celebrate Australian victories at several locations throughout the city that had been equipped with giant screens and accompanied by bands playing live music. Although the people of Turin were indifferent to the competitions at the 2006 Winter Games, they assembled *en masse* every evening near to the site for the medal ceremonies, and filled the streets of the city during the "white nights" (Bianca Notte) organized by the municipality: a simple matter of authorizing unlimited opening hours for the shops for two consecutive Olympic weekends. Beijing 2008 has announced an extremely ambitious program with activities at sites in around 30 Chinese cities during the Games. From this point of view, the Olympic torch relay and the cultural program accompanying the Games, which involve the entire country, offer considerable potential for holding popular events while conveying the Olympic message more effectively.

Over recent years, the IOC has placed great emphasis on the logistical aspects of organizing the Games, notably following the difficulties encountered at the 1996 edition in Atlanta. It has permitted the OCOGs to handle everything related to their "packaging" without a great deal of supervision: ceremonies, cultural and street activities and events, the torch relay, etc. As of 1996, it nevertheless began to develop what is now termed the "look of the Games." This provisional corporate identity is based on colors and motifs used in a multitude of ways, with giant interlaced rings extremely present in order to better promote the "Olympic brand" and blue backgrounds that are more conducive to television rendering. It has also imposed slogans for the Games: "The Millennium Games" in 2000, "Light the fire within" in 2002, "Homecoming Games" in 2004, and "Passion lives here" in 2006.

Such aspects are not sufficient to improve the Olympic experience, however. The IOC has placed too great an emphasis on the television "show," and thus on the broadcasters and the advertisers, whereas it appears essential to take the needs of spectators attending in person and the local population into consideration to a greater extent: they do not necessarily speak English or understand the marketing slogans surrounding the Games. The IOC should, in future, take these festive and cultural aspects in hand, while ensuring that full benefit is derived from the character of the host region and also that the sponsors do not gain the upper hand, as is the case for the torch relay since it has been sponsored by Coca-Cola and Samsung.

The internet and mobile phones should be allowed to play a larger role for reporting the Olympic Games and interacting with their participants. Such new media might revive the interest of young people in the Olympic saga as the Olympic television audience is getting older. The median age of US Olympic television viewers, for example, passed from 38.7 in Barcelona 1992 to 46.2 years of age in Athens 2004.

It is, in fact, by means of the emotions aroused among the genuine participants in the widest sense (athletes, support staff, spectators, the media, young people, etc.) that the Olympic values can best be passed on, and that the Games will preserve their unique value as a cultural heritage for humanity—an aspect that moreover distinguishes them from other major sports events.

6 Governments and the Olympic system

For around 30 years, the Olympic system has needed to handle questions of public order to an ever increasing extent. In other words, the sports order that it has patiently constituted during the twentieth century is now finding itself regularly confronted by public authorities and the juridical orders they engender at a national or international level.

Since the 1960s, the United Nations system has become interested in international sport. As of 1972, boycotts of the Games by certain governments seriously affected the Olympic system. The European Union (EU) and its member states have been particularly active regarding the sports sector since 1995: the year when the Court of Justice of the European Communities rendered its famous "Bosman ruling" (see later in this chapter), although its first decision concerning sport dates from 1974.

The end of the twentieth century was particularly significant for sport thanks to renewed problems of doping, corruption and violence: problems that led states to become increasingly involved in the governance of world sport and to force the Olympic system to adapt and to develop new ways of working with the public authorities.

This chapter thus begins by presenting the links between the IOC and Switzerland, its host state, and then those between the Olympic system and that of the United Nations. Finally, the gradual involvement of European governments in sports-related issues via the Council of Europe and the European Union is described. The various national sport policies are not handled here because they only affect world sport indirectly, and moreover have been the subject of considerable analysis in other works (e.g. Callède in France,[1] Houlihan in the United Kingdom and the Commonwealth,[2] Riordan for the Soviet Union[3]).

IOC and Switzerland

Despite appearances that can at times indicate otherwise, the IOC is not a "real" international organization but a non-governmental organization (NGO) with the legal form of an association under Swiss law pursuant to articles 60 to 79 of the Swiss Civil Code, since its headquarters have been in Lausanne since 1915. This status has been clearly stated in the Olympic Charter since 1970 and makes it a Swiss legal entity. Moreover, in many countries the IOC is cited in legislation on sport as the guardian of the Olympic ideal and/or as the entity that establishes the list of doping substances (a task now entrusted to the World Anti-Doping Agency (WADA), see Chapter 7).

As of 1980, under the presidency of Juan Antonio Samaranch, the IOC constantly improved its level of international recognition, starting with that on the part of its host country.

Following several requests by the IOC during the 1970s, the Swiss Federal Council (its government) finally issued a decree dated 17 September 1981 stating that the IOC had the "specific character of an international institution" and confirming two privileges that it had acquired many years previously: exemption from direct tax on its revenues and the possibility of recruiting staff for its administration without limitations regarding nationality—something important for the IOC given the fact that obtaining work permits was extremely difficult for foreigners in Switzerland at the time.

During the same year, the IOC was designated as owning the commercial rights to the Olympic rings by means of a treaty under international law signed in Nairobi under the aegis of the World International Property Organization (WIPO). The treaty, which obliges state parties to refuse or to invalidate the registration as a mark and to prohibit the use of any sign containing the Olympic symbol, was signed by 46 countries and ratified by around 30 countries, but not by most major commercial powers who often granted this highly lucrative right to their NOC (such as the USA, for example). The year 1981 thus marked Switzerland's recognition of the IOC and to a certain extent that on the part of the international community or at least those that signed the Nairobi Treaty.

This recognition nevertheless remains fragile. More than a quarter of a century after it was granted, the IOC still lacks a headquarters agreement in Switzerland, while non-governmental organizations such as the International Air Transport Association (IATA), the International Committee of the Red Cross (ICRC), and the Global Fund (to fight AIDS, tuberculosis and malaria) were granted such an agreement some years ago. It would seem that the Swiss government wishes to avoid creating a precedent that could be used by the around 30 International Federations headquartered in Switzerland, and even though many of them do not appear to be seeking to obtain such a status.

In 1999, the IOC even preferred to withdraw a claim for exemption from Value Added Tax (VAT) fearing that it could be refused by the Swiss parliament following the scandal surrounding the attribution of the 2002 Salt Lake City Games. Moreover, examination of the exemption request led to the discontinuation of a minor tax exemption for IOC staff members' income that had existed for decades.

To attenuate this failure—also partly one on the part of the Swiss government, which had promised this VAT exemption to the IOC—the new Federal President[4] Adolf Ogi made a commitment to improve the general conditions for the IOC and those IFs headquartered in Switzerland. Close to the world of sport for many years, Ogi had succeeded in having sport included in his Ministry (of Defense) in 1997. He had also been the president of the Candidature Committee of the city of Sion, in Switzerland, for the Winter Games: a candidature that was to fail spectacularly at the 1999 IOC vote. Ogi had also hoped to become an IOC member when his political term in office, intended for the end of 2000, came to an end.

Finally, on 1 November 2000, the IOC signed a document with the Swiss government entitled "Agreement Relating to the Status of the International Olympic Committee in Switzerland." The text, exceptional for several reasons, consisted of 18 articles.[5] It was first of all an agreement between a government and an NGO (the IOC) that could be revised by negotiation, with both parties as equals (or revoked by one year's notice), and disputes were not required to be handled by Swiss courts (Article 15). The situation thus became considerably better than that provided for in the unilateral decree issued by the Federal Council in 1981. Secondly, and even if it only confirms the IOC's existing privileges, it extends them to its foundations (see Chapter 2) and to its pension fund. It grants virtually diplomatic travel privileges for its staff and employees, notably by recognizing the credentials issued by the IOC. Finally, it offers the assistance of Swiss diplomatic and consular services abroad, as it does for the ICRC.

In 2001, the Canton of Vaud (where the Lausanne headquarters are located) and the city of Lausanne—in close collaboration with the Swiss Confederation—drew up particularly favorable conditions for the around 25 International and European Sports Federations that had established headquarters on its territory or were considering doing so and already had an income tax exemption. The conditions concerned questions relating to entering the country, residence and work permits, the acquisition of property, and the taxation (direct and indirect) of the staff of these organizations. An international sport administration complex was built on the shores of Lake Geneva to house smaller federations, while larger ones (UEFA, UCI, FIVB) purchased land and built their own premises as the IOC had done 20 years earlier.

The twenty-first century thus began under excellent auspices for the IOC and the other sport organizations based in Switzerland. The Swiss government welcomed them with open arms, and the country's public authorities provided sufficient flexibility in order for them to function in an unrestricted way as the entities governing world sport. Lausanne was thus fully living up to its title of "Olympic capital" (attributed by the IOC in 1993).

In 2007, a new federal law on the host state was passed by the Swiss parliament in order to regulate relations between Switzerland and the various types of international organizations headquartered there. A special category was included for the IOC and other major IFs. The law also stipulates that the signature of future headquarters agreements falls under the competence of the Swiss Federal Council and not that of the parliament. This law opens the door for a future headquarters agreement for the IOC, the FIFA and a few other IFs. Such agreements would provide additional privileges to these Olympic system organizations such as extraterritoriality of their offices, juridical immunity, duty free imports, etc.

The Olympic system and the United Nations system

As of the 1960s, the IOC decided to approach the United Nations Organization (UN) with a view to enhancing its international recognition. It was moreover as of this period that the UN became interested in sport, through the issue of apartheid. Under pressure from the international community, the IOC excluded South Africa from the Olympic Games beginning from those of 1964 in Tokyo. The team from Rhodesia, a country ruled by a racist regime at the time, was excluded from the 1972 Munich Games despite the team having already arrived. The IFs were also forced to exclude these two countries from their competitions. Some sports, such as rugby and cricket, resisted the exclusion but were subjected to various boycotts and press campaigns

The Supreme Council for Sport in Africa (SCSA)—a body founded in 1965 for the organization of the first all-African Games and linked to some African governments—used the pretext of a tour to South

Africa by the New Zealand rugby team to organize the boycott of the 1976 Montreal Games, even though rugby was not an Olympic sport. Around 30 African countries withdrew from the Montreal Games on the eve of the Opening Ceremony. The following year, the UN adopted a resolution against apartheid in sport that became a convention in 1985. As of that moment, international sporting relations with South Africa virtually ceased. In order to take part in the 1984 Los Angeles Games, the South African miler Zola Budd needed to acquire a British passport thanks to her ancestors' citizenship. In 1988, this type of subterfuge was not longer permitted. It was only a change of political regime that brought South Africa back into the fold, at the 1992 Barcelona Games (with Nelson Mandela in the stands at the opening ceremony), some 25 years after its exclusion from the Olympic system.

The UN also intervenes in the world sport system by means of various embargos that it has imposed as a result of conflicts or civil wars. The one concerning ex-Yugoslavia in the early 1990s particularly affected the Olympic system. Security Council Resolution 757 mentioned sport as the subject of sanctions for the first time, and thus threatened the participation of Yugoslavian athletes (mainly from Serbia) at the 1992 Barcelona Games.

The IOC had recognized the NOCs in Slovenia and Croatia as soon as the countries were admitted to the international community: the participation of athletes of these new nationalities presented no problem from a point of view of the Olympic and international order. Spain, however, as a member of the UN, felt obliged to exclude the Yugoslavian NOC's team from the Games—in complete contravention of the IOC rules that guaranteed access to the Games to all recognized NOCs. Via the UN, the entire international community was thus exerting pressure on the IOC to exclude Yugoslavia. The IOC was thus faced with a similar problem that it encountered in 1976 when the Canadian government had refused access to Taiwanese athletes on the pretext that Canada only recognized the People's Republic of China (admitted to the UN instead of Taiwan in 1971). Possessing better diplomatic skills than his predecessor Killanin, who had ultimately bowed before Canada's decision, IOC President Samaranch found an amicable solution, i.e. the participation of Yugoslavian athletes as "individual athletes" under the Olympic flag.

The above solution had been negotiated with the UN via one of its former staff who had become an advisor to the IOC President: the Ethiopian Fékrou Kidané. This former journalist, extremely well versed in the workings of both the Olympic and UN systems, became Samaranch's Chief of Staff after the Barcelona Games and responsible for a spectacular rapprochement between the two systems. In 1993, he succeeded in having two resolutions passed by the 48th UN General Assembly: one proposing an Olympic Truce with a view to the 1994 Lillehammer Games and the other to designate 1994 as the International Year of Sport and the Olympic Ideal. These resolutions were adopted unanimously after intensive lobbying, and came at an ideal moment since the year 1994 was also that of the IOC's centenary and plans were made to celebrate it at a sumptuous Olympic Congress in Paris.

During ancient times, the Olympic Truce (*Ekecheiria*) protected those traveling to Olympia to take part in the Games, which were considered to be a sacred festival. The Greek city-states were supposed to guarantee them free passage despite their incessant wars. The 1993 UN Resolution revived the principle by calling upon the member states to cease all warlike acts during the 15 days of the Games and one week before and after them. Resolutions similar to that for Lillehammer have been proposed by all host countries of the Summer and Winter Games since 1996 and have been adopted by the UN General Assembly held during the fall prior to the Games. Such resolutions are now part of the symbolic tradition of the Games and of the OCOGs' preparation for them, in liaison with their respective governments. Each resolution very cleverly includes, in its final statement, the fact that the subject will be (again) included on the agenda two years later.

The effectiveness of this mechanism has, however, never really been tested. Many wars have continued during the Games since 1994, including those involving forces from the host country (for example the Italian troops in Iraq during the 2006 Turin Games). It should nevertheless be noted that the United States did not bomb Iraq during the 1998 Nagano Games, and despite the fact that the American president's spokesman had stated that US foreign policy did not take sports events into account.

Furthermore, each successive resolution refers to the IOC and thus confers a certain international role on it. The IOC has moreover, on the initiative of the Greek government, created a specific foundation based in Lausanne and Athens in order to perpetuate the Olympic Truce. It is presided jointly by the IOC President and a former Greek Minister of Foreign Affairs, and is managed by a Greek ambassador. The IOC considers it to be a means of promoting its ideal of peace and its international status.

In parallel to this rapprochement with the UN, the IOC also began signing numerous co-operation agreements with most UN agencies or those affiliated to it as of the 1990s: the United Nations Environment

Programme (UNEP, 1992), the World Health Organization (WHO, 1993), the United Nations Children's Fund (UNICEF, 1994), the United Nations Office on Drugs and Crime (UNODC, 1995), the World Meteorological Organization (WMO, 1996), the World Bank (1996), the United Nations Development Programme (UNDP, 1996), the Universal Postal Union (UPU, 1997), the Food and Agriculture Organization (FAO, 1997), the International Labour Organization (ILO, 1998), the United Nations Educational, Scientific and Cultural Organization (UNESCO, 1998 and 2004), the World Tourism Organization (WTO, 1999), the International Federation of Red Cross and Red Crescent Societies (IFRCRCS, 2003). Joint activities are also undertaken with the High Commission for Refugees, the International Telecommunication Union, the Joint United Nations Programme on HIV/AIDs, etc.

The short distance between Lausanne, the seat of the IOC, and Geneva, the seat of the UN in Europe, has incontestably contributed towards this spate of signatures, which follows a long-standing idea by Coubertin, i.e. the rapprochement of the "little brother in Lausanne and the big sister in Geneva"—the latter being the former League of Nations in which he had officiated as part of the Greek delegation during the 1930s while maintaining personal relations with Albert Thomas, the first director of the International Labour Office.

The texts of these memorandums of understanding, which are usually stated on a single page, are mostly included in Frank Latty's book on the status of the IOC.[6] Beyond the few concrete activities resulting from the agreements, the main result has been a kind of mutual recognition on the part of the two systems. The UN flag flew over all competition sites beside the Olympic flag for the first time at the 1998 Nagano Games. The successive IOC Presidents have been invited to address the UN General Assemblies in 1995 (Samaranch) and 2002 (Rogge). In 2000, 160 Heads of State and of Governments meeting at the UN headquarters in New York for the millennium summit adopted a final resolution including a paragraph that called upon the member states to observe the Olympic Truce and to support the IOC in its efforts to promote peace and mutual understanding through sport and the Olympic ideal. The inclusion of such a paragraph in such a solemn declaration constituted a diplomatic success for the IOC and a form of recognition on the part of the international community.

At the end of 2001, the UN Secretary-General Kofi Annan appointed a special advisor on sport for development and peace: Adolf Ogi, who had left the Swiss Government at the end of 2000. Ogi thus earned his revenge over the IOC members who did not elect him as a member six months previously despite the support of the IOC Executive Board and

President Samaranch. He devoted himself to the task with an enthusiasm typical of his work on sport at a national level.[7] Ogi set up an office at the UN European headquarters in Geneva, on an extremely small budget granted by the Swiss Confederation, and mobilized various components of the UN system within an inter-agency working group on sport that he co-chaired with the Director of UNICEF. In 2003, he organized a first International Conference on Sport and Development at Switzerland's Federal Sports School in Macolin. The event, which was to be his swan song, in fact served to further his position: his period in office was extended for two years, and he was given the title of assistant secretary-general.

At the end of 2003, he had the UN Assembly General vote on a resolution proposed by Tunisia on economic and social development through sport. On this occasion, the work of the inter-agency group on sport was published. In its wake, 2005 was proclaimed as the "International Year of Sport" and a second conference on development through sport was organized in Macolin. Adolf Ogi retired from office at the end of 2007 having assisted with the start-up of the first Office for Sport for Development and Peace at the UN headquarters in New York.

The considerable political progress made by sport within the entire UN system at the end of the twentieth and the early twenty-first century is thus eminently clear. In the 1950s and 1960s, sport was mainly the domain of UNESCO alone since it can be considered as part of both culture and (physical) education—two areas handled by this specialized Paris-based agency. In 1958 for instance, UNESCO favored the foundation of the International Council of Sport and Physical Education (ICSPE)—the International Council of Sport Science and Physical Education as of 1983—as an autonomous entity uniting all organizations interested in co-operating in this area.

It was only after the African Olympic boycotts of 1972 and 1976, however, that UNESCO Director-General Amadou Mahtar M'Bow once again became interested in sport. The first Conference of Ministers and Senior Officials Responsible for Physical Education and Sport (MINEPS I) was organized in Paris in 1976. In 1978, the Intergovernmental Committee for Physical Education and Sport (CIGEPS) and a Fund for the International Development of Physical Education and Sport (FIDEPS) were created, the latter to provide financial assistance for CIGEPS activities. The same year, the UNESCO General Conference (uniting all the member states) adopted an International Charter on Physical Education and Sport. Clearly, the UNESCO was positioning itself as a direct competitor to the IOC and its Olympic Charter. With the help of the IFs and their president, Thomas Keller of Switzerland, the IOC stood firm despite its major political problems, notably the boycotts of Montreal and Moscow in 1976 and 1980 respectively.

President Samaranch managed to smooth matters over by signing a first co-operation agreement with Director M'Bow, who attended the Los Angeles Games in 1984, and also by maintaining particularly cordial relations with his successor and compatriot Frederico Mayor. The second edition of MINEPS held in Moscow in 1988, led to a joint UNESCO–IOC resolution on the subject of doping problems following the Ben Johnson scandal at the Seoul Games the same year. In 1989, the UNESCO General Conference adopted three resolutions related to sport: on the fight against doping, the defense of the universality of the Olympic Games, and the necessity of cooperation between public authorities and sport organizations. Even before the resolutions regarding the Olympic Truce reached the UN as of 1993, these UNESCO resolutions were the first to bestow a kind of international recognition on the IOC.

While the UN began to be seriously interested in sport at the beginning of the 1990s, UNESCO distanced itself from it considerably. MINEPS III, held in Punta Del Este (Uruguay) in 1999, went almost unnoticed. In 2000, the new Japanese Director General reduced the already small credits granted to the sport sector. It was only three years later that UNESCO regained interest in the area by adopting an international convention against doping in 2005 (see Chapter 7).

Europe and sport

Sport was born and originally developed in Europe: in Greece if one goes back to ancient times or in England if we are referring to modern sport. Curiously, European institutions only became interested in sport as a social and economic phenomenon well after their respective foundation. When the Treaty of Rome was signed in 1957, and provided the basis for the Common Market known today as the European Union, sport was not on the agenda despite the fact that Italy had just organized the Winter Games in Cortina d'Ampezzo and Rome was to organize the Summer Games three years later. Admittedly, sport had not yet become a real industry and its international officials at the time—notably IOC President Avery Brundage—wished to have as little as possible to do with governments.

The historical role of the Council of Europe

At the end of the 1960s, however, the Council of Europe started to take an interest in sport. This intergovernmental association, founded in 1949 and based in Strasbourg (France), in fact united all Western European countries: far more than those who adhered to the Treaty of Rome (six at the outset). Even Switzerland, which is neutral, has been a member since its foundation. After the fall of the Berlin Wall, most former iron curtain countries also joined this council, whose criteria for membership are by no means restrictive. In 2007, it counts 47 European countries, including Russia.

The Council of Europe was initially satisfied—regarding sport—with holding regular meetings of senior officials, Secretaries of State and Ministers of Sport who were beginning to appear at the same time within European governmental structures. Eastern Union countries held similar conferences, which President Samaranch attended each year from 1980 to 1988. These conferences were behind the creation in 1973 of the European Sports Conference as an entity of the Conference on Security and Cooperation in Europe—now the Organization for Security and Cooperation in Europe (OSCE)—that was intended to bring about a rapprochement between the Eastern and Western blocs. Given the radical political developments in Europe, however, this entity has completely lost its influence although it continues to exist on paper.

In 1971, as a first concrete action, the Council of Europe supported the creation of a documentation and contact center in Brussels: the Clearing House, which was to close 30 years later having lost its utility but which contributed strongly towards arousing the interest of the European States in sports policies. In 1975, the Council had the sport ministers adopt a "Sport for All" charter that stressed the members' interest in making sport more widely available to the general population since it was beneficial to health, education, social integration, tourism, etc. In 1977, it created the Committee for the Development of Sport to unite governmental representatives and NGOs interested in sport, notably the European Sports Federations that were beginning to develop their structures. As of 1960, for example, the Union of European Football Associations (UEFA) organized a Nations Cup known today as the Euro, one of the world's leading sports events. The Committee for the Development of Sport is based on an ad hoc fund created in 1978 and under the control of the annual Ministerial Conference.

As of this period, the Council of Europe became interested in other aspects of sport. It decided to focus on the problem of doping, which was spreading, and to that end adopted several resolutions and declarations in the 1970s. An Anti-Doping Convention was signed in 1989, and is an international treaty that has since been ratified by numerous countries, including some beyond Europe.

In another area, the Council adopted a Convention on Spectator Violence and Misbehaviour at Sports events in 1985, just a few months after a tragic incident at Heysel Stadium in Brussels leading to around forty deaths during the European Cup Final. Together with legislation adopted in several member states (such as the United Kingdom), this convention helped stem the soaring increase in hooliganism.

In 1992, the Council of Europe adopted a Code of Sports Ethics intended to combat emerging problems in sport (racism, violence, etc.) and to promote fair play. The code is appended to a European Sports Charter also drawn up in 1992 in order to affirm the right to sport and physical education as a factor within human development.

Today, at the beginning of the twenty-first century, the Council of Europe administers its various conventions although the sport sector, which was once a separate directorate but has been downgraded to become a simple department. In 2007, however, the Council established an Enlarged Partial Agreement on Sport (EPAS) to better finance its activities in this domain. In future, the Council's main means of intervention within questions of sport will no doubt be made by the European Convention on Human Rights which has its own court in Strasbourg under the council's aegis. The court is increasingly invoked by athletes when they consider that their fundamental rights have been infringed (notably the right to work or the right to a fair trial).[8]

It is interesting to note that the Council of Europe's policies on sport have developed from those concerning the entire population ("sport for all") towards a greater focus on elite sport, sport as entertainment, and the governance of sport.

Growing interest on the part of the European Union (EU)

As indicated above, sport is not mentioned either in the Treaty of Rome or the various European treaties that have come to complete it, including that of Maastricht signed in 1993 marking an acceleration of European integration and an increase to 15 States under the name of the European Union. The Council of the EU (its "government") has no specific legal basis for proposing, for example, a sports policy for the entire union.

This lack does not, however, prevent European institutions from being interested in sport, or at least since 1974. It was in that year that the Court of Justice of the European Communities (the EU's highest court, based in Luxemburg and also often referred to as the European Court of Justice) issued a ruling (Walrave and Koch versus the International Cycling Union) where it judged that sport falls under European community law if it constitutes a financial activity such as professional cycling.

The ruling was confirmed by a further case in 1976, this time concerning football (Donà versus Mantero). Professional sport as a whole is affected but so, too, is "amateur" sport as soon as it leads to major financial activity that could contravene the fundamental principles of the community law such as the free movement of persons (for example when players and coaches were involved), services (ski lessons, players agents' services) and assets (tickets for competitions, etc.) stipulated in Article 48 of the treaty, or free competition (subsidies to certain clubs, exclusive sponsorship contracts, selling of broadcasting rights, anti-doping rules, etc.) and the prohibition of abuse of a dominant position (Articles 85 and 86).

As of 1983, the European Economic Community (EEC) as it was then called informed the IOC and the sports federations of the possible areas of incompatibility between certain of their practices as financial actors and the aforementioned principles in the Treaty of Rome. Football above all was concerned because of its rules relating to the transfer of players and its restrictions on the number of "foreign" players who nevertheless came from EEC countries. The UEFA and the FIFA were particularly targeted but thought they could avoid community law because they covered a wider area than the EEC.

The IOC did not consider itself directly involved in the issue, although it was gradually opening up the Games to professional athletes, sponsors, and private television channels at the time. In 1993, the German Olympic Committee and the German Confederation of National Sports Federations (DSB) nevertheless reacted by creating a liaison office with the EU in Brussels whose role was to observe and influence its policies and decisions related to sport. Other NOCs and sports confederations supported this effort (France, Austria, the Netherlands, Denmark, Finland, Sweden, and Norway) as did the European Olympic Committees (the continental association of NOCs). Sport, like many other sectors, began lobbying in Brussels. The director of the small liaison office in Brussels was to become the IOC President's Chief of Staff in 2001.

It was only with the famous "Bosman ruling" issued by the European Court of Justice in 1995 that the sports movement became aware that things had changed. The ruling, which was the subject of interminable controversy in the forms of books and articles, condemned Liège Football Club in Belgium (which employed Belgian professional Jean-Marc Bosman whose contract was reaching an end), for claiming a transfer fee to his new French club. Since the French club did not pay the fee, the transfer of Bosman was—under the currently valid sport regulations—rendered null and void, which meant that Bosman was prevented from playing football and thus earning a living. The court ruled that the UEFA's (and indirectly FIFA's) transfer and nationality regulations (i.e. restricting the number of foreigners) did not comply with European law (notably on the free movement of persons within the community).

The case led to a huge uproar within the world of football and incited other footballers to go to court: notably the Hungarian Balog in 2001 with a similar case to Bosman's but for a player from outside the EU. Although the Balog case was resolved at the last moment when Balog withdrew his claim (after an amicable settlement), the UEFA and the FIFA were finally forced to modify their rules regarding international transfers in 2001, after long negotiations, in order to take the court's remarks into consideration. It was the first time that an intergovernmental organization (through its judiciary authorities) forced a sports organization to abandon some of its "sport" rules that had financial consequences. Other federations needed to act similarly, notably the International Basketball Federation (FIBA) following the case of the Finnish player Lehtonen in 2000 (on maintaining the possibility of fixing transfer deadlines). Although the FIBA's position was upheld in that case, it nevertheless decided to delete all the nationality quotas for professional teams, and not only in Europe but throughout the world.

The International Automobile Federation (IAF), which governs Formula 1 races, is another IF that had to bow to the European Commission, represented in this case by the Directorate General for Competition.

The times when sports organizations believed they were not subject to national or international legislation as a result of their world scope are clearly over.

A new case, this time in 2003 and concerning the Slovakian handball player Kolpak, moreover proved that European law also applied to a non-member state (Slovakia was not an EU member at the time) if the said state had signed an association agreement with the EU. At the time, such agreements concerned 24 neighboring countries plus all signatories to the Cotonou agreement, i.e. 48 African countries, 15 in the Caribbean and 14 in the Pacific. The EU's influence on sport was reaching virtually worldwide proportions.

Under the impact of the Bosman ruling, football and other professional sports competitions took a highly financial turn within Europe. In particular, they started to draw the attention of major media groups because the transfer possibilities had multiplied since they were liberalized. Players' salaries soared, and major clubs attempted to outdo each other, placing their finances at risk. Faced with this phenomenon, clubs began to seek new methods of financing (sponsoring, broadcasting rights) that inevitably led them to fall a little further into the clutches of European law and particularly regarding competition.

The illusory "sports exception"

To overcome the adverse effects of EU legislation on the economics of sport, the sports movement promptly called for a "sports exception" to EU law, similar to the cultural exception adopted previously for assets and services related to this important sector of European identity. Many observers made reference to exception from the anti-trust law in the United States, from which several professional American sports have benefited since the 1960s.

For some time, the UEFA and FIFA felt this exception could be their lifeline, despite the fact that the European Court of Justice did not systematically rule against the sports movement for the cases brought before it. We could cite, for example, the Lehtonen case (see above) or that of the Belgian judoka Deliège who contested the decisions of the Belgian Judo Federation based on the nationality criteria that prevented her from taking part in the Atlanta Olympic Games. In 2000, the European judges ruled against the plaintiff and implicitly recognized the possibility for sport organizations to adopt certain organizational rules pertaining to sport, such as the selection of athletes. Several other decisions during the 1990s can even be interpreted as clear support for the specific character of sport, and sometimes to the detriment of the fundamental liberties guaranteed by the EU treaties.

New problems facing sport are nevertheless emerging within the European framework, however. Examples are the status of players' agents, the territoriality of sports competitions, broadcasting rights,[9] public aid to professional sport clubs, the ownership of several clubs by the same entity and, of course, questions of doping, violence, and corruption.

In order to handle these questions more globally, a sport sector was created within the European Commission Directorate General for Education and Culture at the end of the 1980s, following the adoption of the Andonnino Report in 1985 by the European Council meeting in Milan. This report considered sport to be one of the means of constructing a "Citizens' Europe" and of creating a feeling among the population of belonging to the European community.

In 1991, the European Commission set up the first European Sports Forum at the request of the sports movement. A consultative forum, it brings together, more or less every year, non-governmental sports organizations and European public authorities with a view to discussing current, relevant topics.

In 1992, the EU subsidized the Albertville and Barcelona Games so that European symbolism would be present during the Opening and Closing Ceremonies (although it was unable to put the idea of all athletes from EU member countries parading together into practice). A period of dialogue developed, notably when Commissioner Viviane Reding took office at the end of the twentieth century.

In 1997, on the signing of the Treaty of Amsterdam (modifying previous European treaties such as those of Rome and Maastricht) a "Declaration relating to sport" was adopted by the European heads of state and governments, among around 50 others on a wide number of topics. It said:

> The Conference emphasizes the social significance of sport, in particular its role in forging identity and bringing people together. The Conference therefore calls on the bodies of the European Union to listen to sports associations when important questions affecting sport are at issue. In this connection, special consideration should be given to the particular characteristics of amateur sport.

This brief declaration marked the failure to have the "sports exception" inscribed within the treaty itself but nevertheless constitutes a first legal basis for handling sport at a European level in a different way to that of the financial point of view.

In the wake of the declaration, the community presented its global vision of the sector during the European Council meeting in the Finnish capital in December 1999. This "Helsinki report" of around 10 pages clearly states that the "development of sport in Europe risks weakening its educational and social function," and calls for "safeguarding current sports structures" and a clarification of the legal environment of sport in order to restrict the multiplication of conflicts. The report was adopted after two particularly sensitive years for the sports movement because of major doping scandals and corruption involving certain IOC members.

The Helsinki report had a concrete effect in that one year later, on the initiative of the French presidency of the EU and in particular its Minister for Sport, Marie-George Buffet, a new declaration was adopted by the European Council meeting in Nice in December 2000. This "Nice declaration," far longer and more detailed than that of Amsterdam, reaffirms the social importance of sport, which must be accessible to all, and recognizes the central role of the sports federations and of their autonomy for the establishment of sport rules. It calls for preserving the clubs' training capacities and for protecting young athletes. It also recommends that the equity of competitions be guaranteed, and that players' employment contracts be adapted in line with sport's specific characteristics.

Although the Nice declaration was quite detailed, it still failed to provide a legal basis that would be as strong as that of an article within a treaty, such as that on the principles of free movement or free competition.

The sport movement in Europe thus continued to plead for the inclusion of sport in European treaties.

Meanwhile, the opportunity to draw up a European constitution arose in February 2002. At the sports ministers' summit in Almeria, 11 European states supported the idea that sport should feature among the areas within which the EU can intervene in a way that is complementary to that of the individual member states. This was the basis, for example, behind the decision to launch a European Year of Sport with a view to the Euro 2004 in Portugal and the Olympic Games in Athens: two events for which certain infrastructures were financed by the EU.

The draft of a European Constitutional Treaty presented at the Salonika Summit in Greece and adopted in 2004 explicitly mentioned sport in its Article 16 (briefly, and among other areas such as education and culture), and particularly in Article III-182 that links it directly to the said areas.

Although it was ratified by several EU states, the European constitution fell by the wayside following referendums in France and in the Netherlands that resulted in those countries rejecting it. A "simplified" version of it was adopted in December 2007 and must now be ratified by each member state in order to enter into force at the beginning of 2009. Article 149 of the new treaty stipulates that "The Union shall contribute to the promotion of European sporting issues while taking account of the specific nature of sport, its structures based on voluntary activity and its social and educational function." It adds that Union action shall be aimed at (among other points): "developing the European dimension in sport, by promoting fairness and openness in sporting competitions and cooperation between bodies responsible for sports, and by protecting the physical and moral integrity of sportsmen and sportswomen, especially the youngest sportsmen and sportswomen."

When this new wording was published in October 2007, the IOC as well as several IFs governing team sports saw it as a victory.[10] It should nevertheless be stressed that the text that will ultimately be adopted will not permit any deviation from common European legislation as soon as sport engenders financial activities. It will by no means constitute an exception from the law on competition, but will simply enable the EU to take certain specific characteristics of sport into account and to launch joint activities in addition to those of the individual member states.

The Court of Justice of the European Communities has moreover recalled that the "sports exception" is impossible by means of its judgment on the Meca-Medina and Majcen case in 2006. The affair involved two professional swimmers who tested positive for doping at a long-distance swimming event organized by the International Swimming Federation (FINA), and who were suspended for four years in 1999—a sentence reduced to two years by the Court of Arbitration for Sport. The swimmers then appealed against the IOC and the implementing of its anti-doping regulations by the FINA, alleging that their rights regarding European competition law had been breached. Although the case was dismissed by the European Commission and the Court of First Instance of the European Communities, the swimmers nevertheless appealed before the Court of Justice, which acknowledged that the Court of First Instance had committed a legal error. Simultaneously, however, the Court of Justice reversed the decision by the Court of First Instance and thus indicated that the IOC and the FINA had acted rightly.

The case would have been of little interest if the Court of Justice had not taken advantage, when publishing its decision, to reaffirm in a press release that the IOC's anti-doping rules fell within the scope of EU competition law, or in other words that its decision in the Meca-Medina and Majcen affair had been taken on a case-by-case assessment basis and therefore did not constitute a precedent for future decisions. The court thus rejected the former and traditional distinction between sporting rules (under the unique responsibility of the Federations) and rules of law (to be applied by judges).

The publication of the decision immediately caused uproar in the Olympic system, including claims that the court was reversing its jurisprudence and creating legal insecurity for sport organizations, who would not be able to predict the outcome if athletes lodged such complaints. Any rule issued by an IF that can be qualified as a condition within the exercise of a sporting activity now risks falling within the scope of the rules concerning free movement or of competition within the EU, and furthermore—via cooperation agreements between it and other countries—beyond it. Nearly all disciplinary measures for doping, cheating or inappropriate behavior may lead to an athlete being prevented from competing (and thus freely moving and working within professional sport).

The world of football was at the forefront of the criticism against the court. At almost the same moment, however, the Independent European Sport Review was published. The review is a document requested by the

German, British, Spanish, and French governments but financed by the UEFA since it was mainly intended to concern football. José Luis Arnaut, its author and a former Portuguese Minister for Sport, stated that it was impossible, generally speaking, to except sport from EU law and instead proposed that pragmatic, "soft laws" (quasi-legal instruments) be implemented by the European Commission, the Council of the EU and/or the European Parliament in order to improve the legal certainty of sport organizations, i.e. to permit them to guarantee that their rules are compatible with European law.

The review rightly considers that the European judges have other, more important cases to handle that are more in keeping with the real intentions of the EU's founders. It also calls for a formal agreement between the EU and the UEFA. The European Parliament strongly supported Arnaut's views by means of a resolution on the future of professional football in Europe adopted in March 2007.[11]

The IOC and the FIFA were surprised by both the Independent European Sport Review and by the European Court of Justice decision in the Meca-Medina and Majcen case. They counter-attacked by organizing an emergency seminar held in Lausanne in September 2006 that united the IFs and the NOCs to debate on the autonomy of the Olympic and sport movement. The topic was raised again in February 2008 during a second seminar, devoted more specifically to the governance of the Olympic movement, and will be discussed at the 2009 Olympic Congress in Copenhagen, Denmark. In future, it seems that the claim to autonomy is replacing the claim that sport has a specific nature. The Olympic system now claims that sports organizations should preserve their autonomy and should not be indirectly governed by European judges.

On top of this legal frenzy on the specificity and autonomy of sport, the European Commission published its first white paper on sport in the summer of 2007, which had been in preparation for many months. Its objective was to provide strategic direction concerning the role of sport in Europe, and to propose a whole series of initiatives—some more concrete than others—that together constituted the "Coubertin Action Plan" yet without going as far as legislation or rulings.

While reaffirming that "sport activity is subject to the application of EU law" and excluding any overall exemption from that law for sport, the paper acknowledges that two specific characteristics may be accepted: the rules guaranteeing the integrity of sports competition and the pyramidal structure of the Federations, organized on the basis of national entities.

Along with other IFs, the IOC and the FIFA reacted violently to this white paper, by means of a rare joint press release.[12] They stated that the report was "structured in full contradiction with the actual architecture of the Olympic movement, ignoring in particular the regulatory competences of the International Federations." Although they are world organizations, both the IOC and the FIFA stated that they wished to defend the "European model of sport" although the European Commission itself affirmed in its accompanying document to the white paper[13] that it was difficult to characterize such a model and that it could not be applied to all sports with their various specificities, which thus deserved to be handled differently.

The IOC and the FIFA also joined the UEFA, as well as other European team sport federations, in demanding a more stable legal environment for sport in Europe and in particular regarding the sport organizations' discretionary powers concerning their rules. In November 2007, they managed to have the French and Dutch governments co-sign a memorandum to the European Commission asking for more legal certainty concerning professional sport matters. During the same month, reacting to the European Commission concern over violence (hooliganism and racism) and corruption (match fixing and illegal betting) in football, UEFA's President even called for the creation of a "European sport police" in partnership with Europol.

While regretting a lost opportunity with the white paper, the largest world and European sport entities stated that they wished to pursue cooperation with the EU member states,[14] the European Parliament and the European Commission. Such essential cooperation will effectively become the norm for coming years. Europe will continue to exert a strong influence on world sport, whether the global sport organizations like it or not.

Towards a new legal framework for the Olympic system?

In 1999, the problems related to doping and corruption revealed the limitations of the IOC's current status and structures in the eyes of the public authorities. The negative consequences of those issues on the Olympic image that is sold to sponsors and television companies could, over time and despite internal reforms, lead to the downfall of an institution that has existed for over one hundred years and that to date has made it possible to organize—virtually without interruption—peaceful gatherings known as the Olympic Games. Whatever else may be said of the Games, they are part of mankind's heritage and are one of the rare powerful symbols of international cooperation.

Today, sport—often likened to a civilized form of warfare—is placing its top leaders and elite athletes in a moral situation similar to that of the generals and soldiers of the nineteenth century, who fought in wars where anything was permitted. Having witnessed the inhuman carnage at the Battle of Solferino, a certain Henri Dunant of Switzerland founded the International Committee of the Red Cross (ICRC) in 1863, aimed at protecting civilian and military victims of armed conflicts. In doing so, he was inaugurating international humanitarian law aimed at "civilizing" war. It would seem that today, we should take precautions to ensure that sport remains the "civilizing factor" stressed by Elias and Dunning.[15]

The current structures of the International Red Cross and Red Crescent Movement could serve as inspiration for a new legal framework for the Olympic system. They comprise three components united by common "Fundamental principles": the ICRC, the National Red Cross or Red Crescent Societies and the International Federation of those societies (IFRCRCS). An International Conference, usually held every four years, unites the three components and the states parties to the Geneva conventions (four international treaties signed in that Swiss city in 1949 to renew older conventions dating back to the late nineteenth and early twentieth centuries). The conference adopts and modifies the movement's statutes and proposes new protocols to the Geneva conventions (four have been signed since 1949).

Like the IOC, the ICRC is a simple association under Swiss law but has been granted specific, official responsibilities defined in the Geneva conventions and in their additional protocols. It carries out tasks as mandated by the international conference. The 15–25 members of the ICRC are all Swiss citizens.

The ICRC has headquarters agreements with over 50 states including with Switzerland, in Geneva (since 1993 only!). The agreements state its international legal status on the respective territories and grant privileges and immunities usually awarded to inter-governmental organizations and their officials. The ICRC is notably exempt from value added tax (VAT) since its introduction in Switzerland.

In 2007, there were 186 National Red Cross or Red Crescent Societies recognized by the ICRC. They provide a variety of auxiliary services to the national public authorities in matters of health and protection, both during wars and in times of peace, as well as assistance in the case of disasters. Like the American and French Red Cross Societies, for instance, many of them have public or semi-public statutes and/or receive government subsidies.

The IFRCRCS was founded in 1919 with the title of a League. It was an association intended to coordinate international assistance to disaster victims on the part of the national societies and to act as a liaison, support and study entity. Its headquarters are in Geneva.

The ICRC, the IFRCRCS, and the national societies meet every two years within the framework of the Council of Delegates.

Table 6.1 compares the Olympic system and the Red Cross Movement, even though the nature of their respective responsibilities is by no means the same.

The ICRC and its movement benefit from a much more solid legal framework than that of the IOC and the Olympic movement. Beyond the headquarters agreement—from which the IOC does not yet benefit—the major difference is that of international recognition of the ICRC by the Geneva Conventions, international public law treaties ratified by nearly 200 states.

Following a proposal made at the 1981 Olympic Congress in Baden-Baden (Germany), the IOC entered into discussion with the United Nations Organization with a view to drawing up a convention that would protect the Olympic Games. The process was nevertheless halted because of fears that the UN member states would take advantage of it in order to demand structural modifications to the Olympic system such as those called for by the socialist states during the 1950s and 1960s, e.g. the designation of the IOC members by their respective governments on the principle of "one country, one vote." Finally, the IOC decided to settle for limited recognition via successive resolutions concerning the Olympic Truce (see earlier in this chapter) and notably the first of them that proclaimed 1994—the year of the IOC's centenary—as the International Year of Sport and of the Olympic Ideal.

In 1999, the Olympic system formed a partnership with the public authorities to create the World Anti-Doping Agency (see Chapter 7). The WADA currently benefits from better international recognition than the IOC thanks to the 2005 UNESCO Convention against Doping in Sport.

Table 6.1 Comparison of organs: the Olympic system and the Red Cross Movement

Olympic System	Red Cross Movement
Olympic Charter (including Fundamental Principles)	Statutes (including Fundamental Principles)
IOC	ICRC
205 NOCs	186 National RCRC Societies
ANOC	IFRCRCS
IFs	Humanitarian NGOs
Olympic Congress	Council of Delegates
(no equivalent)	RCRC International Conference
(no equivalent)	Geneva Conventions

A vast, new partnership between the Olympic system and the public authorities could be envisaged within the framework of what could be called the "Lausanne conventions" in homage to the particular role of this Swiss city since Coubertin's time. The said conventions should cover all the current, major problems within sport: corruption, doping, and violence. They would incorporate the ethics and anti-doping codes that have been established. Moreover, they should associate the IFs closely with the conventions, since those entities have no real equivalent in the Red Cross model except, perhaps, the many non-governmental humanitarian associations. The two European conventions (on violence at sport events and against doping), which recognize the additional responsibilities of the public authorities and voluntary sport organizations could serve as examples. They have been signed by around 40 European states.

Like the ICRC, the IOC has maintained a central role in its own system. Its future members would not, however, be citizens of a single country like those of the ICRC but could come—for instance—from countries that have hosted the Games and from the IF presidencies. Worldwide representation would be ensured through the ANOC which unites all the NOCs. Wider Olympic Congresses held every eight years would unite delegates from the IOC, the NOCs, the IFs and the states parties to the "Lausanne conventions." Over time, only those countries having signed the said conventions could, for example, be candidates to organize the Games or even to compete at them. Such a wide ranging reform would better ensure the future of the Olympic movement than the current structures which were conceived at the end of the nineteenth century.

7 The regulators

Three institutions play a particular role in the Olympic system at the beginning of the twenty-first century, and were all created on the initiative of the IOC. They are, in chronological order of their creation, the Court of Arbitration for Sport (CAS), the World Anti-Doping Agency (WADA), and the IOC Ethics Commission. The institutions, which are presented in this chapter, constitute the embryonic form of a global regulation of world sport.

The Court of Arbitration for Sport (CAS)

In 1983 the IOC set in motion the creation of an independent judiciary authority in the form of a Court of Arbitration for Sport (CAS). The court's objective was for sport organizations to have the possibility of avoiding appeal processes before state courts, which were often lengthy and expensive. Moreover, such courts are not always well versed in issues relating to sports. The sentences, or "awards," made by the CAS are in principle confidential unless the parties agree that they may be published. It is a private court, and consists of two chambers, or "divisions": one for ordinary arbitration procedures, which examines all disputes regarding sport that are directly and voluntarily lodged with it by the parties, and the other for handling appeals. It is thus the supreme court for final-instance decisions taken by all the NOCs and IFs that recognize its jurisdiction—including virtually all the Olympic IFs except the International Volleyball Federation (FIVB). The IAAF recognized the court in 2001, and the FIFA did so in 2002 despite intending to found its own court of arbitration for some time.

The CAS also plays an extremely specific role at the Olympic Games in that it sets up ad hoc divisions to settle finally, and extremely rapidly, all disputes arising during the seventeen-day period of the Games. Such divisions have functioned at all the Summer Games since those of Atlanta in 1996, at which six cases were handled (15 in Sydney 2000 and nine in Athens 2004) and at the Winter Games since those of 1998. The ad hoc divisions are superposed on the state courts of the host countries, and are intended to avoid the possibility of a dispute hampering the running of the Games: they are tasked with settling disputes within 24 hours. In principle, they do not intervene in the judging of the competitions but their decisions may affect the holding of competitions or their results.

The Court Office of the CAS is in Lausanne, but it has created decentralized offices in Sydney and New York. The law applied is that of Switzerland unless the parties agree otherwise. Arbitration is based on Switzerland's Federal Law on Private International Law (Chapter 12, International Arbitration), on CAS Code of Sports-Related Arbitration, and on detailed procedural rules. The decisions by the CAS are as binding as those issued by civil courts: either the parties accept them in advance by signing an ad hoc CAS arbitration agreement or because pre-existing contractual agreements regarding arbitration, concluded by a sports organization, are in force.

The procedure states that the parties each select an arbitrator and agree upon a third, or for minor cases the president of the CAS may nominate a single arbitrator. The arbitrator, or members of the arbitration panel, are chosen from a list of around 300 individuals from nearly 90 countries (in 2007), designated for their knowledge of arbitration and of law related to sport. A special list exists for arbitrators familiar with matters surrounding football.

After a fairly slow start during the mid-1980s, the CAS currently handles nearly 300 cases each year, 35 percent of them concerning doping, and 40 percent concerning player transfers (mostly within football). Lists of decisions are published frequently and to some extent constitute case law. A work published for the twentieth anniversary of the CAS provides an excellent overview of cases handled and challenges faced.[1]

In 2007, the CAS has a staff of around 12 persons, headed by a Secretary General, and a budget of nearly seven million Swiss francs, of which nearly two-thirds are covered by the founder organizations of the International Council of Arbitration for Sport (ICAS) (see below). The remaining third is covered by the fees charged to the parties for commercial cases. Disciplinary cases remain free of charge at present.

We can affirm that today, the CAS offers a solution that is appropriate for national but above all for international sports-related disputes. It has led to the IFs' regulations becoming more respectful of the athletes' personal rights (to be heard, to defend themselves, etc.). In addition, it has permitted the establishment of a partnership within the civil judiciary between the sport and public authorities, effectively relieving the latter from a certain burden. Arbitration, or mediation prior to court action, is moreover becoming more widespread at an NOC level (in Belgium, the United States, France, etc.).

The CAS awards may not be appealed against except before the Swiss Federal Tribunal (the country's supreme court) and only in the case of a claim that the general conditions for arbitration specified by Swiss law or by the CAS code or rules have not been respected.[2] Following a first appeal of this kind in 1993—the Gundel case—the Swiss Federal Tribunal recommended to the CAS that it become more independent of the IOC in order to be able to judge such cases independently and impartially but nevertheless upheld its decision and rejected Gundel's appeal.

Since 1994, therefore, the CAS has been supervised by the International Council of Arbitration for Sport (ICAS). The ICAS is a foundation under Swiss law and has a board that consists of 20 individuals. Twelve of these experienced jurists are appointed by the IOC, the IFs and the NOCs (four each), and they in turn appoint four others, with the stated intention of safeguarding the interests of the athletes. The 16 members thus appointed then select the four final members, who must be independent of the entities mentioned. Finally the 20-member council elects its president, following a proposal by the IOC, for four years. For over 20 years, it was Kéba M'Baye of Senegal, an IOC member and former judge at the International Court of Justice in The Hague, who chaired the court. After his death, he was replaced in 2008 by Mino Auletta, an Italian lawyer, who closely defeated Richard Pound, the senior IOC member from Canada, who was suddenly sued for libel in a Lausanne court by UCI a few days before the vote.

The ICAS appoints the CAS arbitrators and if it deems appropriate, it can modify the Code of Sports-Related Arbitration. The structure thus provides for a certain degree of independence from the IOC even though the latter continues to provide a considerable proportion of its budget, either directly or indirectly, and also placed premises at its disposal for many years.

The CAS has in fact canceled certain decisions taken by the IOC regarding doping: for example during the Games in Atlanta and Nagano. Nevertheless, most of the CAS arbitrators are extremely closely linked to organizations within the Olympic system: organizations that propose—in confidence—candidates to become ICAS members. This means that the ICAS members are somewhat distanced from the athletes, who can experience problems in selecting a genuinely impartial arbitrator from the long list of those available within the CAS.

It is interesting to note that the only cases of appeal to the Swiss Federal Tribunal against CAS sentences since its foundation—three in total—were lodged by athletes. In 1993 and 2003, Switzerland's supreme court confirmed the CAS sentence and dismissed the appeals by a horse rider and by skiers. In March 2007, however, it canceled a decision concerning Argentinean tennis player Guillermo Cañas, who had been accused of doping with diuretics by the Association of Tennis Professionals (ATP) and condemned to a 15-month suspension. The court considered that the player had not received a sufficiently full hearing regarding the issue and despite the fact that in order to take part in ATP tournaments he had signed a declaration stating that he waived the right to any form of appeal. Moreover, the court even ordered the CAS to re-examine the case. The CAS did so, rewrote its sentence by mentioning all the arguments that were raised by Cañas' lawyer and simply confirmed its decision without elaborating any further. The Argentinean then decided to lodge a complaint before the European Commission Directorate General for Competition against not only the ATP but also the CAS and the WADA. The latter includes the diuretic product used by Cañas on its list of forbidden substances, although the fact that its use by tennis players would constitute a handicap is widely recognized. Cañas, who was banned from competition for 15 months, considers that the ban constitutes financial and moral harm and is thus claiming extremely high damages and interests. The Competition Commissioner is to hear the parties concerned and possibly bring the case before the European Court of Justice (even though the positive test took place in Mexico and the ATP is an American organization). Depending on the outcome, this case could place the entire edifice patiently constructed by the CAS in doubt.

Generally speaking, the fight against doping represents a serious challenge for the CAS which has been designated by the World Anti-Doping Code (see below) as the appeal court for all decisions taken by anti-doping organizations. Some athletes, in fact, no longer accept the jurisdiction of the CAS despite the fact that they must sign documents that they will do so when they take part in any international competition under the supervision of an IF or the IOC.

In November 2007, for instance, the Kazakh cyclist Andrei Kashechkin chose to appeal against his sentence for doping by the UCI (the Cycling IF) not to the CAS but to a Belgian court in Liege, the city where he lives. The court quickly rejected his appeal but his lawyer—who was among those defending Bosman (see Chapter 6)—has stated that he will appeal to the European Court of Human Rights in Strasbourg if intermediate Belgian courts do not rule in his favor.

A similar case involving Spanish cyclist Carlos Roman Golbano was brought before a court in Almeria, Spain. These two athletes and others claim that the current anti-doping controls infringe their worker's right to practice their profession and even their fundamental human rights by forcing them to give urine and blood samples, wherever they are, from six in the morning until ten at night. They claim, moreover, that the athletes are "small fry" within a huge doping industry in which the other actors are never punished. In short, they believe that many juridical errors are made to protect the interests of international sport and that state courts should intervene more often to ensure that the global sports organizations respect the law.

The World Anti-Doping Agency (WADA)

The World Anti-Doping Agency, created in 1999, is a relatively new entity on the Olympic scene. Its history merits some description, as does placing it within the context of the fight against doping in sport: a far older phenomenon. It is important to note that this fight was originally a completely private affair that was mainly handled by the IOC, but it currently impacts relations between states, (inter-)governmental organizations, and non-governmental sports entities such as the IFs and the NOCs.

After a brief historical overview of the fight against the use of doping substances in sports competitions, we shall describe the composition and the missions of WADA and its actions during its first ten years of existence. A comparison with international organizations of a similar nature but of longer standing will follow, with a view to analyzing the possible evolution of the WADA's juridical nature and role. In conclusion, we shall cover the issues at stake for the future regarding the regulation of doping within world sport.

A brief overview of the fight against doping in sport

The use of doping substances or methods to improve sports performance may well be as ancient as sport itself. Doping—as it is now known—began to emerge as a problem during the 1950s and mainly in cycling. The death of the Danish cyclist Jensen at the 1960 Games in Rome led to the creation by the IOC of a Medical Commission a year later, although it was to remain virtually inactive for several years.

In 1967, the British cyclist Simpson died during the Tour de France. In the same year, Prince Alexandre de Mérode, a young IOC member from the Belgian nobility, was appointed as chairman of the Medical Commission, and was to remain in office for 35 years until his death in 2002. He began his work by organizing the first anti-doping controls—

and gender tests—in 1968 at the Winter Games in Grenoble and the Summer Games in Mexico City, thus making the IOC the first entity to get to grips with the problem of doping on an international level. The work was however restricted to the period of the Games, and the use of doping substances subsequently developed between each edition of them, despite the number of substances prohibited at the Games being increased on each occasion.[3] For their part, the IFs only followed the IOC's example at their own competitions gradually; they were reluctant to do so because of the financial and organizational problems the testing caused and the harm to their image when controls were positive.

In parallel, some countries began to study the problem and introduced ad hoc legislation: notably Austria (1962), Belgium (1965), France (1965), Italy (1971), and Turkey (1971). In 1966, the Council of Europe adopted a Resolution against Doping, and ten years later it included a clause in the European Charter on Sport for All denouncing the use of medication for the purpose of improving performance. In 1978, it formulated an anti-doping recommendation at a Conference of Ministers of Sport of its member states (around thirty countries at the time, excluding Eastern Europe). The end of the 1970s also saw the introduction of controls outside competitions by several countries such as Norway. Some of the larger IFs, such as the International Association of Athletics Federations (IAAF), also began to implement serious doping controls. In 1981, at the Olympic Congress in Baden-Baden, the athletes invited to take part called for extremely serious sanctions for those using doping: disqualification for life.

The various developments resulted, in 1984, in the Council of Europe adopting an Anti-Doping Charter for Sport based on the outcomes from a working group chaired by Prince de Mérode. Co-operation between the Olympic movement and European governments was at its apogee. The charter was then recognized by the General Association of International Sports Federations (GAISF), the Association of European Olympic Committees, the European Commission, the World Health Organization (WHO) and UNESCO.[4] In June 1988, all these efforts led to the adoption of an International Anti-Doping Charter, very similar to that of the Council of Europe, during a conference held in Ottawa and co-chaired by the Canadian government and the IOC. The following October a resolution was adopted at the second International Conference of Ministers and Senior Officials Responsible for Physical Education and Sport organized by UNESCO in Moscow, recommending that the International (and henceforth Olympic) Anti-Doping Charter be applied by all the member states. These various charters are based on the list of forbidden substances and methods progressively established by the IOC Medical Commission, whose legitimacy was thus confirmed.

All these juridical documents unfortunately failed to halt the continuing increase of doping or even to prevent it from being carried out on a major scale. Documentation confirming the practices has today come to light and notably thanks to archive materials from former Eastern European countries. The most striking incident nevertheless remains the disqualification of the Canadian sprinter Ben Johnson at the 1988 Seoul Games.

A period of suspicion and of tension then dawned between the Olympic movement and governments. Canada, directly concerned, set up an enquiry commission chaired by Judge Charles Dubin, the Chief Justice of Ontario: a choice highly criticized by national and international sports organizations, which had always preferred self-regulation to state intervention.

In 1989, the Council of Europe converted the charter into a convention, which was progressively ratified by most of its member states, including those of Eastern Europe who had joined the council following the fall of the Berlin Wall and also by others beyond Europe such as Australia, Canada, and Tunisia.

The convention, which has the force of a treaty, aims to promote the development of national anti-doping policies and their harmonization on an international level. By 2007, it had been ratified by 49 states and signed by two others. It is also worthy of note that several major countries such as South Africa, China, the United States, and Japan are permanent observers to the convention.

In the 1990s, governments started to be heavily involved in the fight against doping. For example, Australia created the Australian Sports Drug Agency (ASDA) in 1990, following revelations regarding substance abuse within its own National Institute of Sport. The first World Anti-Doping Conference, held in Ottawa in 1988, became "permanent," and was followed by those of Moscow (1990), Bergen (1991), and London (1993): the events contributed towards growing awareness of the problem on the part of governments. In their wake, an International Anti-Doping Arrangement (IADA) was created in 1995 on the basis of an inter-governmental agreement first concluded by Australia, Canada, France, Norway, New Zealand, and the United Kingdom but later joined by Denmark, Finland, the Netherlands, and Sweden (France was to withdraw in 1996).

In parallel, the IOC developed a network of around 20 accredited doping control laboratories around the world and attempted to have a unified system of penalties applied by the sports federations. Numerous cases were brought before the civil courts by incriminated athletes, which frequently reversed the decisions taken by the sport organizations and at times required them to pay major sums for damages and interests (one such example being the case of Butch Reynolds who was awarded 27 million US dollars against the IAAF, which never paid the sum).

The 1990s were also marked by increasingly sophisticated doping techniques and the emergence of new products such as erythropoetine (EPO) and growth hormones, which were difficult to detect reliably and thus delayed their inclusion by the IOC on the list of forbidden substances. Gas chromatography and mass spectrometry provided a way forward but was costly for the accredited laboratories, mostly located in Europe and North America. The IOC attempted to mobilize the IFs at several summit meetings in 1993, 1994, and 1995 held to discuss the emerging threats. Some countries in which sport was under state control, such as Russia (some of whose athletes used Bromantan at the 1996 Atlanta Games) and China (some of whose swimmers were detained by customs when arriving in Perth for the 1998 World Swimming Championships for possession of forbidden substances), appeared to be condoning the use of doping and even facilitating access to it.

By the end of the decade, the Tour de France that took place in July 1998 gave rise to a major, public scandal similar to that surrounding Ben Johnson ten years earlier. Following an arrest warrant obtained by the French customs services, who had found forbidden substances in the car trunk of a therapist from the Festina team, the team was forced to withdraw from the race. The interrogation of other cyclists, therapists and executives turned the race into chaos. The French daily newspaper "Le Monde" unsuccessfully called for it to be halted. The IOC Executive Board, at its meeting in 1998, requested explanations from Jean-Claude Killy, president of the company organizing the race (ASO) and a member of the IOC in France. It then decided to convene a World Anti-Doping Conference in Lausanne in February 1999. At the same time, the coach to the Italian football team AS Roma made stunning revelations regarding the proportions taken on by doping within his sport and country.

Two months prior to the conference, the scandal surrounding the corruption of several IOC members regarding the awarding of the Winter Games in Salt Lake City erupted (see Chapter 5 on this subject and also later in this chapter under the section on the IOC Ethics Commission). When the World Anti-Doping Conference opened at the beginning of February 1999, the IOC found itself under attack. Government representatives—notably the German Minister of the Interior—scorned the IOC and accused the Olympic movement of being at best immobile and at worst of complicity in the failure of the fight against doping.

The Conference resulted, after laborious efforts, in the "Lausanne declaration."[5] The first of the two most significant points therein was a wide definition of doping that went beyond the presence of forbidden substances from the IOC's list in the athletes' bodies and included the "use of an artifice, whether substance or method, potentially dangerous to athletes' health and/or capable of enhancing their performances." The second concerned the creation of an "independent international agency" to handle the problem.

The initial plan for an agency, presented at the conference, was however rejected by the delegates since it was seen as too closely linked to the IOC, which had in fact promised to allocate US$25 million towards creating it. The IOC intended to have several stakeholders such as sponsors, the sporting good industry, and the pharmaceutical industry in the agency Board, but not the governments. It was after some ministers' protests that government representatives got half the seats (and had to pay half the budget).

A working group composed of delegates from the Olympic movement, governments and various intra-governmental organizations was therefore tasked by the conference with defining the future agency's structures, missions, and financing within three months. The group took longer than the time allocated for its work, and the entity in question was only formed on 10 November 1999 in Lausanne, under the name of the World Anti-Doping Agency (WADA).

To summarize, the fight against doping in sport has taken place in four successive phases. During the 1960s, the IOC instigated controls at the Games and some countries adopted anti-doping legislation but without any coordination among them. As of the 1970s, the Council of Europe focused on the problem and collaborated closely with the IOC in the 1980s with the result being a charter, which became international in 1988. The 1990s were marked by a loss of confidence on the part of governments regarding the way in which the sports organizations—and notably the International Federations (IFs)—were regulating the phenomenon. The IFs were not always prepared to follow the rules issued by the IOC regarding forbidden substances and the minimum suspension period for athletes taking them. As of 2000, a new agency in which governments and the Olympic movement had parity representation—the WADA—was placed in charge of handling the problem.

The nature and missions of the WADA

The WADA is a Swiss private law foundation pursuant to Articles 80 to 89 of the Swiss Civil Code. According to its statutes, signed before a notary in Lausanne, it has extremely wide and ambitious objectives:

1 To promote and coordinate at international level the fight against doping in sport in all its forms; [...]
2 To reinforce at international level ethical principles for the practice of doping-free sport and to help protect the health of the athletes;
3 To establish, adapt, modify and update for all the public and private bodies concerned, *inter alia* the IOC, IFs and NOCS, the list of substances and methods prohibited in the practice of sport; [...]
4 To encourage, support, coordinate and, when necessary, undertake, in full cooperation with the public and private bodies concerned [...] the organization of unannounced out-of-competition testing;
5 To develop, harmonize and unify scientific, sampling and technical standards with regard to analysis and equipment, including the homologation of laboratories, and to create a reference laboratory;
6 To promote harmonized rules, disciplinary procedures, sanctions and other means of combating doping in sport and contribute to the unification thereof, taking into account the rights of the athletes;
7 To devise and develop anti-doping education and prevention programs at international level, in view of promoting the practice of doping-free sport in accordance with ethical principles;
8 To promote and coordinate research in the fight against doping in sport.[6]

The IOC is the founder of the WADA. It provided it with an initial capital of five million Swiss francs and paid its operating costs for 2000 and 2001 (around 20 million Swiss francs in total) in accordance with the promise made during the 1999 Conference.

As is the case for all Swiss foundations, the Foundation Board is the highest organ. That of the WADA consists of at most 40 members, half from the Olympic movement and the other half from the public authorities. Their period in office is three years, renewable twice (thus nine years maximum). Nominations and renewals must maintain the parity between the Olympic movement and the public authorities "to the extent that the annual allocations or contributions to the budget of the Foundation [...] are equivalent" according to the statutes. The members of the board may be represented by a nominated deputy if they are unable to attend. This possibility has been used frequently, which at times has meant that the board's composition has been far from homogeneous from one meeting to the next. Inter-governmental organizations such as the World Health Organization (WHO) and the International Criminal Police Organization (Interpol) have observer status. The WADA, as a Swiss law foundation, is placed under the control of the Swiss Federal Authority for Supervision of Foundations (Federal Department of Home Affairs).

The board chooses, by majority vote, an Executive Committee of 12 members elected for a one-year term, who are responsible for the management and administration of the agency. There are six members from the Olympic movement and six from the public authorities (one per continent except for Europe, which has two). The committee usually meets on the day before the board in order to prepare decisions. Its members are entitled to an annual indemnity in addition to reimbursement of their expenses, unlike those of the board who receive no such payment. The board has also created five other specialized committees with the following titles: Athletes, Education, Finance & Administration, Health, Medical and Research, and an Ethical Issues Review Panel. Each consists of experts and is chaired by one of its members or attached staff.

The WADA president, from its foundation until the end of 2007, was Canadian IOC member Richard Pound. He was designated to the position by the IOC on a provisional basis but was nevertheless re-elected by the board in December 2001 after a first period in office of two years—and also following his failure to be elected as the IOC President. Apparently, during discussions between the IOC and the European Union (EU) prior to the foundation of the WADA, it was believed in some circles that the presidency should alternate between the Olympic movement and the public authorities every three years. Pound's period in office was nevertheless extended until the end of 2004 in order for the World Anti-Doping Code to be adopted and applied for the Athens Games in August of that same year. It was again extended, until 2007, to cover the first revision of the code. The decision to maintain Pound was facilitated by the promise to elect, in compliance with the Statutes, a vice president from the public authorities.

At its meeting in Madrid on November 2007, the WADA Foundation Board elected John Fahey, former Finance Minister of Australia and Premier of South New Wales during the Sydney 2000 Games, yet with no particular knowledge of doping, as its president. The French vice-president—a former Olympic medalist and minister of sport who expected to be elected—appears to have forgotten that lobbying is more important for obtaining such a position than possessing qualifications. Moreover, a further influencing factor was that too many international sport presidencies are occupied by Europeans. Professor Arne Ljungqvist, member of the IOC, chairman of WADA's Health, Medical and Research Committee and representing the Olympic movement, was chosen as the new vice president.

In 2007, the Foundation Board consisted of 38 members (34 on its creation): the president and vice president, 18 representatives of the

Olympic movement (4 for the IOC, 5 for the IFs, 4 for the NOCs, 4 for the IOC Athletes Commission, 1 for the International Paralympic Committee) and 18 representatives from the public authorities (3 for Africa, 4 for Asia, 2 for Oceania and 5 for Europe, of which 3 are designated by the EU and two by the Council of Europe). The choice of the countries and their continental representatives is made by an International Intergovernmental Consultative Group on Anti-Doping in Sport (IICGADS) created in 1999.

The president or vice president, as appropriate, is designated by the IOC President from among the IOC members. The five IF members are appointed as follows: three by the Association of Summer Olympic International Federations (ASOIF), one by the Association of International Olympic Winter Sports Federations (AIOWSF) and one by the General Association of International Sports Federations (GAISF). In 2007, three out of the five IFs' representatives were IOC members. The four NOC representatives are designated by the Association of National Olympic Committees (ANOC): in 2007, two of them were IOC members. The four representatives of the athletes are designated by the IOC Athletes Commission, whose members are nearly all elected by their peers during meetings at the Olympic Village during the Summer or Winter Games. In 2007, they were all IOC members. It can thus be affirmed that the IOC is particularly well represented on the WADA Board (15 out of 38 members) and even more so on the Executive Committee (six out of 12).

When it was founded in 1999, the WADA's headquarters were provisionally established in Lausanne despite the fact that several governments believed that its seat should not be in the same city as the IOC. The following year, a call for candidates to host a permanent headquarters was made by the IOC among the NOCs and their Ministries of Sport, to be submitted by October 2000. Around 10 cities considered responding, and six submitted a bid: Bonn (Germany), Lausanne (Switzerland), Lille (France), Montreal (Canada), Stockholm (Sweden), and Vienna (Austria). Lille was eliminated since it failed— by one day, and as a result of poor service by an express courier service—to meet the bid deadline. The five other candidatures were examined by an ad hoc evaluation committee that deemed the bids by Lausanne, Montreal, and Vienna to be more appropriate but without recommending any of them in particular.

Discreet lobbying took place for the cities and their countries. Switzerland's Federal Council (its government) signed an agreement with the WADA that exempted it and its non-Swiss staff from direct and indirect taxes as well as customs taxes, pending a future headquarters agreement,[7] thereby granting it a status that was virtually one of an international organization: one not yet achieved by the IOC. The city of Lausanne did everything in its power to ensure that the WADA would stay there, notably including a promise to pay its rent for two years. The Swiss Confederation offered to pay the costs of its installation. The ASOIF recommended that Lausanne be chosen, as did the new IOC President elected one month prior to the decision. The European Commissioner for Education, Culture and Sport, Viviane Reding and the French Minister for Sport, Marie-George Buffet, had been calling for the WADA's location to move away from Lausanne since its foundation, and they thus supported Vienna, which city highlighted its country's membership of the EU (unlike Switzerland) as an asset. Canada, through its own Minister for Sport Denis Coderre, who was a member of the WADA Board at the time, intervened strongly with the public authorities and notably visited the African representatives in their countries and the IOC President. Canada offered the WADA the status of an international organization, with several privileges and immunities, if it became registered under Canadian law. The city also offered 15 million Canadian dollars over ten years to pay the lease on the new offices, plus tax advantages for WADA employees.[8]

In August 2001, the WADA Board elected Montreal on the fourth round (with 17 votes) over Lausanne (15). Bonn was eliminated after the first round (no votes) and Stockholm after the second (one vote). Vienna was beaten in the third round with six votes versus 11 for Lausanne and 15 for Montreal, but—it would seem—without all European votes being cast in favor of Lausanne in the following round. If a single vote previously cast for Montreal had been used for Lausanne in the final round, there would have been an equal number of votes and the casting vote would be that of the Canadian president of the WADA, who had decided to abstain from voting until that point.[9] It is impossible to be certain regarding which member voted for which city since the board had opted for a secret ballot prior to the vote. In addition to the Canadian Minister for Sport, however, it is probable that the two members representing the Olympic movement who are Canadian citizens or live in the country (not including the president) voted for Montreal and thus tilted the balance since the European voters were not aligned. Even on a level of the EU, there were three bids (including the rejected one by Lille). It is moreover worthy of note that there were no Austrian, Swiss or German members of the board to support the bids from those countries. A firm of lawyers from Lausanne that maintains a close relationship with the WADA president had stated the opinion that a conflict of interest could not be claimed for the board members if they had no direct personal or financial advantages regarding the outcome of the vote.[10]

Following the choice of its headquarters, the WADA decided to create regional offices for the various continents: in Johannesburg (South Africa) for Africa, Tokyo (Japan) for the Asia-Pacific region, and in Montevideo (Uruguay) for Latin America. Lausanne was maintained as the European office.

A logo was created: it is a green "equal sign" representing equity and fairness in a black square denoting the customs and rules that must be respected. The "tag line" is "Play true."

The WADA administration is headed by a Director General (originally from Finland and replaced by David Howman, of New Zealand, in 2003). There are ten directorates: science; standards and harmonization; education; communications; legal affairs; African office; Asia/Oceania office; European office; Latin American office; medical, with the last five being located outside Montreal. There is a staff of around 50, with members from around 15 nationalities in order to reflect the WADA's multi-cultural aspirations. A certain desire for transparency has led to numerous documents (including minutes of meetings) being placed on the agency's Internet site (www.wada-ama. org) and by permitting the media to attend the Foundation Board meetings. A strategic plan drawn up in July 2001 and revised twice in 2005 and 2007 guides the daily work. After stating a vision, "a world that values and fosters doping-free sport" and a mission, "to promote, coordinate, and monitor the fight against doping in sport in all its forms," the 2001 plan had eight general priorities stated in the form of activities and performance indicators:[11]

1 To be an independent organization that follows and leads in the development of best practices in its administration, finance, and general operations to ensure the success of its mandate.

2 To be an organization recognized as an anti-doping leader on behalf of sport and athletes.

3 To have a universal Anti-Doping Code covering all sports and countries.

4 To have internationally harmonized rules and regulations governing the operation of national anti-doping programs.

5 To coordinate a worldwide program for in- and out-of-competition testing.

6 To develop anti-doping education and prevention programs at the international level aimed at promoting the practice of doping-free sport according to ethical principles.

7   To establish and manage targeted research programs relating to detection of doping and protection of athletes' health.
8   To establish and implement a laboratory accreditation program.

The early days of the WADA (2000–2002)

In line with its objectives, the WADA's first three years of operation were driven by four major areas of action: the organization of out-of-competition testing; observation of anti-doping tests at the Olympic Games; the launch of research and prevention programs; and drafting the World Anti-Doping Code.

The organization of unannounced out-of-competition tests required the signature of agreements with all the Olympic IFs in order for them to authorize and make it mandatory for their athletes to undergo controls outside their national and international events. Within record time, the International Paralympic Committee (IPC) and all the IFs signed the agreements and the subsequent amendments thereto, with the exception of the FIFA (football) and the ITF (tennis), notably because of the potential implications for their professional players. Most of the tests (3,639 in 49 countries from January 2001 through February 2002, of which 27 were positive) were entrusted to a consortium composed of the Australian Sports Drug Agency (ASDA), the Canadian Centre for Ethics in Sport (CCES), and the Norwegian Confederation of Sport. The consortium sub-contracted controls throughout the world to the Swedish company IDTM (International Doping Tests and Management), which has been active in the sector since 1991. Extremely precise statistics were drawn up, providing the first overview of tests carried out and their results for each (Olympic) sport.[12]

As soon as it was founded, the WADA gave priority to ensuring that the Anti-Doping Code was adhered to at the Games in order to verify the quality of tests carried out in this reference event and to make sure that no positive cases were recorded, as some feared. To do so, the agency designated a group of observers for the Sydney Games (September 2000) and another for those of Salt Lake City (February 2002). With the agreement of the IOC, the observers monitored the procedures that were put in place by the IOC and the respective OCOGs. After the Games, the observers published reports containing recommendations for the future. The group working in Sydney notably raised the alarm regarding the large number of athletes using certain medicines on the list of products to be declared, even though the practice practice (called Temporary Use Extensions, TUE) complied with the Olympic Anti-Doping Code.[13] The Salt Lake group highlighted the slow, opaque work of the laboratory temporarily installed on site by Professor Catlin of the University of California Los Angeles (UCLA). Previously, anti-doping procedures had been under the full responsibility of the IOC Medical Commission at the Games, so independent observers gave rise to a certain degree of tension between that commission and the WADA.

In parallel to the out-of-competition testing and observing the Games, the WADA launched research and prevention funds using its own funds and thanks to contributions from the EU. Grants were awarded to researchers, and a conference on genetic doping was organized in New York. A total of US$4.5 million was attributed to that area in 2001. The WADA's stated objective was to invest 30 percent of its budget in scientific research.

In the area of education and prevention, an "Athlete passport" was launched for the Salt Lake Games in 2002 in the form of a document (and an Internet site) that included all the controls undergone. A similar system had been used by the International Weightlifting Federation since 1995. Five hundred athletes adopted the passport at Salt Lake City, which was the forerunner of the later ADAMS system (see later in this section). An e-learning website covering various aspects of doping was also opened during the Games, and was intended to be an entertaining and educational tool within a program aimed at preventing doping among young people and athletes.[14]

The WADA's primary objective in its early years nevertheless remained the creation of a World Anti-Doping Code. The project was entrusted to a small team, with the assistance of consultants. The code was intended to replace that of the Olympic movement, adopted in 1999 and entirely under the responsibility of the IOC Executive Board—although not well accepted by governments. The WADA code included a list that expanded upon that of the IOC regarding prohibited substances and methods. Aimed to encompass both amateur and professional sport, the code clearly separated what was prohibited during competitions from what was also forbidden out of competition. It also stated the norms for accrediting specialized laboratories and for the control procedures.

It was necessary for the code to be compatible with existing national legislations, and to serve as a legal basis in countries without such legislation and that could find it easier and quicker to adhere to an international convention based on the code than to have their own legislation drawn up and enacted.

In order for the code to be adopted as rapidly as possible, consultations took place with the governments of France, China, Norway, and

Canada and with national anti-doping organizations and IFs.[15] In fact, the consultation process was almost more laborious than the provisions of the code. The aim, however, was to be ready for the 2004 Athens Games (see below).

While being financed by the IOC for the start-up years of 2000 and 2001 (around US$20 million), the WADA was financed on a parity basis as of 2002 by the Olympic movement (from the portion of broadcasting rights for the Games previously shared by the IOC, the IFs, and the NOCs) and by public authorities. The scale adopted by the public authorities for the latter portion had been decided by the IICGADS in May 2001: 47.5 percent for Europe, 29 percent for the Americas, 20.46 percent for Asia, 2.54 percent for Oceania and 0.5 percent for Africa. As of later in 2001, however, the scale was contested by the EU representative, Commissioner Viviane Reding, who felt that Europe should have veto rights on budgetary matters (to avoid mandatory contributions being imposed) and/or additional seats on the Board because of its large contribution. She believed, moreover—as did others in the IOC—that the WADA's expenses lacked transparency, were not well justified and too high. The issue was all the more sensitive since the agency had stated its intention of accountability since its very foundation, along with its objective of independence and transparency.[16]

Viviane Reding's attempts were unsuccessful but in order to save face, she insisted that the WADA's financial operations were incompatible with the budgetary rules of the European Commission so she preferred to resign from the board (and did so in May 2002).

The WADA budget of US$18.27 million submitted to the board in 2001 was indisputably somewhat sketchy, as was the financial plan for 2003–6 that forecast an annual budget increase of 7 percent.[17]

The European contribution towards the 2002 budget was finally collected for payment to the WADA via a fund specially created by the Council of Europe on the basis of the contributions scale normally used for its member states. In all, the public authorities contributed US $8.5 million and the IOC contributed the same amount. In addition, and despite the disputes mentioned above, the EU paid US$1.2 million to finance three pilot projects: e-learning, the Athlete passport, and training for independent observers. Regarding expenditure for 2002, the WADA budgeted US$5 million for scientific research, US$3.3 million for out-of-competition tests, and US$1.25 million for activities related to drawing up the code.

For the following years, the European Sports Ministers, meeting in Almeria, Spain in May 2002, reached an agreement regarding European WADA financing as of 2003.

Several countries, notably the USA, Italy, and those in South America, did not respect their commitments to pay and the WADA was forced to reduce its target budget. The 2003 budget had been established at US $20.2 million, but only 78 percent was covered by governmental contributions. By the end of the first half of 2003, the WADA was virtually without means, so the IOC in turn decided to pay its contribution in installments as and when the governments respected their commitments. The WADA was therefore obliged to cut its annual expenditure and threaten countries that had failed to pay with somewhat unrealistic sanctions such as being deprived of the right to use their flag at the Olympic Games or a refusal to take their candidatures to host sports events into consideration.

In short, during its first three years of operation, the WADA took over most of the work that the IOC Medical Commission had undertaken outside the Games since the 1970s, with a view to effectively fighting doping at all sports competitions: drawing up a universal list of forbidden substances, accreditation of control laboratories, research, prevention, etc. The WADA had considerably larger resources to do so than the IOC Medical Commission, which had depended too highly on the voluntary input by its scientific members, many of whom saw the role as a prestigious one. The commission was, however, far from being independent from the IOC because like all the other commissions its members were appointed by the IOC President.

The period from 2003–2007

The World Anti-Doping Code was officially adopted during a conference specifically convened for the purpose in Copenhagen, Denmark, in March 2003. The organizations that were its signatories (IOC, IFs, NOCs, and the IPC) formally undertook to have it adopted by their highest organs before the 2004 Athens Games opened in August 2004, and the governments made a commitment to insert it within their respective legislations prior to the Turin Games in February 2006. The extremely short deadlines were imposed with the threat of being suspended from the Olympic movement for any IFs and NOCs who did not meet them. Governments failing to comply were threatened with the non-acceptance of candidatures for the Games or other international competitions.[18]

In the end, the code was accepted for the 2004 Athens Games by all the NOCs and all the Summer and Winter Olympic IFs—including by the FIFA in May 2004 and at the very last moment, in August, by the International Cycling Union (UCI). Twenty-six out of the other

28 Federations recognized by the IOC and 13 of the further 20 member federations of the GAISF also adopted the Code, as did nearly 500 other national and international sport organizations including the IOC, by decision of its 2003 Session. Certain IFs, highly reluctant to comply with the requirements because of the minimum two-year ban required for doping, were finally convinced to accept the code following the inclusion within it of a clause stating that "exceptional circumstances" could be taken into consideration to reduce the two-year ban. The significant change of attitude on the part of the United States should also be noted: the US president specifically mentioned the fight against doping in his State of the Union speech in January 2004. As of that moment, the United States Anti-Doping Agency (USADA) began to actively pursue doping offenders, to the point of depriving the American team of several star athletes at the Athens Games and investigating medalists of the Sydney Games, notably the famous sprinter Marion Jones. (Jones was later convicted of perjury and served some time in jail, a first for an Olympic athlete in relation to a doping matter.)

On the eve of the Athens Games, the code had been signed by 133 governments, although the signatures did not make this document drawn up by a private entity legally enforceable, even though governments had parity representation on the WADA Board. For that to become the case, it would be necessary to adopt an international treaty that would permit states that ratified it to incorporate it within their national legislation, policies or regulatory texts.

In January 2003, UNESCO agreed to prepare such an international legal instrument in the form of a convention inspired by that of the Council of Europe but that explicitly referred to the new code and at the same time recognized the role of the WADA as the entity responsible for applying the said code on an international level. The convention was adopted at the UNESCO General Conference in October 2005 and came into force on 1 February 2007 after ratification by a 30th member state, i.e. one year later than the stated objective of the 2006 Turin Games. The process was nevertheless completed in record speed for inter-governmental organizations and the diplomatic sector. It should also be acknowledged that ratifying the convention required countries that had already implemented national laws or regulations to adapt them accordingly. At the end of 2007, the International Convention against Doping in Sport has been ratified by 74 member states (out of 191 signatories). After 1 January 2010, acceptance of the convention should become a condition for presenting a candidature for world championships and the Olympic Games (as of those of 2018).

After the adoption of the code in 2003, the strategy and structure of the WADA underwent major revision in order to focus on five objectives:

1 To implement, support, oversee, and monitor compliance of the World Anti-Doping Code.
2 To educate and inform signatories to the code, governments and athletes as well as support personnel about the dangers and consequences of doping abuse.
3 To lead, coordinate and support an effective anti-doping scientific, laboratory, and research program of the highest quality.
4 To increase the capability of anti-doping organizations to implement anti-doping rules and program to ensure compliance with the code.
5 To be a world leading organization whose corporate operating activities reflect international standards of best practices.[19]

Several of the five new objectives group together some of those in the preceding ones. As an example, the important issue of laboratory accreditation—formerly the eighth objective—was linked to the implementation of the code by the WADA (henceforth the first objective). On the other hand, and on the basis of its new strategy, the WADA decided to withdraw completely from anti-doping controls in- and out-of-competitions, despite having focused intensively on that area at the outset (formerly the fifth objective). That work was delegated, in accordance with the code, to the national and regional anti-doping organizations such as USADA in the USA, the CNLD in France, the Swiss Anti-Doping Agency, and a number (70 in 2007) of other new bodies created as of that moment in countries having ratified the UNESCO convention. The decision had considerable strategic impact: today, the effectiveness of the fight against doping varies greatly from one country to another. Certain athletes, and in particular those in developed countries, are monitored very closely and tested out of competition, while those from less developed countries—which have other priorities—are subjected to far fewer controls. Doping controls are expensive, and cannot always be carried out in the country concerned, even if that country has signed the International Convention.

In order to address this problem and facilitate the work of all the stakeholders in the fight against doping, the WADA has set up an Anti-Doping Administration and Management System (ADAMS). Based on an extranet, it permits users to manage tests in and out of competition, to enter temporary use exemptions (TUEs), to supply details regarding the whereabouts of athletes' training sites, to provide and consult the test results, and other important information such as a clearing house function.

After a two-year consultation procedure among the stakeholders, the World Anti-Doping Conference held in Madrid in November 2007 adopted a second version of the World Anti-Doping Code which will enter into force on 1 January 2009 (well after the Games in Beijing). The major change is the possibility afforded by the new code to extend (for aggravating circumstances) or reduce (for mitigating circumstances) the overall suspension period of two years imposed on an athlete for a first positive test by the 2003 version of the code, with the maximum suspension set at four years. This change was made to accommodate contradictory requests by the IAAF (athletics) and FIFA (football) federations for longer or shorter suspension periods respectively. The change was also implemented to adapt the wordwide code to a standard requirement by most judicial systems that sentences should be proportional to circumstances and thus respect the fundamental rights of athletes. In fact, from 2003 to 2007, the CAS was called upon to study almost sixty suspension decisions and reduced their length in most cases. Doped athletes who are ready to help an inquiry will also receive a reduced sentence. An information-sharing agreement with Interpol to facilitate the implementation of the new code had been prepared to be signed in Madrid but fell through at the last minute because of the lack of interest from most of the international police body member states.

Apart from implementing the new code, the new WADA president's task will be to consolidate the WADA after eight years of highly rapid development with Richard Pound at its head, and to ensure that the fight against doping remains on governmental agendas. One major landmark will be the publication, scheduled for November 2008, of the WADA's evaluation of the compliancy achieved by the various stakeholders having ratified the code. A preliminary document presented to the 2007 IOC Session states that only 22 Olympic IFs out of 35 and 21 NOCs out of 205 are compliant. Much work remains to be done.

Comparison between the WADA and other sectors of international relations

Many problems that arise on an international level require collaboration between governments and the sectors involved. There are nevertheless few international organizations that, like the WADA, unite the public and private sector in a balanced way within a single structure. Most registered inter-governmental organizations grant observer status to various other organizations that share their mission. Similarly, non-governmental organizations (NGOs) often invite governments to take part in their work. Organizations that fully integrate governmental authorities and NGOs in the manner adopted for the WADA are extremely rare.

Two examples can be cited, however: the World Conservation Union (formerly the International Union for the Conservation of Nature and Natural Resources and still frequently known as the IUCN today), and the International Red Cross and Red Crescent Movement (IRCRCM). We shall present the two organizations briefly and then compare them with the WADA.

Founded in 1948, the IUCN is a vast alliance of public and private organizations from 181 countries that are dedicated to protecting the environment. Its stated mission is to "influence, encourage and assist societies throughout the world to conserve the integrity and diversity of nature and to ensure that any use of natural resources is equitable and ecologically sustainable." Its legal structure is that of an association under Swiss law pursuant to Article 60 et seq. of the Swiss Civil Code. It admits members of three categories: A: State members and governmental agencies; B: NGOs; and C: affiliated members (without the right to vote). In 2007, the IUCN's membership consisted of 84 states, 108 governmental agencies, 82 international NGOs and 749 national NGOs, plus 33 affiliates. It employs a staff of over 1,000 in around 40 regional offices, and around 100 employees work at the headquarters in Gland, between Lausanne and Geneva. The IUCN notably facilitates the conservation of nature in developing countries by making experts available and by organizing conferences and carrying out local projects.[20] It is financed by means of bilateral agreements (two-thirds of the total), multilateral agreements, membership fees, and various other sources (donations, publications, etc.). Its work is based on various international conventions related to the environment that have been adopted since the 1970s: on wetlands (1971), the protection of world natural heritage sites (1972), international trade in endangered species (CITES, 1973), migratory species (1979), climate change (1992), biodiversity (1992), the fight against desertification (1994).

The IUCN's organs are: the World Congress (the general assembly of the IUCN as an association in the sense of the Swiss Civil Code); its council; its regional committees, the voluntary experts' commissions established by the congress, and the secretariat headed by a Director General. The congress usually meets every three years. Most decisions are taken by simple majority of the votes cast by A and B category delegates. State members have three votes, governmental organizations from a non-member state have one collective vote, international NGOs have two votes and national NGOs one vote. The council, elected at each congress, is an executive organ consisting of the president, the treasurer, the commission chairs (6), regional advisors (25), and up to 6 additional councilors.

The International Red Cross and Red Crescent Movement (IRCRCM) is, according to its website,[21] a term that unites the International Committee of the Red Cross (ICRC, an association under Swiss law created in 1863), the International Federation of Red Cross, and Red Crescent societies (IFRCRCS), an association founded in 1919, and all the 186 national societies that are recognized by the ICRC and that thus form part of the IFRCRCS. The movement's purpose is to facilitate cooperation among its members and the states that have signed the Geneva Conventions (1949), consecrating what is known as "international humanitarian law." It works on the basis of seven fundamental principles: humanity, impartiality, neutrality, independence, voluntary service, unity, and universality.

The highest organ of the movement is an international conference that is held every four years, and that consists of a delegate for each of the following: the ICRC, the IFRCRCS, the 186 national societies, and the 188 States that have signed the Geneva Conventions. Each delegate has one vote.[22] It should be noted that the states participate fully in the conference without being formal members of the IRCRCM. A Standing Committee meets every six months to manage the movement, and consists of two ICRC delegates, two from the IFRCRCS and six delegates elected by the international conference, usually representing states and national societies who are often under the aegis of the public authorities. (See also Chapter 6.)

Table 7.1 summarizes some elements for comparison between the WADA, the IUCN, and the IRCRCM. There is a certain sharing of power within the highest bodies of all three entities between NGOs and state organizations or governments. This public–private parity nevertheless remains somewhat theoretical, since certain national Red Cross or Red Crescent societies are virtually governmental agencies, as are many NOCs. Furthermore, the states are not members of the WADA Board as they can be in the highest organs of the IUCN and the IRCRCM, since the WADA Board consists of continental representatives appointed by the International Intergovernmental Consultative Group on Anti-Doping in Sport (IICGADS). Finally, the WADA Board takes important decisions by qualified two-thirds majority and not simple majority (with some exceptions), unlike the other two bodies where decisions are by simple majority.

Table 7.1 Elements for comparison between the WADA, the IUCN, and the IRCRCM

	WADA	IUCN	IRCRCM
Date of foundation	1999	1948	1919
Area of work	Fight against doping	Conservation of nature	Humanitarian action
Main components	Olympic Movement (IOC, IFs, NOCs)/public authorities	Environmental NGOs/states and government agencies	ICRC, IFRCRCS and national RCRC societies/signatory states*
Highest organ (frequency of meetings)	Foundation Board (every six months)	World congress (every three years)	International conference (every four years)
Executive organ	Executive Committee	Council	Standing Committee
Legal form	Private foundation under Swiss law	Private association under Swiss law	None stated in the statutes
Basic text	Statutes	Statutes and rules	Statutes and rules of procedure
Inter-governmental conventions	2005 international convention adopted by UNESCO in order to apply the World Anti-Doping Code (2003 and 2007)	Various international conventions relating to the environment (1971 to 1994)	Geneva conventions (1949) and additional protocols

Note
* The signatory states to the Geneva conventions take part in the international conference of the Red Cross without being—according to the statutes—IRCRCM members.

It is in fact difficult to compare the highest organs of the three organizations since their size and the frequency of their meetings are different. Those of the IUCN (World Conservation Congress) and the IRCRCM (International Conference of the Red Cross and Red Crescent) are summit meetings uniting states and numerous other delegates, held every three or four years respectively. The WADA Board has only 38 members and meets twice or three times a year without the official presence of the member states. The IOC does convene Olympic Congresses (every eight years according to the Olympic Charter but recently in 1973, 1981, and 1994, and planned for 2009) that unite its members, the IFs and many sports organizations, either inter-governmental or recognized by the IOC. The WADA will no doubt be invited to the next edition, planned in 2009, in Copenhagen (Denmark). The Olympic Congresses do not, however, constitute adequate representation for the states and are moreover of a consultative nature only.

The WADA's Executive Committee can be more easily compared to the executive organs of the UICN (Council) or the IRCRCM (Standing Committee). Table 7.2 shows a more balanced distribution of powers in those bodies.

Given the situation described, the most viable solution for parity representation within the fight against doping would seem to be a regular international anti-doping conference of which the WADA would become the secular arm. The "permanent" world conferences of Ottawa (1988), Moscow (1990), Bergen (1991), and London (1993) were convened jointly by the IOC and the government of the host

Table 7.2 Voting rights in the executive organs of the WADA, the IUCN, and the IRCRCM

In 2007	*WADA Executive Committee*	*IUCN Council*	*IRCRCM Standing Committee*
Votes by non-governmental members	6 (including the vice president or president)	13 (1 president, 1 treasurer, 6 commission chairs, 5 experts)	4 (2 from the ICRC and 2 from the IFRCRCS)
Votes by governmental members	6 (including the president or the vice president)	25 (24 regional councilors (3 per region) + 1 representative of the Swiss Confederation)	6

country (see earlier in this chapter). The world conference in Lausanne in February 1999 was convened by the IOC only, and the International Summit on Drugs in Sport held in Sydney in November of the same year was convened jointly by the Australian and Canadian governments.

Today it is the WADA that convenes an international conference every four years in compliance with the mandate stated within the World Anti-Doping Code. The first took place in Copenhagen (2003) and the second in Madrid (2007). The main power attributed to the conferences is to ratify the evolution of the code.

The idea defended by the French Minister for Sport in the early days of the WADA, i.e. of changing its private nature to become a genuine inter-governmental organization, appears to have been abandoned. The change is moreover unnecessary as proven by the ICRC's legal status of an association supported by the Geneva Conventions or that of the UICN, partially mandated by the various inter-governmental conventions relating to the environment. In addition, and according to Swiss legal experts, a foundation under Swiss law such as the WADA may have its seat outside the country.[23] Whatever the WADA's precise status, however, it will remain an extremely unusual international organization.

Challenges for the future regarding the regulation of the Olympic system

Like environmental protection and humanitarian action, the fight against doping requires a partnership between the public authorities and the private organizations concerned. This necessity is the result of a certain failure on the part of the market to resolve these complex problems alone— problems that demand coercion on a national and international level that can come from states alone (police, customs, intelligence, courts). For a century, international sport regulated itself at a world level by means of the private, monopolistic system of the IFs and the IOC as global sport organizations. The massive development of doping has revealed the limits of those bodies and the necessity for the public authorities to intervene. There can be no question of moving towards full regulation of doping by the public authorities since doing so would lead to placing sports activity under the power of the states. The solution of creating an independent agency was thus selected, and lends credibility on a world level to the fight against doping. By means of the WADA World Anti-Doping Code and the UNESCO Intergovernmental Convention, the stakeholders have provided it with the rules and regulatory powers required.

After several decades during which the fight against doping was by no means effective—because the extent of the problem had been poorly assessed and/or the appropriate measures were not taken—the global sports organizations finally saw the need to form an alliance with the public authorities in 1999 to combat the scourge that is doping. At the end of the twentieth century, however, sport has seen two other scourges appear on the horizon: violence and corruption.

Violence in sport, which at one time mainly concerned spectators (hooliganism), now also affects athletes, either between players or against judges and referees—a fact that can be easily seen from televised sport.[24] What television spectators do not see, however, is the violence in sport that is also affecting younger athletes, who may be subjected to psychological or even physical violence on the part of their coaches or even of their parents, who want them to become stars.[25] A charter concerning the rights of children in sport was for instance drawn up in Geneva, in 1988. This violence naturally goes against the educational benefits of sport, which can thus become a bad example to children.

Corruption within sport—once exceptional—appears to have become common among athletes and sport executives. The cases of the IOC and the FIFA reached the headlines in 1999 and 2002 respectively. The massive sums that circulate in the sport sector can lead executives to become deceitful and/or to commit reprehensible acts (bankruptcies, the use of false passports for athletes, etc.). Corruption is also reaching the sports field, and distorting results. "Fixed" matches have shed doubt on the outcome of football championships in many countries. The phenomenon affects not only football, however, but also athletics, boxing, cricket, cycling, Formula 1 racing, gymnastics, judo, ice skating, sailing, tennis, etc., in particular when betting is involved. The cases have at times been flagrant, including at the Games. The NGO Transparency International called for football and ice skating to be removed from the Olympic program as a result of corruption.

Doping, violence and corruption thus constitute an infernal trio frequently cited by the IOC President,[26] and are also a cause for concern at government level. The Council of Europe adopted a European Convention on Spectator Violence and Misbehavior at Sports Events in 1985 following a drama resulting in multiple deaths at the Heysel Stadium in Belgium. Members of the Organisation for Economic Co-operation and Development (OECD) signed a Convention on Combating Bribery of Foreign Public Officials in International Business Transactions in 1997 that has not yet been applied to sport but could prove appropriate to the extent that sports competitions can be seen as business transactions between public and private organizers, athletes and sponsors, from several countries.

Just as doping is considered to be a public health problem by numerous governments (since it affects many young people as well as elite athletes), violence and corruption could be increasingly seen as problems affecting public order or public moral values. The Council of Europe's Committee of Ministers moreover proposed a Code of Sports Ethics in 1992 that provided a definition of fair play and recalled the responsibilities on the part of governments and sports organizations regarding this ideal that is essential for "all sports activity, sports policy and management" (stated in the "Aims of the Code").

It should not be forgotten that any increase in doping, violence or corruption could also, over time, lead to the public authorities deciding to reconsider their financing of sport. Spending public money is mainly legitimized by a desire to promote health, education, and sustainable development.

In its introduction, the WADA's World Anti-Doping Code justifies the fight against doping because of the ethical, educational, and social values of sport—and those values are placed at risk as a result of violence and corruption as described above.

In Canada, the agency handling the national anti-doping program is the Canadian Centre for Ethics in Sport (CCES) in Ottawa. Its mandate is, however, wider, and serves the ideals of sport in general.[27] Many of the WADA's political and administrative leaders maintain close links with the centre, quite apart from their geographical proximity. It could be possible that in a few years' time, the WADA could turn its focus to issues other than doping. Once it has brought that issue under control it could—at the instigation of governments—become a kind of organization to regulate world sport in order to prevent it from becoming entrenched in its darker side.

Should that be the case, however, it would find the IOC blocking its path, since the IOC sees itself as the guardian of sports ethics and has moreover created a commission for that purpose during the same year that it came together with governments in order to create the WADA.

The IOC Ethics Commission

Since its foundation in 1894, the IOC has presented itself as the guardian of the ethics of sport, as the Olympic Charter was to affirm one hundred years later: "Olympism seeks to create a way of life based on the joy of effort, the educational value of good example and respect for universal fundamental ethical principles."[28] Historically, the IOC has always defended a certain idea of sport, which has led it to sanction some athletes. Until 1972, and a case involving the Austrian skier Karl

Schranz at the Sapporo Winter Games and money he received from equipment manufacturers, it focused on those who infringed the rules of amateurism. As of 1968, it concentrated mainly on those convicted of doping.

Starting from the 1970s, the Olympic Games began to take on an increasingly important role within the phenomenon of sport, and indeed became the pinnacle within an athlete's career. The business interests at stake soared for both participants and organizers. After the sporting and financial success of the 1984 Los Angeles Games, cities flocked to submit candidatures for Summer and Winter Games alike, and the IOC's membership included more and more well-known individuals from the world of sport and beyond it. From 91 members in 1984, the figure rose to 110 in 1998.

It was within the framework of the ethical scandal surrounding the candidature of Salt Lake City for the 2002 Winter Games that the IOC founded the Ethics Commission in 1999 among other major structural reforms (see Chapter 2).

Although relatively recent, the Ethics Commission has played a significant role within the functioning of the Olympic movement at the beginning of the twenty-first century. It is thus of interest to examine its composition, rules, and decisions in order to gain a better understanding of its current directions and to evaluate its contribution towards regulating the Olympic system. Comparisons with similar organizations are made, as are proposals with a view to improve the commission's functioning. Finally, its actions are placed in relation to the question of the governance of world sport, considering sport as a public good to be preserved for future generations.

Foundation and composition

In November 1998, some of the media in the US State of Utah denounced various practices by the Salt Lake City Candidature Committee.[29] It was moreover not the first time that allegations were made regarding favors accepted by IOC members from candidate cities: an entire book detailing practices was published in Sweden following the defeat of Falun as a candidate for organizing the Winter Games. English journalists produced two best-sellers in 1992 and 1996 describing the unethical behavior of numerous leading figures in the IOC and world sport.[30] In December 1998, however, the suspicions surrounding Salt Lake City were confirmed to the media for the first time, and by Marc Hodler, a senior member of the IOC Executive Board during one of its meetings in Lausanne.

This eminent Swiss IOC member had, since 1986, been tasked by IOC President Samaranch to draw up and monitor rules of good conduct for candidate cities following the elections of the 1992 host cities (Albertville and Barcelona), since there had been rumors of corruption regarding all bids.[31] Hodler's statements, which accused several members and several cities, rapidly reached the four corners of the globe. The NOC of the USA (USOC), the Salt Lake Olympic Organizing Committee (SLOOC) and the US Congress rapidly set up enquiry commissions, as did the IOC as an emergency measure. Its own commission, chaired by IOC Vice-President Richard Pound, published a report in January 1999 whose recommendations were accepted in March of the same year at an Extraordinary Session (general assembly) of the IOC. Of the 110 members at the time, six were the object of a virtually unanimous vote of exclusion, and a further ten received reprimands of varying degrees of severity. Three members had already resigned or had died since the events.[32]

At the same Session, the IOC created an Ethics Commission under pressure from the US media and some of its sponsors (notably the life insurance company John Hancock). President Samaranch immediately nominated the commission members, as is the practice for all other IOC commissions. He entrusted its chair to his long-standing friend from Sénégal, Kéba Mbaye: a former judge at the International Court of Justice in the Hague, member of the IOC from 1973 and president of the Court of Arbitration for sport (CAS) since its foundation in 1983. Mbaye remained the commission's chairman until his death in 2007, although he had become an honorary member of the IOC in 2003 after reaching the age limit.

The other commission members fell into two categories: those belonging to the IOC (three) and those outside it (four). In 1999, those from the IOC were Chiharu Igaya (Japan), Charmaine Crooks (Canada) and Kevan Gosper (Australia). The others were Robert Badinter (France, former Minister of Justice and Chairman of the French Constitutional Council), Howard Baker (United States, American Senator); Kurt Furgler (Switzerland, former President of the Swiss Confederation), and Javier Pérez de Cuéllar (Peru, former UN Secretary-General).

The composition evolved over the years as certain members resigned. In 2000, for instance, Kevan Gosper left the commission following an enquiry relating to a visit by his family to Salt Lake City during its candidature, and even though the enquiry exonerated him from any misdemeanor.[33] He was replaced by Ninian Stephen, a former governor general of Australia and a judge at its supreme court.

The original idea was for the number of commission members from outside the IOC to be greater than that of those within it. The spirit of the rule was, however, not respected at the outset since its chairman was an IOC member (honorary as of 2002) and Kurt Furgler became a member of honor of the IOC as of 2000.

Today, according to its new statutes,[34] the commission consists of nine members of which five are not IOC members. At least one of the four IOC members is an elected member of the Athletes Commission. The members are designated by the IOC President, but must be approved by the IOC Executive Board. The term in office is four years and is renewable. Members may be removed from office by a two-thirds majority vote of the IOC Executive Board. As of 2007, it has been chaired by Youssoupha Ndiaye of Senegal, IOC member and chairman of the Senegal Constitutional Council.

Since the commission was created, its chairman has been assisted by a secretary whose role is somewhat unclear. The daily work is coordinated by a special representative: first François Werner, a former French cabinet official and since 2002, Pâquerette Girard Zappelli, a Franco-Swiss lawyer. The commission's offices are located in the "Villa du centenaire" a magnificent property owned by the IOC and directly neighboring the Olympic Museum in Lausanne.

The commission's independence from the IOC is questionable. Despite stating its independent nature in its statutes, it cannot avoid the provisions that moreover constitute part of those same statutes. For instance, the commission reports exclusively to the IOC Executive Board, which approves the members designated by the IOC President. Its composition is announced each year in the same press release that contains details of the other IOC commission members designated by the IOC President. Its annual budget is submitted for the approval of the IOC Executive Board. Its offices are within the IOC's premises. Its Internet site is a section within that of the IOC (along with the sections for the other commissions). Its members and staff are included within the list of commissions and staff of the IOC Administration, etc.

In order to affirm its independence more firmly, however, and notably on a financial level, the commission organized the creation of a private foundation under Swiss law, under the name of the "Foundation for Universal Olympic Ethics" (FUOE) in accordance with Articles 80 et seq. of the Swiss Civil Code. The Foundation Council (which has full powers, pursuant to Swiss law) consists of the commission members and is headed by its chairman. It also includes the IOC's Director of Finance, since the IOC provided the capital for the foundation. This extremely unusual juridical structure recalls that adopted by the Court of Arbitration of Sport (CAS), which is headed by an International Council of Arbitration for Sport (ICAS) (see earlier in this chapter). The ICAS members are however nominated by the various components of the Olympic movement, which is not the case for the FUOE whose members are designated by the IOC.

The rules applied

The primary concern of the commission and in particular that of its first chairman, a senior jurist, was to establish a certain number of texts on which to base its actions. These are of course only "sporting rules" that have no civil or penal implications.

Pursuant to the stipulations in the Olympic Charter, it was first necessary to create the commission by means of an article (called a "rule") in the said charter. In June 1999, the IOC Session held in Seoul thus adopted a new rule (initially number 25 but now separated into two separate rules numbered 22 and 23), stating the commission's two main roles:

"It is charged with defining and updating a framework of ethical principles," and "it investigates complaints raised in relation to the non-respect of such ethical principles [...] and if necessary proposes sanctions to the IOC Executive Board." The commission has also taken on a "mission of prevention and advising the Olympic parties on the application of the ethical principles and rules."[35] This mission is not (yet) explicitly stated in rule 22 of the Olympic Charter.

Decisions regarding sanctions proposed by the commission may either be taken by the IOC Executive Board or, at its recommendation, by the Session. The sanctions apply to the IOC members, the IFs, the NOCs, and the OCOGs, and consist of withdrawing their Olympic prerogatives temporarily or permanently (IOC membership, participation on the Olympic program and recognition for an IF, organization of the Games or of IOC meetings). During the Games, the sanctions also concern all individuals accredited, in particular the athletes, officials, and other "participants" who may have their accreditation or eventual medals withdrawn.

At the same time as introducing the rule relating to the founding of the commission, the 1999 IOC Session adopted the Code of Ethics and the commission's statutes. The code was revised in 2007. It forms an integral part of the Olympic Charter, and lists six major principles within the framework of Olympic activities:

1 Dignity and integrity of the individual who must not be subjected to any form of discrimination, doping, harassment, betting, or security risks.

2 Integrity on the part of individuals regarding remuneration, gifts, excessive hospitality, conflicts of interest, and behavior likely to tarnish the reputation of the Olympic Movement or association with persons whose activity is inconsistent with the principles of the Olympic Charter.
3 Resources used in a transparent manner, that can be audited and that are in keeping with Olympic purposes, without interference on the part of sponsors and broadcasters.
4 Candidatures that respect the IOC's rules of conduct for the candidate cities.
5 Harmonious, neutral relations with state authorities in accordance with the respect of human rights, the environment, and the Olympic ethical principles.
6 Refraining from revealing confidential information entrusted by Olympic stakeholders or by others if the intent is to harm or for personal gain.

The code also indicates that implementing provisions may be set out by the commission, and that breaches of the code should be reported to the IOC President.

This extremely vast and somewhat tangled set of principles is applied to the "Olympic parties," defined as the IOC and its members, the NOCs and the cities wishing to organize the Games. It is interesting to note that the IFs are not explicitly stated as such parties, while sanctions are foreseen against them in rule 23 of the Olympic Charter. The IFs may voluntarily adopt the code in order to avoid the costs of setting up their own ethics commission, but they tend to remain autonomous.

In 2004, the FIFA and the International Federation of Associated Wrestling Styles (FILA) adopted their own codes of ethics, applied by their own ethics commissions. FILA's code is almost identical to that of the IOC. FIFA's code was revised in 2006 to create a new independent ethics committee which constitutes FIFA's third judicial body. The first chairman of this committee is Lord Sebastian Coe of the United Kingdom. In 2007, the International Amateur Boxing Association (AIBA) also created an ethics commission following a change of president and Secretary General, accused of corruption. The International Cycling Union (UCI) put a code and a commission in place several years ago, as did FITA (Archery IF).

According to rule 23 of the Olympic Charter, the sanctions may also be based on the World Anti-Doping Code (see above) or "any other decision or applicable regulation issued by the IOC or any IF or NOC [...] or any applicable public law or regulation."

In 1999, the IOC had wished to adhere to the OECD's Convention on Combating Bribery and had taken steps to do so, but without results.[36] The civil and penal conventions against corruption signed by the Council of Europe member states in 1999, or the Code of Sports Ethics adopted by the same council in 1992 could be possible reference regulations.

Implementing provisions, revised in 2007, complete the commission's statutes and state the rules of procedure. Anyone may send a written complaint or denunciation, but the submission of a case to the commission is decided upon by the IOC President alone, if he deems it appropriate.

The commission also provides advice to Olympic organizations that so request. Before formulating its recommendations regarding measures or procedural rules, the commission may: request any pertinent documents; hear the parties or the witnesses; designate experts; appoint a secretary within its number for a specific case, etc. The investigation work is carried out by the commission's special representative, who has taken on a significant role within the functioning of the Olympic system, and is often among the 10 leading Olympic personalities in the list drawn up annually by an insider information bulletin.[37]

The commission's Code of Ethics and its statutes have been completed over the years by various other implementing texts: rules of conduct applicable for all cities wishing to organize the Olympic Games;[38] directives concerning the election of the IOC President; rules relating to conflicts of interest affecting the behavior of the Olympic parties; implementing provisions of the Code of Ethics regarding the definition of "participants" at the Olympic Games; implementing provisions regarding the special representative.

Rule 22 of the Olympic Charter states that all the texts and rules emanating from the IOC Ethics Commission are submitted for the approval of the IOC Executive Board. The rules concerning conflicts of interest were finally adopted in August 2002 after lively discussion at the IOC Session in Salt Lake City, based on a first draft submitted by the Executive Board.[39] These rules were further modified in 2006.

When reading all these texts, in part redundant and reworked over the years, the impression gained is one of a juridical tangle that is difficult for common mortals to grasp. It should be noted in any case that the commission unites the powers of a legislator and a prosecutor, since it draws up its own rules and investigates cases submitted to it under the ultimate supervision of the IOC Executive Board, which acts as the judge for its recommendations and may submit more serious cases to a "popular jury" consisting of all the IOC members (the Session).

Cases and decisions

No complete list of all cases brought before the commission exists, although the cases are numbered by year. The highest numbers of cases whose details were published are: two for 2001, eight for 2002, three for 2003, five for 2004, seven for 2005, five for 2006 and two for 2007. Several of them are well known thanks to the media and, since 2004, to the commission's website. They are gradually creating a form of jurisprudence. The cases handled can be classified into four categories corresponding to four potential "clients": the candidature committees, the IOC members, the NOCs and the IFs.

Cases concerning candidature committees

The candidature committees for organizing the Games constitute the primary target of the IOC Ethics Commission, since it was founded after the actions by that of Salt Lake City.

In September 1999, the IOC President submitted a report by the firm King and Spalding to the commission regarding abuse that could have taken place during Atlanta's candidature for the 1996 Games.[40] In May 2000, after eliminating allegations concerning persons who were no longer IOC members, the commission proposed halting work on the dossier with the exception of alleged actions on the part of a member, and which were eventually deemed to be venial.[41]

In September 2001, the IOC seized the commission with regard to statements made by businessman André Guelfi, who claimed he had influenced the election of Beijing over Paris for the 2008 Games. The outcome of the enquiry is not known, but the commission refused to become involved in the issue of attributing the 2008 Games to the Chinese régime, as the International Federation for Human Rights requested of it.

As of 2002, the commission has also been used for advisory purposes, both by the IOC department responsible for candidatures and by the candidature committees themselves, the latter with the aim of avoiding any blunders that could exclude them from the process. In July 2003, it was called upon to handle a case of possible conflict of interest on the part of the chairman of the IOC Evaluation Commission for the candidatures for 2010, which was finally dismissed.

It was as of the highly disputed competition for the 2012 Summer Games, involving five major world capitals (London, Madrid, Moscow, New York, and Paris), that the commission was called upon to play a real "policing" role in 2004 and 2005. Notable issues that it handled were: invitations to French embassies for IOC members by the Paris candidature (forbidden after a complaint by Madrid); last-minute financial proposals by the New York candidature to the IFs (accepted because they were already stated in the candidature dossier); those offered to the NOCs and athletes by London (which preferred to officially withdraw them for fear of sanctions); a presentation by London to an assembly at the Commonwealth Games (forbidden); a project for a debate on British Broadcasting Corporation (BBC) television between those in charge of the five candidatures (forbidden).

Certain cities criticized the commission for a lack of impartiality because its special representative was French. This reproach caused the commission to be somewhat hesitant to take action in June and July 2005, towards the end of the race finally won by London despite—or thanks to—direct criticisms towards the Parisian candidature from other bids that were in principle forbidden by the rules. The chairman of the IOC Ethics Commission did not, in fact, travel to the city where the elections took place, and British Prime Minister Tony Blair was able to intensively lobby many IOC members during the hours preceding the vote.

A similar scenario took place at the 2007 IOC Session, where the presidents of the Russian Federation and of Korea and the Austrian prime minister also acted in the same way in order to defend the candidatures of Sochi, Pyeongchang and Salzburg respectively for the 2014 Winter Games. Since then, the IOC is envisaging the solution of forbidding the heads of state or of the governments of the cities concerned from taking part at the Session where the city is elected.

The most delicate matter on which the commission was called upon to issue judgment regarding the 2012 candidatures was without doubt that of a report by BBC television broadcast a few days prior to the Athens Games in August 2004. It showed, thanks to a hidden camera, Bulgarian IOC member Ivan Slavkov ready to negotiate a "contract" aimed at making the IOC members vote for London.[42] Four other persons, who were not IOC members, were also denounced as intermediaries or agents prepared to facilitate the purchase of votes. The names of the agents in question had been widely circulated at the time of the Salt Lake City scandal. According to rumors in press circles, the BBC was also in possession of elements incriminating eleven further IOC members but preferred not to use them for fear of an attack for libel. The situation was therefore extremely serious for the IOC, which—a few days prior to the opening of the Games in Athens— feared that a scandal similar to that surrounding Salt Lake City could erupt. On the day following the broadcast, the IOC Ethics Commission recommended that Ivan Slavkov be immediately suspended, and the accreditations for the Games issued for the four agents in question be withdrawn. In passing, it exonerated the London candidature. The IOC Executive Board immediately accepted the recommendations but no enquiry was opened regarding the rumors relating to other IOC members because of lack of proof.

At the same time—on the eve of the 2004 Games—the commission failed to intervene when the president of the Athens OCOG (and her husband Theodoros Angelopoulos) were the subject of a criminal case filed by her brother-in-law and brother for the embezzlement of 24 million euros from the family fortune with a view to obtaining the Games seven years previously.[43] In fact, Mr. Angelopoulos quite unexpectedly received the Olympic Order in July 2005, and his wife had already received it at the closing ceremony of the 2004 Games.

Cases concerning IOC members

The IOC members are the second target of the commission, in relation to their behavior surrounding candidatures or other areas. Two have already been excluded since the commission was founded, and several have resigned or been reprimanded. On each occasion, they were brought to task for having infringed the ethical principles of the Olympic Charter or the Code of Ethics and thus seriously damaging the reputation of the Olympic movement.

The first case concerned Mohamad Hasan, an Indonesian IOC member imprisoned for several years in his country for corruption not related to Olympism. The commission recommended his exclusion[44] in 2002, which was finally approved only at the Athens Session in August 2004.

Following the suspension of Ivan Slavkov because of the BBC report (see above), the Commission carried out an enquiry and heard Slavkov. In October 2004, it recommended to the Executive Board that he be excluded, and the board in turn submitted the proposal to the IOC Session in July 2005. Having heard Slavkov, the Session adopted the proposal by 82 votes in favor, 12 against and 5 abstentions. In 1999, Ivan Slavkov had already been the subject of a denunciation on the part of the candidature by Cape Town (South Africa) for the 2004 Games, but the case had been dismissed because of insufficient proof.[45] After his exclusion, he stated that he wished to appeal to the Court of Arbitration for Sport but did not do so.

The most important IOC member that the commission has been called upon to handle was without doubt Kim Un Yong of Korea, who at the moment of the facts was a vice president of the IOC, president of the NOC of South Korea, of the International Taekwondo Federation and of the General Association of International Sport Federations (2005), and a member of parliament in his country. As was the case for Hasan and Slavkov, the commission proceeded in two stages. It began by recommending suspension in 2004 and then exclusion in February 2005.[46] The suspension of Kim's rights and prerogatives as an IOC member was based on the fact that he had been convicted and sentenced by a Seoul district court for giving and receiving financial favors in relation to his sports responsibilities. The accusations within Korea arose following the non-election of the city of Pyeongchang to host the 2010 Winter Games (obtained by Vancouver with a two-vote margin). Certain Korean political circles believed at the time that Kim had preferred to favor his own election as an IOC vice president over that of the Korean candidature that had taken place the previous day and could have affected his chances. Accusations of corruption against Kim had in fact been circulating for some time within Olympic circles, but had never been proved. In 1999, after the Salt Lake City scandal, the IOC had in fact reprimanded him severely, but this had not prevented him from running for the IOC presidency two years later and coming second with 23 votes.[47]

Once Kim had been finally sentenced by the Korean justice system (having exhausted all possible appeal procedures), the commission recommended his exclusion to the IOC Executive Board in February 2005. The board in turn brought the matter before the IOC Session. Kim's daughter, assisted by lawyers who invoked the lack of respect for human rights on the part of the Korean judiciary and a politically motivated sentence, made a last attempt to reverse the decision. Under pressure from the Korean government, which was supporting a new candidature by Pyeongchang for the 2014 Winter Games, Kim Un Yong resigned from the IOC in May 2005. This avoided the Session having to take a decision regarding his exclusion. Certain observers believed, however, that the two-thirds majority required for such a decision would not have been obtained if Kim had been able to defend himself in person.

Although the commission has stressed on several occasions in its decisions that the ethical character of behavior is independent from its penal implications, it nevertheless preferred to await the final sentence issued on the suspended IOC members in order to avoid being accused of basing its recommendations on unproven allegations. One of the reasons for doing so is that the commission has no real investigatory powers. It can study documents submitted to it, hear the parties and witnesses but under no circumstances force them to appear before it. Neither Kim nor Hasan were able to defend themselves in person because they were in prison—and in fact used the situation as an argument to delay the Session's decision.

In April 2005, the commission adopted the same attitude regarding Yoshiaki Tsutsumi of Japan, an honorary IOC member imprisoned for having provided false information to companies quoted on the stock exchange and falsifying accounting information. The matter was not related to Olympism. Tsutsumi nevertheless resigned immediately, which halted the procedure before the commission. It is worthy of note, however, that he was a real estate promoter and a driving force behind the candidature of Nagano for the Winter Games. At the time, he and business associates had given the IOC several million US dollars towards the Olympic Museum (where his name remains engraved in the wall of marble plaques showing the donors).

Henry Kissinger, also an honorary IOC member for services rendered at the time of the 1999 crisis, fared better than Tsutsumi. In December 2003, the commission decided not to follow up a complaint lodged by the Swiss association Track Impunity Always (TRIAL), which called for his exclusion because of some of his actions as a major figure within American foreign policy. The commission stated that the actions in question had taken place prior to his nomination to the IOC and had never been the subject of a decision by the judiciary. TRIAL stressed that the commission's argument opened the IOC's doors to individuals with troubled pasts as long as they had not been sentenced by courts, and that it also contradicted the commission's affirmation that it distinguished between unethical behavior and actions punishable by law.

The commission also handled cases whereby IOC members were investigated in their countries: notably the Italian Franco Carraro in 2006, the Korean Park Yongsung in 2005 and Frenchmen Guy Drut in 2004 and Henry Sérandour in 2007. Park and Drut, despite being pardoned by their respective state presidents, received a reprimand and were suspended from participation in IOC commissions for five years. Park resigned his Judo IF presidency a few months later and thus lost his IOC seat. Carraro, accused of having taken part in the Calciopoli scandal (football match fixing for betting) but exonerated of all blame by the Italian sport authorities, was also exonerated by the commission. Sérandour escaped a reprimand because he reached the IOC age limit in 2007.

In 2007, the commission requested the Canadian member Richard Pound to demonstrate greater restraint in his public statements regarding athletes' reputations.[48] Pound had insinuated that Lance Armstrong had not won the Tour de France without resorting to doping. This minor reprimand was the result of a complaint by Armstrong regarding the WADA president, but was intended for Pound as an IOC member rather than as the head of the WADA: the commission acknowledged it was not mandated to take action regarding matters concerning the WADA.

Cases concerning the NOCs

The NOCs are the third of the Olympic parties that fall within the commission's remit, but to date have been relatively unaffected by its decisions probably because very few cases are brought to its attention. Only three cases are known: the NOCs of Iraq, Somalia, and Ethiopia.

Following the American intervention in Iraq in March 2003, the commission examined the complaint filed by the British NGO Indict at the end of 2002, notably regarding torture inflicted on players in the national football team by one of Saddam Hussein's sons, the president of the Iraqi NOC. The commission proposed that the NOC be dissolved and a new one created, ensuring that none of its new members belonged to the former committee.[49] The proposal was accepted by the IOC, which organized elections early in 2004 and the participation of an Iraqi team at the Athens Games. Such a decision could in fact have been taken without the intervention of the commission, as had been the case on several occasions within Olympic history (such as recently for the NOC of Afghanistan, suspended for the 2000 Sydney Games and reinstated for Athens 2004).

The case of Farah Addo, president of the Somali NOC, is the result of a complaint by the FIFA following Addo's ten-year ban from the world of football because of embezzlement of funds intended for sport projects in the country. Since Addo was accredited for the Athens Games (for which the national football team had qualified), the FIFA called for his accreditation to be withdrawn. The commission's recommendation to comply with the request was rapidly accepted.[50] It should be noted that Farah Addo had also accused the FIFA president of grave misconduct prior to his re-election to the federation in 2002.

The Chef de Mission of the Ethiopian NOC at the 2006 Turin Games was banned from all future Olympic Games for illicit trade in accreditation. The CAS ultimately reduced the ban to the Games of 2008 and 2010.

An abusive complaint by the president of the International Triathlon Union (ITU) against the president of the British Olympic Association

(and IOC member) for his active support to an unsuccessful female candidature for the ITU presidency was not taken up by the commission.

Cases concerning the International Federations

The commission has also studied the case of at least one IF: that of
volleyball (FIVB) and even though the IFs are not considered to be
Olympic parties in its statutes. The case was mainly the result of the
FIVB President being an IOC member in Mexico at the time. The
case—a fairly complex one—took place in three stages.

Initially, FIVB President Ruben Acosta lodged a complaint against
Mario Vásquez Raña, another Mexican IOC member, for statements
that were damaging to the reputation of the FIVB and its president at
the 2003 Panamerican Games in San Domingo. Vásquez Raña, who is
the president of the Pan American Sports Organization (ODEPA) that
supervises these continental games, attempted to have an Argentinean
volleyball team take part in the said games, despite the fact that the
country's national federation and its president had been suspended by
the FIVB following financial problems resulting from the world championships held in Buenos Aires in 2002. In December 2003, the commission decided only to remind the parties of the "spirit of mutual
comprehension, friendship and solidarity [that] must be respected
within the Olympic Movement."[51]

In the meantime, in August 2003, the ODEPA lodged a complaint
against the FIVB for an alleged violation of the right—fundamental
according to the Olympic Charter—to take part in sports competition:
in that case the Argentinean volleyball players at the Panamerican
Games. The Argentinean professional beach volleyball team was at the
same time authorized to play on the circuit. While recognizing the
independence and autonomy of each IF regarding the administration
of its sport, the commission proposed that the IOC remind the FIVB
of this right to participate and that the FIVB be given a warning.[52]
The IOC Executive Board retained only the first part of the recommendation at its meeting in December 2003.

This combat between the two Mexican IOC members took place
against the backdrop of a third complaint, dating from March 2003, by
Mario Goijman, former president of the Argentinean volleyball federation, against the FIVB and its president. The complaint to the commission was made in parallel to one lodged with a Swiss regional court
in Lausanne (located in the Canton of Vaud, where the FIVB has its
seat). The allegation was of falsified documents and disloyal management
(the so-called "Volleygate affair"). Cautious, the commission decided in

December 2003 to await the decision by the Vaud court. It recalled, however, that "the axiom 'the money from sport must go to sport' constituted an ethical principle binding upon everyone within the Olympic movement; for sports leaders in particular, apart from just compensation for legitimate expense or 'loss of earning,' this principle must be applied." Through this sibylline statement, the commission was targeting the large commissions received by Ruben Acosta for negotiating the broadcasting rights for the FIVB competitions. The commission sums in question, of around 10 percent of the amount of some contracts, are however authorized under the FIVB Rules.

Early in 2004, Mario Goijman provided the media with information concerning the complaint lodged with the court, and was sentenced by the Lausanne court for violating confidentiality regarding the investigation. In parallel, the commission drew up a draft recommendation aimed at sanctions against the FIVB and Ruben Acosta. Acosta was nevertheless re-elected by a vast majority in May 2004 at the FIVB Congress in Porto (Portugal), which also confirmed the rules relating to the attribution of the commission payments that were the subject of the dispute and again approved the accounts that Goijman claimed had been falsified.

However, while a whole series of IOC and IF meetings were being prepared in Lausanne in May 2004, rumors were circulating that the IOC Executive Board, influenced by Vásquez Raña who was a member thereof, could adopt sanctions upon the recommendation of the IOC Ethics Commission. Ruben Acosta then resigned as an IOC member, since in any case he had reached the age limit of seventy. The IOC President wrote him a letter including a phrase stating the IOC's "acknowledgement for your highly-appreciated support and contribution."[53]

Some, however, did not appear satisfied with the outcome reached. The IOC Executive Board, meeting in Athens on the eve of the 2004 Games, studied the commission's decision.[54] In the end, it decided on a simple public reminder to the FIVB and its president of the principle of "the money from sport must go to sport" and published its decision of 21 October 2003 that established this new principle on the IOC's website.

In December 2004, the Vaud examining magistrate pronounced the case brought by Goijman dismissed.[55] Goijman appealed to the cantonal court. In March 2005, the appeal judges confirmed the dismissal of the case with the exception of one point. They ordered the examining magistrate handling the case to reopen it and indict Ruben Acosta and two other executives of the FIVB for false information on commercial companies and falsified documents.[56] This meant that the appeals judge referred the three persons indicted to the police court. In March 2006, the police court found them not guilty of the final accusation but did award part of the costs to Ruben Acosta.

During the case, which took place over nearly four years, it is difficult to refrain from thinking that the commission was made use of within a vendetta between two Mexican IOC members.

It has, in fact, refrained from intervening in other similar cases affecting IOC members. Sepp Blatter, president of the FIFA and an IOC member in that capacity, was accused of embezzlement by five of his seven vice presidents and his Secretary General.[57] A criminal lawsuit was filed in Zurich without the commission launching an enquiry. Similarly, it did not react to a complaint lodged with a New York court in December 2003 by the World Skating Federation against the International Skating Union (ISU) and its president, Ottavio Cinquanta, for unethical practices.[58] In the case of Hein Verbruggen, the president of the International Cycling Union (UCI) until September 2005 and also an IOC member, the commission was called upon to issue recommendations following two complaints concerning the irregularities surrounding the election of his successor,[59] but its verdict was not made public.

The fact that the IFs are not "Olympic parties" has no doubt prevented the commission from intervening in the case of suspected corruption regarding the judging of certain competitions at the Salt Lake City Games (figure skating)[60] and Athens (boxing, fencing, gymnastics, wrestling, and taekwondo). The IOC settled for holding bilateral meetings with the IFs concerned, while the media protested about the "mafia of judges" within sport.[61] On the other hand, in the case of boxing, the IOC suspended the payment of the balance of the Athens television rights to the IF concerned. In 2006, the president of that IF, considered to be corrupt by numerous observers, was not re-elected and was replaced by a Taiwanese IOC member strongly supported by the IOC.

Comparisons and recommendations

The IOC Ethics Commission is an entity inspired by US public practices but has virtually no equivalent in the world of international NGOs, of which the IOC is one.

We recall that the creation of the commission was suggested by US sponsors and its media when the scandal surrounding the attribution of the Games to Salt Lake City erupted. They based their call for such a body on the recommendations of the Salt Lake City OCOG Ethics

Commission and of an ad hoc commission appointed by the US Olympic Committee (USOC), chaired by Senator Mitchell. It was also at that time that the Senate and the House of Representatives launched hearings on the functioning of the US and international Olympic movement. The hearings and also the governance and ethical problems within the USOC—which changed both its president and Director General four times between 1999 and 2004—obliged the USOC to initiate reforms at all levels. The USOC, which is a non-profit corporation founded by a congressional act, thus created a permanent ethics commission consisting of five independent members (with the exception of its chairman who is a an ex officio member of the board of directors) and assisted by an ethics officer.[62] An ethics code was also adopted for its employees, volunteers (including executives), and member organizations (national federations).

Similar structures have existed for far longer within the US Congress and in the legislative assemblies of most of the 50 US states and large towns, as well as within federal executive and judicial sectors. Ethics commissions also exist in many European countries, notably in the areas of medicine, politics, and university education. Professional ethics codes also exist in various fields.

In the area of sport, the end of the twentieth century saw the creation of several national organizations dedicated to ethics in sport, often linked to the question of doping. Some notable examples are the Canadian Centre for Ethics in Sport (CCES),[63] the St James Ethics Centre that was active at the moment of the Sydney Games,[64] the Lausanne Foundation MOVES (Movement for Ethics in Sport),[65] and the Institute for Diversity and Ethics in Sport in Orlando (USA).[66] Some NOCs, such as that of Switzerland, have also launched initiatives to promote ethics in sport. All of the above, however, are organizations that are mainly active in a single country.

Among international NGOs comparable to the IOC, it should be noted that neither the International Committee of the Red Cross (ICRC) nor the World Conservation Union (UICN) have a permanent ethics commission. As of 1999, the NGO Transparency International began to take great interest in the IOC and in sport in general. It held a debate on the subject at its 10th International Anti-Corruption Conference in Prague, in 2001. The IOC Ethics Commission's special representative took part in the debate, although the cooperation envisaged at the time has not moved forward.

Finally, within the United Nations system, the High Commission for Refugees (HCR) has a code of conduct for its salaried staff[67] and the World Health Organization (WHO) has set up an ethics commission for its activities and staff.[68] These are two of the very few inter-governmental organizations to have ethics structures.

The IOC Ethics Commission is thus a fairly original construction although largely inspired by the United States. It is well positioned to become a reference within sport, although it would be preferable for it to rely more heavily on specific expertise and on work already carried out by specialists or organizations that preceded it, on a national or international level, and even from outside the sport sector. It should also be more independent, as is the case for some of the above-mentioned commissions.

The commission will also need to contend with a multiplication of ethics codes within the IFs and NOCs and to work towards a harmonization of rules, which is reminiscent of what the WADA has achieved for doping with the World Anti-Doping Code.

The IOC Ethics Commission is an entity that has already developed considerably since its foundation in 1999. Created at the end of Samaranch's presidency as a rapid response and a palliative to pressure on the part of the US Congress and media, it has changed since 2001 under President Rogge to become a strong tool responsible for imposing a "zero tolerance" regime regarding ethics within the Olympic movement.

While the WADA, also created in 1999, is handling doping—a scourge within sport and notably for ethical reasons—the IOC Ethics Commission is handling corruption within the world of Olympism in a wider sense. Like doping, corruption in sport has taken on considerable proportions. The Central Department for the Prevention of Corruption (SCPC) within the French Ministry of Justice stresses in its 2003 report that corruption benefits clubs, executives and intermediaries.[69]

President Rogge is fully aware of the risk to the Olympic movement of doping and corruption. At the end of 2007, he also singled out illegal betting as a new form of sporting corruption. Constantly in the eyes of the media, and even more so during the period of the Games, the IOC simply cannot allow itself the slightest blunder without it being immediately spread throughout the planet by the media. At the opening of the IOC Session immediately before the 2004 Athens Games, Rogge was to state: "The Olympic Movement believes in the educational role of sport. This is why it preaches the values of tolerance, fair play and respect for the rules. Sport has a duty to set an example. Let us respect and ensure respect of strict ethics, and sanction the athletes and leaders who do not do so."[70]

It now remains only for the IOC Ethics Commission to be irreproachable regarding its organization and the way it handles the cases submitted to it. By doing so, it can emerge as the world's highest authority on sporting ethics, a little like the Court of Arbitration for Sport (CAS) has become the reference for arbitration related to sport over the 20 years since its creation.

If, however, corruption within Olympic sport soars in the same way as doping, the states could be tempted to intervene in the form of a public entity as they did regarding the creation of the WADA. The states could, in fact, consider the Olympic Games and more generally Olympic sport as being a cultural heritage that should not be regulated by simple associations like the IOC or the IFs. The IOC Ethics Commission would then be reduced to a first step within a supranational specialized organization intended to provide good governance of world sport.

8 Olympic governance

Some conclusions

For over a century, international sport has mainly been governed by a network of non-profit associations centered round the Olympic Games and the World Championships in various sports. This network has adopted the name of "The Olympic Movement," and its leading actor is the International Olympic Committee (IOC): a club of individuals that co-opts its own members and that was founded in 1894 by Pierre de Coubertin.

Despite the considerable evolution of sport during the twentieth century and the increasing scale of the Summer and Winter Games, the IOC continued to exist without major changes to its structure throughout what proved to be a century beset by upheavals of all kinds. It was only in 1999 that the very foundations of the IOC suddenly shook, as a result of around twenty of its members being involved in a corruption scandal related to the awarding of the Olympic Winter Games to Salt Lake City. It was also around this time that doping, violence and illegal betting at sports events began to constitute a serious concern for governments, who realized that the Olympic movement was unable to keep those issues under any real control. And so, at the end of the last century, the IOC suddenly found itself confronted with doubts regarding its legitimacy on the part of the general public and the public authorities.

We can situate the emergence of the term "governance" within Olympic circles around this same period, notably thanks to the influence of American journalists and sponsors. It was officially introduced within the Olympic Charter in 2004 (Rule 19.3.2) although in a marginal manner. This focus on governance is a result of the dysfunctions mentioned above but also, as of the 1980s, of the growing professionalism within Olympic organizations and the increasing interest on the part of the various stakeholders—and particularly nation states, the European Union and the sponsors—in how the Olympic system functions.

Although this system was one of the oldest ways of self-government by means of a network, with its consensual, horizontal co-ordination mechanisms, its fragile equilibrium became threatened at the end of the past century as a result of new types of public or commercial actors (sponsors, media companies, professional leagues) that wished to take part in its governance.

The question how the IOC is governed remains central within the new organization of world sport at the dawning of the present century, which is why we have focused considerably on the IOC in this work. We shall conclude by outlining the IOC's five levels of governance and by proposing five principles for the governance of the Olympic system and of world sport.

Levels of governance for the IOC

The IOC's governance can be summarized by using a five-level model developed by Pérez[1] and its interpretation by Chappelet.[2]

Management

On a first level, this means managing the "IOC Group"[3] and the resources available to it effectively and efficiently on a day-to-day basis. This is the role of the IOC's administration in Lausanne, headed by a Director General and 13 directors, who manage a staff of over four hundred. The administrative management is under the close control of the IOC President, who has chosen to live and work in Lausanne. This approach started by Samaranch has been continued by his successor Jacques Rogge, meaning the role is one of an executive president despite the fact that the position is not remunerated.

Corporate governance

The second level is one of control over the IOC's top management: a task that—according to the Olympic Charter—falls to the IOC's Session (its annual general assembly of members) and to the Executive Board elected from among its number, which meets four to five times a year. The board, consisting of 15 members, is the real source of power within the IOC: in theory, no major decision may be made by the IOC President (who chairs it) without its agreement or at times its ratification after the event. It is completed by around 25 specialized commissions consisting of members and experts nominated by the president, which monitor the activities of the various directors within the administration. Certain commissions, such as those handling finance, television, and Olympic Solidarity, are more important than others wherein the members fulfill a more honorary role. The highest powers within the IOC are the prerogative of the Session, which can modify the Charter, add or remove sports from the Olympic program, elect the president and the members of the Executive Board and designate the host cities of the Games.

Governance management

The third level of governance is one of ensuring that the IOC members who constitute the Session and the various commissions are capable and worthy of fulfilling their role. This ultimate surveillance is the responsibility of the Nominations Commission and the Ethics Commission, created only in 1999. The former commission studies and proposes eligible candidates prior to a vote by secret ballot on the part of existing members. The latter recommends sanctions for members who have failed to respect the Olympic Code of Ethics—sanctions that can be as severe as exclusion. The IOC Athletes' Commission also plays a specific role within governance management, since 12 of its members are elected by athletes taking part in the Summer and Winter Games, and thus automatically become IOC members.

Harmonization

This, the fourth level, concerns the provision of mechanisms in the case that the IOC's decisions are contested, and to harmonize the said mechanisms with those of other sport or juridical bodies. Since the IOC is an association under Swiss law, it is the Swiss legal system that constitutes a first national mechanism, but the IOC has rarely appeared before Swiss courts. It has been cited far more frequently outside of Switzerland, notably regarding doping cases. The World Anti-Doping Agency (WADA) was founded among other goals to harmonize the fight against doping on the part of sport organizations and governments on an international level, by means of a code. The Court of Arbitration for Sport (CAS) handles appeals for all cases of doping lodged by various parties. The appeals are stated as being the final recourse in the world of sport, yet Swiss and above all European courts have been charged with examining numerous "final" sentences issued by the CAS, notably regarding the free movement and competition laws within the European Union.

Metagovernance

On this, the fifth and final level, the IOC's role is to respect and promote the fundamental principles of universal morals and human rights stated in numerous international constitutional texts and treaties (such as the European Convention on Human Rights), and to place sport "at the service of the harmonious development of man, with a view to promoting a peaceful society concerned with the preservation of human dignity" as the preamble to the Olympic Charter affirms.

Since 1993, the IOC has received support for its vision from the United Nations, whose General Assembly has adopted the custom, prior to each edition of the Games—Winter or Summer alike—to adopt a Resolution on the Olympic Truce at the request of the host country. This albeit symbolic Resolution to some extent forces the IOC to take its corporate social responsibility extremely seriously and to ensure that sport makes a positive contribution to society and endeavors to eliminate its main scourges (doping, violence, and corruption).

Principles for the governance of world sport

It goes without saying that the IOC cannot assume such a responsibility for world sport alone. As we have seen, many other public, nonprofit or purely private organizations now play an important role within the Olympic system. It is now not so much a question of the governance of IOC but of Olympic governance as a whole.

To put such a form of Olympic governance in place, it is necessary to implement five major political and management principles within all the Olympic organizations and of course including the IOC. The principles described below could serve as a framework of the "good governance" of world sport.[4]

The principles are also inspired by rules that are to an increasing extent required by those national or supranational governments with which the Olympic system must cooperate in order to organize the Olympic Games, and more generally in order to promote a certain philosophy of sport, known under the name of "Olympism."

Transparency

The Olympic system needs clear rules and procedures, and must publish regular, detailed reports on its activities that include financial statements. It must communicate with the public on a regular basis, via the Internet and via the media, to which its meetings should be opened wide. Its archives must be easily accessible.

Since the early days of the Olympic system, the Olympic Charter has served as both the IOC's statutes and the procedural rules for the movement it coordinates. Since 2000, the IOC has been publishing a full report on its program and accounts every two years. It also maintains an extremely comprehensive website and invites journalists to its meetings. The debates at its Sessions are even broadcast by closed circuit television. The IOC's archives are available at the Olympic Museum, although the minutes of its meetings are subject to a lengthy embargo. Nevertheless, many sport organizations would benefit from being as transparent as the IOC.

Democracy

The Olympic system must take its decisions democratically, based on procedures laid down in advance and by means of secret ballots, with votes cast by members representing the main stakeholders within their respective sports. The executives' periods in office must be limited in time. Minorities must be respected. Equality according to sector needs to be improved.

Since its foundation, the IOC has functioned on the principle of "one member, one vote" but it was only after the 1999 reform that its membership has really reflected the main components of the Olympic system: athletes, NOCs, and IFs. Periods in office are now limited to eight years, but are still too easily renewable. Women represent barely 10 percent of the members, and Europe has almost as many representatives as all the other continents together. In the area of democracy, the IOC and many sport organizations have a great deal of work to do.

Accountability

The Olympic system must be accountable to its stakeholders: athletes, parents, coaches, officials, fans, host cities, sponsors, broadcasters, etc. It must moreover be able to show that the human and financial resources available to the Olympic sport organizations have been used to promote sport in general and/or their specific sport objectives. Their members must be irreproachable in that regard.

In 1999, the IOC created an Ethics Commission to monitor the behavior of the Olympic parties. Several NOCs and IFs have created their own such commissions although that could lead to problems of harmonization. Most of the IOC's financial revenues—92 percent—is redistributed to the OCOGs, to the IFs (directly) and to the NOCs (via Olympic Solidarity). The IOC does not, however, control precisely how those funds are used. The athletes have their own commission within the IOC, as they do within many NOCs, but rarely influence decisions that are made. The World Olympians Association, which unites athletes having taken part in the Games at least once, has a seat on the Athletes' Commission and is at times consulted by the IOC. The other stakeholders are, however, rarely or never consulted. The situation is very similar within most Olympic organizations.

Autonomy

The Olympic organizations must preserve their autonomy from their corporate or governmental backers, but must nevertheless respect the legislation of the countries or groups thereof in which they operate. Their autonomy must be as wide as possible within the legal framework of the country or region where they are headquartered and, of course, in line with the overall principles of natural justice.

Since its foundation, the IOC has been affirming this principle of autonomy for itself, the NOCs and the IFs. Many NOCs nevertheless experience great difficulty in remaining independent of their respective governments, and even though they currently receive considerable funding from Olympic Solidarity. Moreover, for around the last 20 years the sporting rules drawn up by the IOC or the IFs and the parameters for the competitions—including the Games—have evolved considerably under the influence of the media and the sponsors. At times, those rules have potentially contradicted certain laws, notably on a European level. The IOC and the IFs for (professional) team sports have been calling for a "sports exception" within EU legislation (see Chapter 6), but their attempts are doomed to remain unsuccessful since sport has become a major industry that cannot be exempted from the rules of world or European economics.

Social responsibility

The Olympic organizations ensure that their activity serves the society in which they operate, thus contributing towards solidarity and sustainable development for humanity.

In this regard, the IOC has stated highly ambitious, idealistic objectives since its foundation, including peace, multi-cultural education, and human dignity through sport. As of the 1990s, it began to focus strongly on protecting the environment within the framework of organizing the Olympic Games. In 1999, it adopted a vast Agenda 21 for the Olympic movement. The terms "sustainable development" and "legacy" were introduced into the Olympic Charter. Various projects aiming to use sport as a tool for development and peace were launched, often in cooperation with United Nations agencies. Programs for Olympic education, culture, career development for athletes, and sport for all were created in conjunction with sponsors. These activities, dating from the 1990s, should be pursued and reinforced by the IOC and widely emulated by other Olympic organizations.

Respect for the five principles mentioned above depends to a large extent on the Olympic system continuing to develop the self-regulation that it put in place over the entire twentieth century. If it fails to do so, it is probable that governments will attempt, to an increasing extent, to intervene in the governance of world sport with a view to preserving public health, public moral and public order in the face of excesses that could take on even more alarming proportions.

As of the 1970s, at the time when the IOC encountered political problems leading to boycotts to the Games, UNESCO attempted to assume a certain degree of leadership within sport thanks to the adoption of the International Charter on Physical Education and Sport. In 2005, UNESCO adopted an ad hoc convention to render the World Anti-Doping Code operational in all countries that had signed it. In the future, UNESCO could tighten its grip on world sport or contribute toward the creation of another specialized inter-governmental organization attached to the United Nations system. There is discussion, in some quarters, of a United Nations program for sport, similar to that created for the environment.

For the Olympic movement, one alternative would be to use the structures of the International Red Cross Movement as inspiration (see Chapter 6). To do so, it would be necessary to convene a diplomatic conference for instance in the Olympic Capital City, which would result in the signature of what could be termed the "Lausanne Conventions" by as many countries as possible. Such conventions would be administered by the IOC just as the Geneva Conventions are managed by the International Committee of the Red Cross, with—for example— a world conference uniting governments and Olympic organizations held every four years with the aim of preserving sport as a global public good, and the Olympic Games as a world heritage.

It is naturally difficult to predict the form that the Olympic system will take in the future, since so many factors are involved, ranging from political, legal, environmental, social, and financial issues, etc.

Simply continuing along its current path, however, would not appear to be the ideal one for permitting the Olympic system to survive and flourish. Although the creation of a specialized UN agency for sport and the signature of "Lausanne Conventions" could appear to be somewhat far-fetched notions, these moves could prove to be the only viable, long-term solutions for fighting the very real threats to the credibility of sport: doping, violence, and corruption.

Notes

1 A brief overview of the Olympic system

1 Jean-Loup Chappelet, *Le Système olympique* (Grenoble: Presses universitaires, 1991).
2 An Olympiad spans four years, i.e. the period between one edition of the Olympic Games and the next.

2 International Olympic Committee

1 *IOC Final Report 2001–2004* (Lausanne: IOC, 2005), 109.
2 *Catalyst for Collaboration, IOC Interim Report 2005–2006* (Lausanne: IOC Communication Department, 2007), 10.
3 The documentary also showed surgeon and future President Jacques Rogge interrupt a surgical procedure to take a telephone call from Samaranch, and the Korean Kim Un-Yong state, untruthfully, that he had never visited the candidate cities for the organization of the Olympic Games.
4 *Catalyst for Collaboration, IOC Interim Report 2005–2006* (Lausanne: IOC Communication Department, 2007), 78.
5 This is however a small amount compared to the professional leagues' revenues. Formula 1's revenues amounted to US$3.9 billion (in 2007), National Football League's revenues to US$6.5 billion (in 2006), Major League Baseball's revenues to US$5.1 billion (in 2006) and English Premier League clubs' combined revenues was US$3 billion (in the 2006–07 season). Source: Sports Business Group at Deloitte.
6 Sources: Jean-Loup Chappelet, *Le Système olympique* (Grenoble: Presses universitaires, 1991) and IOC, *2006 Marketing fact file* (Lausanne: IOC internal publication, 2006).
7 *Olympic Market Research: Analysis Report* (Lausanne: IOC internal publication, 1997). Sport equipment manufacturers' logos were not included in the study.
8 Sources: Holger Preuss, *Economics of the Olympic Games: Hosting the Games 1972–2000* (Sydney: Walla Walla Press, 2000) and *Final report on the XXVII Olympiad 1997–2000* (Lausanne: IOC internal publication, 2006).
9 *Final report on the XXVII Olympiad 1997–2000* (Lausanne: IOC internal publication, 2001).

10 *Final report on the XXVII Olympiad 1997–2000* (Lausanne: IOC internal publication, 2001), The Museum, 6.
11 *Final report on the XXVII Olympiad 1997–2000* (Lausanne: IOC internal publication, 2001), The Foundation, 6.

3 National Olympic Committees

1 MEMOS, a French acronym meaning Executive Masters in Sports Organization Management.
2 Andrew B. Bernard and Meghan R. Busse, "Who Wins the Olympic Games: Economic Resources and Medal Totals," *Review of Economics and Statistics* 86, no. 1 (2004): 413–17.

4 International Sports Federations

1 John Forster and Nigel K. Pope, *The Political Economy of Global Sporting Organisations* (London: Routledge, 2004).
2 *Olympic Programme Commission, Report to the 117th IOC Session* (Lausanne: IOC, May 2005); and *Olympic Programme Commission, Report to the 119th IOC Session* (Lausanne: IOC, July 2007).
3 Among the IFs that are to date recognized by the IOC but are not Olympic, that of rugby (IRFB) was also founded prior to the IOC, in 1886. Rugby was moreover an Olympic sport on four occasions: 1900, 1908, 1920 and 1924. It should also be noted that other international groupings, which have today disappeared or been replaced, existed before the IOC: The International Yachting Union (1875), the International Club for Equestrian Competitions and the International Cyclist Association, for example.
4 Football reappeared on the program as of the 1936 Games but with complete amateurs only. Today, although Olympic football still does not benefit from the world's best players, the reason is not the rules regarding amateurs—which have disappeared—but because the FIFA wishes to preserve the unique prestige of its World Cup.
5 John Forster and Nigel K. Pope, *The Political Economy of Global Sporting Organisations* (London: Routledge, 2004), 102.
6 Itself contested by the International Men's Tennis Association (IMTA), founded in 2003.

5 Organising Committees of the Olympic Games

1 The president and vice-president of the Salt Lake City Candidature Committee were indicted in 1999 but found not guilty by a Utah court in 2003.

6 Governments and the Olympic system

1 Jean-Paul Callède, *Les politiques sportives en France* (Paris: Economica, 2000).
2 Barrie Houlihan, *Sport, Policy and Politics* (London: Routledge, 1997).
3 James Riordan, *Sport in Soviet Society* (New York: Cambridge University Press, 1977).
4 The Swiss Federal Presidency rotates annually among the seven members of the Federal Council (Swiss government).

5 This document and other agreements between the IOC and various international organizations can be found in Frank Latty, *Le Comité international olympique et le droit international* (Paris: Montchrestien, 2001).

6 Frank Latty, *Le Comité international olympique et le droit international* (Paris: Montchrestien, 2001).

7 Prior to becoming Minister for Defense and Sport in 1997, Adolf Ogi had served as the Director of the Swiss Ski Federation from 1972 to 1988, which was a golden era for Swiss skiers. He also chaired the Swiss candidature of Sion for the 2006 Winter Games.

8 Human rights can also be invoked in other continents. For instance, Canadian female ski-jumpers complained to the Canadian Human Rights Commission because they are excluded from the Games in Vancouver 2010 (only the male ski jump is on the Olympic program) and consider that it is a discriminatory practice.

9 The main area in which the IOC could be affected by EU law is that of television broadcasting rights, which until 2002 were not really the subject of open tenders. During the mid-1990s for example, the IOC signed long-term agreements covering four editions of the Games (2000 to 2008) for most financially significant territories but without really permitting potentially interested television channels to compete for the rights. For Europe, the IOC signed an agreement with the European Broadcasting Union (EBU), the continent's grouping of non-encrypted, free-to-air channels, in 1995. Doing so protected it for several years from the European "Television without Frontiers" directive that permits every EU member state to ensure that major sports events—naturally including the Games—are accessible free of charge to all spectators. The exclusive EBU contract was nevertheless for a long period of time and as such could have led to reactions on the part of the European Commission. In 2004, an agreement was again signed with the EBU (71 public channels from 51 countries, including the 25 EU Member Countries at the time) for the 2010 and 2012 Games, but this time following an open tender. The EBU is said to be prepared to subcontract part of its broadcasting rights.

10 IOC Press Release, *Sport in the EU Reform Treaty*, Lausanne, 19 October 2007.

11 The European Parliament already intervened in sports matters on one occasion, in April 2004, by inviting the Commission to collaborate with the International Labour Organization, which had launched a campaign entitled "Red Card to Child Labour." The aim was to ensure that the IOC demanded—as a contractual condition within its licensing, sponsorship and marketing agreements—that the working conditions involved in products marketed under the IOC's brand complied with internationally recognized labor norms.

12 IOC-FIFA Joint Declaration, *EU White Paper on Sport: Much work remains to be done*, Lausanne, 11 July 2007.

13 Commission Staff Working Document, *The EU and Sport: Background and Context*, Accompanying document to the White Paper on Sport, Brussels, 2007, 41–43.

14 A meeting of the IOC with 8 European sport ministers took place in Lausanne in January 2008.

15 Norbert Elias and Eric Dunning, *Quest for Excitement: Sport and leisure in the civilizing process* (Oxford: Blackwell, 1986).

7 The regulators

1 Ian S. Blackshaw, Robert C. M. Siekmann, and Janwillem Soek, eds., *The Court of Arbitration for Sport, 1984–2004* (Cambridge: University Press, 2006).

2 Or the cantonal court of Vaud if the two parties are domiciled in that canton. This state of affairs, which has arisen on at least one occasion, is somewhat bizarre when the case is one relating to international issues.

3 For the evolution of the list of substances, see Albert Dirix and Xavier Sturbois, *Trente ans de Commission médicale au CIO* (Lausanne: Olympic Museum, 1999), 59.

4 Barrie Houlihan, *Dying to Win* (Strasbourg: Council of Europe Publishing, 1999), 139.

5 *Lausanne Declaration on Doping in Sport*, adopted by the World Conference on Doping in Sport, Lausanne, Switzerland (4 February 1999).

6 *Statutes of the World Anti-Doping Agency*, published on the WADA website www.wada-ama.org.

7 Agreement between the Swiss Federal Council and the World Anti-Doping Agency to stipulate the fiscal status of the agency and of its staff in Switzerland (5 March 2001).

8 Report by the Commission for the Evaluation of Candidatures for the Seat of the WADA, 75, 78.

9 Of the 35 members of the board, one from India was absent or not represented. The president did not vote and the two Nigerian members had a single vote, i.e. 32 voting members of the WADA Board.

10 Minutes of the meeting of the WADA Foundation Board, Tallinn, Estonia (21 August 2001), 6.

11 *WADA Strategic Plan*, internal document (July 2001), 4.

12 *WADA Out-Of-Competition Testing Program Report*, Foundation Board meeting (8 February 2002).

13 WADA, Office of the Independent Observer, *Sydney Olympic Games 2000, Executive Summary Report* (14 November 2000).

14 Website www.truegame.org (2 May 2002).

15 Minutes of the meeting of the WADA Executive Committee, Lausanne (2 December 2001), 4.

16 Montreal declaration, adopted at the IICGADS meeting (16–18 February 2000), 1.

17 Minutes of the WADA Foundation Board meeting, Lausanne, Switzerland (3 December 2001), 12.

18 Kuala Lumpur Declaration on Anti-Doping in Sport (24–26 April 2002), 2.

19 WADA, Strategic Plan 2004–9, 3 et seq.

20 www.iucn.org (October 2007).

21 www.redcross.int (October 2007).

22 *Statutes and the Rules of Procedure of the International Red Cross and Red Crescent Movement*, adopted by the 25th International Conference of the Red Cross, Geneva (23–31 October 1986), www.icrc.org

23 Minutes of the meeting of the WADA Executive Committee, Lausanne (2 December 2001), 16

24 John Leizman, *Let's Kill ' Em: Understanding and Controlling Violence in Sports*, (University Press of America, 1999); Dominique Bodin (eds.) *Sports et violences* (Paris: Chiron, 2001).

25 Fred Engh, *Why Johnny Hates Sport* (New York: Square One, 2002).
26 For example Mike Rowbottom, "Rogge's war on 'doping, corruption and violence,'" *Independent*, 17 June 2001.
27 www.cces.ca.
28 Fundamental principle 1, *Olympic Charter*, version in force from 1 September 2004, Lausanne, IOC, 9. Note: unless indicated otherwise, the aforementioned version of the charter is used for extracts in this chapter.
29 For a more detailed description of this case, see Pascal Duret and Patrick Trabal, *Le sport et ses affaires* (Paris: Métaillé, 2001), Chapter 6.
30 Vyv Simson and Andrew Jennings, *The Lords of the Rings* (London: Simon & Schuster, 1992). Andrew Jennings, *The New Lords of the Rings* (London: Simon & Schuster, 1996).
31 Jaume Boix, Arcadio Espada and Raymond Pointu, *Juan-Antonio Samaranch: l'héritage trahi* (Paris: Romillat, 1994).
32 Jean-Loup Chappelet, "Le Système olympique et les pouvoirs publics face au dopage et à la corruption: partenariat ou confrontation?" in *Sport et ordre public*, ed. Jean-Charles Basson (Paris: La documentation française, 2001), 215–34.
33 IOC press release (15 May 2000). Kevan Gosper also intervened in a manner considered to be inappropriate by the media early in 2000 with a view to his daughter being the first Australian torch-bearer in the Olympic Torch Relay for the Sydney 2000 Olympic Games.
34 *Statutes of the IOC Ethics Commission.* Text adopted by the IOC Executive Board, Beijing (26 April 2007).
35 See www.olympic.org/fr/organisation/commissions/ethics/index_uk.asp (consulted on 1 October 2007).
36 IOC press release (1 October 1999).
37 ATR Golden 25, special edition, *Around The Rings* (1 January 2005), 7.
38 The said rules are revised for each new call for candidatures. They contain business considerations relating to the logos that have no relation to ethical issues.
39 Press release (2 February 2002): note the differences between the proposed draft and the text that is in force.
40 IOC press release (27 September 1999).
41 Press release (28 June 2000).
42 The commission's decisions D/3/04 (5 August 2004) and D/2/04 (25 October 2004) are published on the website: www.olympic.org/fr/organisation/commissions/ethics/index_uk.asp.
43 Karl-Heinz Huba, *Sport Intern* 36 (20 August 2006).
44 Decision D/01/02 (7 May 2002).
45 IOC press release (15 May 2000).
46 Decisions D/01/04 (22 January 2004) and D/01/05 (4 February 2005).
47 On the day prior to the election, the commission had moreover expressed its displeasure regarding Kim's electoral promise to have the members paid by the IOC for their "office expenses" to the extent of US$50,000 per year, and which could be perceived as a manner of buying their votes.
48 Decision D/01/07 (2 February 2007).
49 Decision D/01/03 (28 April 2003).
50 Decision D/4/04 (7 August 2004).
51 IOC press release (5 December 2003).

52 Decision D/03/03 (21 October 2003).
53 Letter dated 17 May 2004, published on the FIVB website, consulted in May 2004.
54 Decision D/02/04 (14 May 2004).
55 Press release by Judge Nicolas Cruchet (11 December 2004).
56 Pierre Dubath, "Trois inculpations à la FIVB," *24 Heures*, Lausanne, 23 March 2005. Under Swiss law, an indictment does not indicate an accusation.
57 Sylvain Cypel, "Les opposants lancent l'offensive contre la gestion de Joseph Blatter," *Le Monde*, Paris, 28 May 2002.
58 www.worldskating.org/news/isu-complaint-12dec2003.shtml consulted on 5 April 2004.
59 Stéphane Meier, "Les zones d'ombre d'une campagne conflictuelle," *Le Temps*, Geneva, 22 September 2005.
60 Pierre Ceaux and Piotr Smolar, "Le scandale du patinage aux JO d'hiver relancé par l'arrestation d'un membre de la mafia russe," *Le Monde*, Paris, 3 August 2002.
61 IOC press release (26 November 2004).
62 Bye-Laws of the United States Olympic Committee, Section 5.4, 15.
63 www.cces.ca, consulted on 24 April 2006.
64 www.ethics.org.au consulted on 24 April 2006.
65 www.moves-ch.org consulted on 24 April 2006.
66 www.bus.ucf.edu/sport consulted on 24 April 2006.
67 UNHCR, *Code of Conduct & Explanatory Notes*, June 2004.
68 www.who.int/ethics/en consulted on 24 April 2006.
69 *Rapport d'activité pour l'année 2003*, Paris, 2004. See Chapter III: "Le blanchiment: les implications pour le sport." See also Eric Decouty, "Comment le sport sert à blanchir l'argent sale," *Le Figaro*, 13 July 2004.
70 IOC press release (10 August 2004).

8 Olympic governance: some conclusions

1 Robert Pérez, *La gouvernance de l'entreprise* (Paris: La Découverte, 2003).
2 Jean-Loup Chappelet and Brenda Kübler, "The Governance of the International Olympic Committee," in Milena Parent and Trevor Slack (eds.) *International Perspectives on the Management of Sport* (Amsterdam: Elsevier, 2007), 207–27.
3 All of the organizations controlled by the association that is the IOC, notably the Olympic Foundation, the Olympic Museum Foundation, IOC Television and Management Services SA, Olympic Broadcasting Services SA, Olympic Television Archive Bureau, etc.
4 In February 2008, the IOC proposed seven "Basic Universal Principles of Good Governance of the Olympic and Sport Movement": vision, mission and strategy; structures, regulations and democratic process; highest level of competence, integrity and ethical standards; accountability, transparency and control; solidarity and development; athletes' involvement, participation and care; harmonious relations with governments while preserving autonomy. The seven principles will be discussed until the 2009 Olympic Congress for final approval.

Select bibliography

John Bale and Mette Krogh-Christensen, eds., *Post-Olympism? Questioning Sport in the Twenty-first Century* (Oxford: Berg, 2004). A series of highly critical articles on the Olympic movement and the Games.

Robert K. Barney, Stephen R. Wenn, and Scott J. Martyn, *Selling the Five Rings: The IOC and the rise of Olympic commercialism* (Salt Lake City: University of Utah Press, 2002). An in-depth history of the advent of sponsors and broadcasters within the Olympic System.

John E. Findling and Kimberly D. Pelle, eds., *Encyclopedia of the Modern Olympic Movement* (Westport, CT: Greenwood Press, 2004). Devotes a chapter to the history of the IOC, to each edition of the Summer and Winter Games, to the various IOC Presidents and to various other Olympic subjects. Each chapter includes a useful bibliographical essay.

John Forster and Nigel K.Ll. Pope, *The Political Economy of Global Sporting Organisations* (London: Routledge, 2004). This book analyzes the evolution of modern sport, examining the ways in which sporting organizations, such as the IOC, FIFA, and the ICC (International Cricket Council), have adapted over the years to accommodate changing environments.

John R. Gold and Margaret M. Gold, eds., *Olympic Cities: Urban planning, city agendas and the world's Games, 1896 to the present* (London: Routledge, 2006). Reviews the effect of the Olympic Games on the cities that have organized them and the organizational challenges that they involved. Around a dozen essays on emblematic Olympic cities complete the work.

Allen Guttmann, *The Olympics: A history of the Modern Games* (Chicago: University of Illinois Press, 2002). One of the best reference works on the history of the modern Games. The same author wrote a biography of Avery Brundage, IOC President from 1952 through 1972 (*The Games Must Go On*).

Christopher Hill, *Olympic Politics* (Manchester: University Press, 1996). The work shows how and why politics have always been central to the organization of the Games and the development of the Olympic system.

Barrie Houlihan, *Dying to Win: Doping in sport and the development of anti-doping policy* (Strasbourg: Council of Europe Publishing, 1999). A detailed history of the fight against doping prior to the creation of the World Anti-Doping Agency.

Fernand Landry and Madeleine Yerlès, *One Hundred Years. The idea, the presidents, the achievements. Vol. III: The presidencies of Lord Killanin and Juan Antonio Samaranch* (Lausanne: CIO, 1996). The history of the IOC during the last quarter of the twentieth century. Despite being an official work, the text includes extremely interesting statistics that reveal the striking growth of the IOC and the Games during the period. Vols. I and II cover the periods 1896–1942 and 1943–72.

Helen Lenskyj Jefferson, *Inside the Olympic Industry: Power, Politics and Activism* (New York, SUNY Press, 2000). A very critical panorama of the Olympic system.

John J. MacAloon, *This Great Symbol: Pierre de Coubertin and the Origins of the Modern Olympic Games* (Chicago: University Press, 1981). A seminal work in order to understand the renovator of the Games and the beginnings of the Olympic movement. MacAloon has also recently published a fascinating book on the evolution of the Olympic Flame Relay.

Michael Payne, *Olympic Turnaround: How the Olympic Games stepped back from the brink of extinction to become the world's best known brand* (London: Praeger, 2006). The book describes the introduction of marketing techniques in the Games for the greater benefit of Olympic finances and the glory of its author, who was the IOC's marketing director for 15 years.

Richard Pound, *Inside the Olympics: A behind-the-scenes look at the politics, the scandals, and the glory of the Olympics* (London: Wiley, 2004). An account of the last 20 years of the IOC and the Games by a Canadian member who was a candidate to succeed Samaranch and the first president of the World Anti-Doping Agency. Pound has written several other books on various aspects of Olympic history and the fight against doping.

Holger Preuss, *The Economics of Staging the Olympics: A comparison of the Games 1972–2008* (Cheltenham, UK: Edward Elgar, 2004). An impressive series of financial and economic statistics regarding the organization of the Games since those of Munich in 1972.

Alfred E. Senn, *Power, Politics, and the Olympic Games: A history of the power brokers, events, and controversies that shaped the Games* (Champaign, IL: Human Kinetics, 1999). A synthesis written by a historian of the Cold War that shows the evolution of the IOC since its foundation.

Eleni Theodoraki, *Olympic Event Organization* (Amsterdam: Elsevier, 2007). This work focuses on the recent Organising Committees of the Olympic Games and those of other major events.

Kevin Young and Kevin B. Wamsley, *Global Olympics: Historical and Sociological Studies of the Modern Games* (Amsterdam: Elsevier, 2005).

Index

Note: page numbers in *italic* indicate the entry is part of a box, table or figure.